Celebrate Recovery®

LEADER'S GUIDE

John Baker is the founder of Celebrate Recovery®, a ministry born out of the heart of Saddleback Church. Over the last twenty years, more than 11,500 individuals have gone through this Christ-centered recovery program at Saddleback. The Celebrate Recovery program is now being used in over 20,000 churches nationwide. In 1993, John and Pastor Rick Warren wrote the Celebrate Recovery curriculum which has been published and translated into twenty-three languages.

John began serving at Saddleback as a lay pastor in 1991. In 1992, he was asked to join the Saddleback Church staff as the Director of Small Groups and Recovery. In 1995, his responsibilities increased as he became the Pastor of Membership. In this position, John's responsibilities included pastoral counseling, pastoral care, Celebrate Recovery, support groups, small groups, family, singles, and recreation ministries. In 1996, he developed Saddleback's lay counseling ministry.

In June 1997, John became the Pastor of Ministries, responsible for the recruitment, training, and deployment of church members to serve in one of the more than 156 different ministries at Saddleback.

In 2001, Rick Warren asked John to become the Pastor of Celebrate Recovery. This is John's shape, his passion, and his calling. In addition, he serves as one of the five elders at Saddleback. John is a nationally known speaker and trainer in helping churches start Celebrate Recovery ministries. These ministries, in thousands of churches, reach out not only to their congregations but also to their communities in helping those dealing with a hurt, hang-up, or habit.

John and his wife, Cheryl, have been married over forty years and have served together in Celebrate Recovery since 1991. They have two adult children, Laura and Johnny. Laura and her husband, Brian, have twins. Johnny and his wife, Jeni, have three children.

A PURPOSE DRIVEN® RECOVERY RESOURCE

John Baker

FOREWORD BY RICK WARREN

Celebrate Recovery®

A recovery program based on eight principles
from the Beatitudes

LEADER'S GUIDE

ALCOHOLISM • DIVORCE • SEXUAL ABUSE • CODEPENDENCY • DOMESTIC VIOLENCE
DRUG ADDICTION • SEXUAL ADDICTION • FOOD ADDICTION • GAMBLING ADDICTION

CELEBRATE RECOVERY
20
ANNIVERSARY
1991-2011

Z ZONDERVAN®

ZONDERVAN.com/
AUTHOR**TRACKER**
follow your favorite authors

AUTHOR'S NOTE:

Because I have picked up a variety of quotes and slogans from numerous recovery meetings, tapes, and seminars, I have not been able to provide some sources for all of the material here. If you feel that I have quoted your material, please let me know and I will be pleased to give you the credit.

ZONDERVAN

Celebrate Recovery Leader's Guide, Revised Edition
Copyright © 1998, 2005, 2012 by John Baker

Requests for information should be addressed to:
Zondervan, *Grand Rapids, Michigan 49530*

ISBN 978-0-310-68965-2

Cover design: Brand Navigation
Cover photography: David Robbins / Getty Images
Interior design: Michelle Espinosa

Printed in the United States of America

12 13 14 15 16 /PHP/ 20 19 18 17 16 15 14 13 12 11 10 9 8 7 6 5 4 3 2 1

This book is dedicated to my Lord and Savior, Jesus Christ.

*To my wife, Cheryl, and my children, Laura and Johnny,
for loving me no matter what.*

*To Pastors Rick Warren and Glen Kreun,
for trusting and believing in me.*

To the Saddleback Church staff, for their support.

*To the thousands of courageous men and women who have celebrated
their recoveries with me over the last twenty years!*

CONTENTS

PART 1

Principle 1: Realize I'm not God. I admit that I am powerless to control my tendency to do the wrong thing and that my life is unmanageable.

"Happy are those who know they are spiritually poor."

PART 2

Principle 2: Earnestly believe that God exists, that I matter to Him, and that He has the power to help me recover.

"Happy are those who mourn, for they shall be comforted."

PART 3

Principle 3: Consciously choose to commit all my life and will to Christ's care and control.

"Happy are the meek."

PART 4

Principle 4: Openly examine and confess my faults to myself, to God, and to someone I trust.

"Happy are the pure in heart."

PART 5

Principle 5: Voluntarily submit to every change God wants to make in my life and humbly ask Him to remove my character defects.

"Happy are those whose greatest desire is to do what God requires."

PART 6

Principle 6: Evaluate all my relationships. Offer forgiveness to those who have hurt me and make amends for harm I've done to others, except when to do so would harm them or others.

"Happy are the merciful." "Happy are the peacemakers."

PART 7

Principle 7: Reserve a daily time with God for self-examination, Bible reading, and prayer in order to know God and His will for my life and to gain the power to follow His will.

PART 8

Principle 8: Yield myself to God to be used to bring this Good News to others, both by my example and by my words.

"Happy are those who are persecuted because they do what God requires."

THE ROAD TO RECOVERY

Eight Principles Based on the Beatitudes
By Pastor Rick Warren

1. **R**ealize I'm not God. I admit that I am powerless to control my tendency to do the wrong thing and that my life is unmanageable.

   "Happy are those who know they are spiritually poor." (Matthew 5:3)

2. **E**arnestly believe that God exists, that I matter to Him, and that He has the power to help me recover.

   "Happy are those who mourn, for they shall be comforted."
   (Matthew 5:4)

3. **C**onsciously choose to commit all my life and will to Christ's care and control.

   "Happy are the meek." (Matthew 5:5)

4. **O**penly examine and confess my faults to myself, to God, and to someone I trust.

   "Happy are the pure in heart." (Matthew 5:8)

5. **V**oluntarily submit to every change God wants to make in my life and humbly ask Him to remove my character defects.

   "Happy are those whose greatest desire is to do what God requires."
   (Matthew 5:6)

6. **E**valuate all my relationships. Offer forgiveness to those who have hurt me and make amends for harm I've done to others, except when to do so would harm them or others.

   "Happy are the merciful." (Matthew 5:7)
   "Happy are the peacemakers." (Matthew 5:9)

7. **R**eserve a daily time with God for self-examination, Bible reading, and prayer in order to know God and His will for my life and to gain the power to follow His will.

8. **Y**ield myself to God to be used to bring this Good News to others, both by my example and by my words.

   "Happy are those who are persecuted because they do
   what God requires." (Matthew 5:10)

Twelve Steps and Their Biblical Comparisons[1]

1. We admitted we were powerless over our addictions and compulsive behaviors, that our lives had become unmanageable.

   "For I know that good itself does not dwell in me, that is, in my sinful nature. For I have the desire to do what is good, but I cannot carry it out."
   (Romans 7:18)

2. We came to believe that a power greater than ourselves could restore us to sanity.

   "For it is God who works in you to will and to act in order to fulfill his good purpose." (Philippians 2:13)

3. We made a decision to turn our lives and our wills over to the care of God.

   "Therefore, I urge you, brothers and sisters, in view of God's mercy, to offer your bodies as a living sacrifice, holy and pleasing to God—this is your true and proper worship." (Romans 12:1)

4. We made a searching and fearless moral inventory of ourselves.

   "Let us examine our ways and test them, and let us return to the LORD."
   (Lamentations 3:40)

5. We admitted to God, to ourselves, and to another human being the exact nature of our wrongs.

   "Therefore confess your sins to each other and pray for each other so that you may be healed." (James 5:16)

6. We were entirely ready to have God remove all these defects of character.

   "Humble yourselves before the Lord, and he will lift you up."
   (James 4:10)

7. We humbly asked Him to remove all our shortcomings.

   "If we confess our sins, he is faithful and just and will forgive us our sins and purify us from all unrighteousness." (1 John 1:9)

8. We made a list of all persons we had harmed and became willing to make amends to them all.

   "Do to others as you would have them do to you." (Luke 6:31)

9. We made direct amends to such people whenever possible, except when to do so would injure them or others.

   "Therefore, if you are offering your gift at the altar and there remember that your brother or sister has something against you, leave your gift there in front of the altar. First go and be reconciled to them; then come and offer your gift." (Matthew 5:23–24)

10. We continued to take personal inventory and when we were wrong, promptly admitted it.

    "So, if you think you are standing firm, be careful that you don't fall!" (1 Corinthians 10:12)

11. We sought through prayer and meditation to improve our conscious contact with God, praying only for knowledge of His will for us and power to carry that out.

    "Let the message of Christ dwell among you richly." (Colossians 3:16)

12. Having had a spiritual experience as the result of these steps, we try to carry this message to others and to practice these principles in all our affairs.

    "Brothers and sisters, if someone is caught in a sin, you who live by the Spirit should restore that person gently. But watch yourselves, or you also may be tempted." (Galatians 6:1)

1. Throughout this material, you will notice several references to the Christ-centered 12 Steps. Our prayer is that Celebrate Recovery will create a bridge to the millions of people who are familiar with the secular 12 Steps (I acknowledge the use of some material from the 12 Suggested Steps of Alcoholics Anonymous) and in so doing, introduce them to the one and only true Higher Power, Jesus Christ. Once they begin that relationship, asking Christ into their hearts as Lord and Savior, true healing and recovery can begin!

FOREWORD BY RICK WARREN

The Bible clearly states "all have sinned." It is my nature to sin, and it is yours too. None of us is untainted. Because of sin, we've all hurt ourselves, we've all hurt other people, and others have hurt us. This means each of us needs repentance and recovery in order to live our lives the way God intended.

You've undoubtedly heard the expression "time heals all wounds." Unfortunately, it isn't true. As a pastor I frequently talk with people who are still carrying hurts from thirty or forty years ago. The truth is, time often makes things worse. Wounds that are left untended fester and spread infection throughout your entire body. Time only extends the pain if the problem isn't dealt with.

What we need is a biblical and balanced program to help people overcome their hurts, hang-ups, and habits. Celebrate Recovery® is that program. Based on the actual words of Jesus rather than psychological theory, this recovery program is unique, and it is more effective in helping people change than anything else I've seen or heard of. Over the years I've witnessed how the Holy Spirit has used this program to transform literally thousands of lives at Saddleback Church and to help people grow toward full Christlike maturity.

Most people are familiar with the classic 12-Step program of AA and other groups. While undoubtedly many lives have been helped through the 12 Steps, I've always been uncomfortable with that program's vagueness about the nature of God, the saving power of Jesus Christ, and the ministry of the Holy Spirit. So I began an intense study of the Scriptures to discover what God had to say about "recovery." To my amazement, I found the principles of recovery—in their logical order—given by Christ in His most famous message, the Sermon on the Mount.

My study resulted in a ten-week series of messages called "The Road to Recovery." During that series my associate pastor John Baker developed the participant's guides, which became the heart of our Celebrate Recovery program. I believe that this program is unlike any recovery program you may have seen. There are seven features that make it unique.

1. *Celebrate Recovery is based on God's Word, the Bible.* When Jesus taught the Sermon on the Mount, He began by stating eight ways to be happy. Today we call them the Beatitudes. From a conventional viewpoint, most of these statements don't make sense. They sound like contradictions. But when you fully understand what Jesus is saying, you'll realize that these eight principles are God's road to recovery, wholeness, growth, and spiritual maturity.

2. *Celebrate Recovery is forward-looking.* Rather than wallowing in the past or dredging up and rehearsing painful memories over and over, Celebrate Recovery focuses on the future. Regardless of what has already happened, the solution is to start making wise choices now and depend on Christ's power to help make those changes.

3. *Celebrate Recovery emphasizes personal responsibility.* Instead of playing the "accuse and excuse" game of victimization, this program helps people face up to their own poor choices and deal with what they can do something about. We can-

not control all that happens to us, but we can control how we respond to everything. That is a secret of happiness. When we stop wasting time fixing the blame, we have more energy to fix the problem. When we stop hiding our own faults and stop hurling accusations at others, then the healing power of Christ can begin working in our mind, will, and emotions.

4. *Celebrate Recovery emphasizes spiritual commitment to Jesus Christ.* The third principle calls for people to make a total surrender of their lives to Christ. Lasting recovery cannot happen without this step. Everybody needs Jesus. Celebrate Recovery is thoroughly evangelistic in nature. In fact, the first time I took our entire church through this program, over 500 people prayed to receive Christ on a single weekend. It was an amazing spiritual harvest. And during the ten-week series that I preached to kick off this program, our attendance grew by over 1,500! Don't be surprised if this program becomes the most effective outreach ministry in your church. Today, nearly 73 percent of the people who've been through Celebrate Recovery have come from outside our church. Changed lives always attract others who want to be changed.

5. *Celebrate Recovery utilizes the biblical truth that we need each other in order to grow spiritually and emotionally.* It is built around small group interaction and the fellowship of a caring community. There are many therapies, growth programs, and counselors today that operate around one-to-one interaction. But Celebrate Recovery is built on the New Testament principle that we don't get well by ourselves. We need each other. Fellowship and accountability are two important components of spiritual growth. If your church is interested in starting small groups, this is a great way to get started.

6. *Celebrate Recovery addresses all types of hurts, hang-ups, and habits.* Some recovery programs deal only with alcohol or drugs or another single problem. But Celebrate Recovery is a "large umbrella" program under which a limitless number of issues can be dealt with. At Saddleback Church, only one out of three who attend Celebrate Recovery are dealing with alcohol or drugs. We have several other specialized groups too.

7. *Finally, Celebrate Recovery is a leadership factory.* Because it is biblical and church-based, Celebrate Recovery produces a continuous stream of people moving into ministry after they've found recovery in Christ. Eighty-five percent of the people who've gone through the program are now active members of Saddleback Church, and an amazing 42 percent are now using their gifts and talents serving the Lord in some capacity in our church.

In closing, let me say that the size of your church is no barrier to beginning a Celebrate Recovery ministry. You can start it with just a small group of people and watch it grow by word of mouth. You won't be able to keep it a secret for long!

I'm excited that you have decided to begin a Celebrate Recovery ministry in your church. You are going to see lives changed in dramatic ways. You are going to see hopeless marriages restored and people set free from all kinds of sinful hurts, hang-ups, and habits as they allow Jesus to be Lord in every area of their lives. To God be the glory! We'll be praying for you.

Dr. Rick Warren
Senior Pastor,
Saddleback Church

FROM MY HEART TO YOURS

My name is John Baker, and I'm a believer who struggles with alcoholism. In 1992, I joined the Saddleback Church staff as the Director of Small Groups and Recovery. Over the years, I have also have had the honor of serving as the Pastor of Membership and Ministry. In 2001, I became the Pastor of Celebrate Recovery. That's what I do, but God is really more interested in who I am, when there is no one else around. He's interested in my character, my values.

So as a way of introducing who I am, I would like to share my testimony by relating my experiences, as I have traveled my personal "road to recovery."

I was raised in a Christian home in the Midwestern town of Collinsville, Illinois, population 10,000. I had a so-called "normal" childhood, whatever that is. My parents were members of a small Baptist church pastored by a very young Gordon MacDonald. I asked Christ into my heart at age thirteen. In high school I was class president and lettered in basketball, baseball, and track. I felt called into ministry at age sixteen and applied to several Christian universities. Up to this point, everything sounds normal — almost boring.

But I had a problem: I had to be the best in everything. Deep down inside I never felt good enough for my parents, my teammates, my girlfriends, or anyone. If I wasn't good enough for them, I wondered how I could ever be good enough for God. I must have missed the Sunday sermons on God's mercy and Jesus' unconditional love and undeserved and unearnable grace. I was a walking, talking paradox — a combination of the lowest possible self-esteem and the world's largest ego. Believe me, that's not a very comfortable feeling inside. The best way that I can describe the feeling is a burning emptiness — a hole — right in the gut.

I wrestled with God's call and judged myself unworthy to enter the ministry. Instead, after high school I went to the University of Missouri. When I packed for my freshman year, I took my nonexistent self-esteem with me. I joined a fraternity and soon discovered the solution — or what I believed to be the solution — for my life's pain: alcohol. It worked! I fit in! For the first time in my life, I felt like I belonged.

While attending the university as a business administration major (with a minor in partying), I met my wife, Cheryl. We were married during my senior year. Because the Vietnam War was in full swing, we knew that after college I would be called into the service. Little did Cheryl know what else the next nineteen years would have in store.

In 1970 I graduated from college, joined the Air Force, and was chosen to be a pilot. I attended Officers' Training School, and in ninety days learned how to act like an officer and drink like a gentleman. I continued to abuse alcohol, viewing it as a cure for my pain, certainly not a sin!

In the service, I quickly found the proper use for 100 percent oxygen — a cure for hangovers! The service is a great place to discover one's talents. Soon I was selected as my squadron's social officer. Perfect! A job that required a lot of hours planning functions at the officers' club bar. Then the war ended, and I was assigned to a reserve unit.

After the service, I joined Scott Paper Company. I earned my MBA degree at night school and God gave us our first child, a daughter, Laura. Two years later we were blessed with our son, John Jr.

I was promoted eight times in the first eleven years of my business career. I was the vice president of sales and marketing for two large consumer food manufacturers. I had reached all my life's career and financial objectives and goals by the time I was thirty! Along with all this business success, however, came several relocations. Moving every two years made it difficult for us to establish a home church, but as my drinking continued, church became less and less important to me. I knew that if I died I was saved, but my Christianity was not reflected in my lifestyle, business practices, and priorities.

Still, I thought my life appeared normal to casual observers. I was a leader in my church's Awana ministry for youth. I thought nothing of leaving work early to stop by a bar before the Wednesday night meeting so I could relax and relate better to the kids. Didn't everybody do that? I was also my son's Little League coach for five years, but I always stopped by the pizza joint with my assistant coach for a few pitchers of beer after every game. Again, didn't everybody? Talk about insanity!

Slowly I became more and more uncomfortable with the lifestyle I was leading. I faced a major decision. I had a choice: do it my way—continue drinking and living by the world's standards—or surrender, repent, and do it God's way. I wish I could tell you that I saw the light and did it God's way, but the truth is, I chose my way. My drinking increased and I turned my back on God. Proverbs 14:12 (TLB) says, "Before every man there lies a wide and pleasant road that seems right but ends in death."

I was on that road. I was what is known as a functioning alcoholic. I never lost a job, never got arrested for drunk driving. No, the only things my sin-addiction cost me were my close relationships with the Lord and my family. Cheryl and I separated, after nineteen years of marriage. I lost all purpose for living. You see, what I had considered the solution for my life's problem, alcohol, *became* the problem of my life!

My life was out of control. I had created my own hell on earth! On an October morning, I was in Salt Lake City on a business trip when I woke up and knew I couldn't take another drink. But I also knew that I couldn't live without one! I had finally hit my bottom. I was dying physically, emotionally, mentally, and most important, spiritually. I was at **Principle 1**.

Principle 1: Realize I'm not God. I admit that I am powerless to control my tendency to do the wrong thing and that my life is unmanageable.

"Happy are those who know they are spiritually poor." (Matthew 5:3)

Step 1: We admitted we were powerless over our addictions and compulsive behaviors, that our lives had become unmanageable.

"For I know that good itself does not dwell in me, that is, in my sinful nature. For I have the desire to do what is good, but I cannot carry it out." (Romans 7:18)

When I got back home from that business trip, I went to my first AA meeting. But that was only the beginning. All in all, I went to over ninety meetings in ninety days. As time passed, I was ready for **Principle 2**.

Principle 2: Earnestly believe that God exists, that I matter to Him, and that He has the power to help me recover.

"Happy are those who mourn, for they shall be comforted." (Matthew 5:4)

Step 2: We came to believe that a power greater than ourselves could restore us to sanity.

"For it is God who works in you to will and to act in order to fulfill his good purpose." (Philippians 2:13)

This is where I found my first glimmer of hope! God loves me unconditionally. I was finally able to understand Romans 11:36 (TLB): "Everything comes from God alone. Everything lives by His power."

Today my life with Christ is an endless hope: my life without Him was a hopeless end! My own willpower left me empty and broken, so I changed my definition of willpower. Now I know that true willpower is the willingness to accept God's power for my life.

This led me to **Principle 3**.

Principle 3: Consciously choose to commit all my life and will to Christ's care and control.

"Happy are the meek." (Matthew 5:5)

Step 3: We made a decision to turn our lives and our wills over to the care of God.

"Therefore, I urge you, brothers and sisters, in view of God's mercy, to offer your bodies as a living sacrifice, holy and pleasing to God— this is your true and proper worship." (Romans 12:1).

In working the first three principles I said, "I can't, God can," and I decided to let Him. One day at a time. If we don't surrender to Christ, we will surrender to chaos! I thought the first three principles were hard, but now came **Principle 4**.

Principle 4: Openly examine and confess my faults to myself, to God, and to someone I trust.

"Happy are the pure in heart." (Matthew 5:8)

Step 4: We made a searching and fearless moral inventory of ourselves.

"Let us examine our ways and test them, and let us return to the LORD." (Lamentations 3:40)

Step 5: We admitted to God, to ourselves, and to another human being the exact nature of our wrongs.

"Therefore confess your sins to each other and pray for each other so that you may be healed." (James 5:16)

At this point I had to go back to visit the young John Baker, to face the hurts, hang-ups, and habits I had attempted to drown with alcohol. I had to face the loss of my infant brother. I had to accept my part in all the destruction that my alcoholism had caused to all those who were once close to me. After I 'fessed up, I was able to face the truth and accept Jesus' forgiveness and healing, which led me out of the darkness of my secrets and into His wonderful light!

I thank God for providing me with a sponsor who helped me stay balanced and didn't judge me during the sharing of my inventory. I cannot begin to tell you the burden God lifted off me when I completed the instructions found in James 5:16! I now knew I was forgiven by the work of Jesus Christ—the one and only true Higher Power—on the cross and that all the sins and wrongs of my past were no longer a secret. Now I was finally willing to have God change me. I was ready to submit to any and all changes God wanted me to make in my life. You see, not much changed in my life—just everything changed!

Principle 5 made me realize that it was time to "let go and let God." By this time, I was happy to do so! I had seen enough of myself to know that I was incapable of changing my life on my own.

Principle 5: Voluntarily submit to every change God wants to make in my life and humbly ask Him to remove my character defects.

"Happy are those whose greatest desire is to do what God requires." (Matthew 5:6)

Step 6: We were entirely ready to have God remove all these defects of character.

"Humble yourselves before the Lord, and he will lift you up." (James 4:10)

Step 7: We humbly asked Him to remove all our shortcomings.

"If we confess our sins, he is faithful and just and will forgive us our sins and purify us from all unrighteousness." (1 John 1:9)

For me, completing Principle 5 meant three things: (1) I allowed God to transform my mind—its nature, its condition, its identity; (2) I learned to rejoice in steady progress—patient improvement that allowed others to see the changes in me that I could not see; (3) God rebuilt my self-worth based on His love for me rather than my always trying to measure up to the world's standards.

During this time God gave me His definition of humility: "My grace is all you need, for my power is greatest when you are weak" (2 Corinthians 12:9, GNT). Then I could say with the apostle Paul, "I am most happy, then, to be proud of my weaknesses.... For when I am weak, then I am strong" (vv. 9–10, GNT).

I was now ready to work on **Principle 6**, my favorite:

Principle 6: Evaluate all my relationships. Offer forgiveness to those who have hurt me and make amends for harm I've done to others, except when to do so would harm them or others.

"Happy are the merciful." (Matthew 5:7)
"Happy are the peacemakers." (Matthew 5:9)

Step 8: We made a list of all persons we had harmed and became willing to make amends to them all.

"Do to others as you would have them do to you." (Luke 6:31)

Step 9: We made direct amends to such people whenever possible, except when to do so would injure them or others.

"Therefore, if you are offering your gift at the altar and there remember that your brother or sister has something against you, leave your gift in front of the altar. First go and be reconciled to them; then come and offer your gift." (Matthew 5:23–24)

I said this is my *favorite* principle, but certainly not the easiest! I had quite a list of names on my amends list. They ranged from former employers and employees to friends and neighbors. But my most special amends were to my family, especially to my wife, Cheryl. We were still separated. I told her that my drinking was not her fault. I was truly sorry for the pain I had caused in her life, that I still loved her, and that if I could ever do anything for her—anything—she only had to ask.

Over the months of separation, Cheryl had seen the changes God was making in my life, changes that occurred as I worked my program. (This is where it really gets interesting!) She and the kids had started attending a church that met in a gym. It was called Saddleback. One Saturday night I was visiting the kids and they asked me to join them on Sunday morning. Much to their surprise, I said yes! It had been five years since I had last attended a church service, but when I heard the music and Pastor Rick Warren's message, I knew I was home. Cheryl and I began to work in earnest on our problems and five months later, God opened our hearts and we renewed our marriage vows. Isn't that just like God!

As a family we were baptized and later took all the church's classes: 101 Membership, 201 Maturity, and 301 Ministry. In Class 301, I found one of my life's verses:

"You have been chosen by God himself—you are priests of the King, . . . you are God's very own—all this so you may show to others how God called you out of the darkness into his wonderful light. Once you were less than nothing; now you are God's own." (1 Peter 2:9–10, TLB)

As Pastor Rick Warren says, "God never wastes a hurt." All the pain and heartache of my addiction finally made sense!

However, at my AA meetings I was mocked when talking about my Higher Power—the only true Higher Power, Jesus Christ. And at church I couldn't find a small group where individuals could openly relate to my struggle with my sin-addiction to alcohol. I knew they had to be there because in a church the size of Saddleback, I couldn't be the only one struggling with a hurt, hang-up, or addictive habit.

So I wrote Pastor Rick Warren a short, concise, thirteen-page, single-spaced letter outlining the vision that God gave me—

The vision of Celebrate Recovery, a Christ-centered recovery program.

The next thing I knew, Pastor Rick called me into his office and said, "Great, John—you do it!" From that meeting Celebrate Recovery was born.

I finally was able to accept God's call. I entered Golden Gate Baptist Seminary and committed my life to God, to serve Him wherever and whenever He chose.

I have dedicated my life to serving Jesus Christ. I intend to work the last two principles on a daily basis for the remainder of my time on this earth.

Principle 7: Reserve a daily time with God for self-examination, Bible reading, and prayer in order to know God and His will for my life and to gain the power to follow His will.

Principle 8: Yield myself to God to be used to bring this Good News to others, both by my example and my words.

"Happy are those who are persecuted because they do what God requires."
(Matthew 5:10)

Step 10: We continued to take personal inventory and when we were wrong, promptly admitted it.

"So, if you think you are standing firm, be careful that you don't fall!"
(1 Corinthians 10:12)

Step 11: We sought through prayer and meditation to improve our conscious contact with God, praying only for knowledge of His will for us and power to carry that out.

"Let the message of Christ dwell among you richly." (Colossians 3:16)

Step 12: Having had a spiritual experience as the result of these steps, we try to carry this message to others and to practice these principles in all our affairs.

"Brothers and sisters, if someone is caught in a sin, you who live by the Spirit should restore that person gently. But watch yourselves, or you also may be tempted." (Galatians 6:1)

God has blessed me richly, and I gratefully pass on these blessings to you. It is my prayer that this book will help your church start a Celebrate Recovery program where your people can safely work together on their hurts, hang-ups, and habits—a program where Christ's love, truth, grace, and forgiveness are demonstrated in all things.

In His steps,
John Baker

Getting Started

The purpose of Celebrate Recovery is to encourage fellowship and to celebrate God's healing power in our lives as we work our way along the road to recovery. We are changed as we share our experiences, strengths, and hopes with one another. In addition, we become willing to accept God's grace and forgiveness in solving our life's problems.

By working through the principles, we grow spiritually, and we are freed from our hurts, hang-ups, and habits. This freedom creates peace, serenity, joy, and most importantly, a stronger personal relationship with others and our personal, loving, and forgiving Higher Power, Jesus Christ.

On November 21, 1991, Celebrate Recovery held its first meeting at Saddleback Church, Lake Forest, California. The program not only has survived, but has been truly blessed and continues to grow beyond our greatest expectations. More than 11,500 courageous individuals have worked through their hurts, hang-ups, and habits at Saddleback Church since the ministry began.

We have tried a variety of new ideas and concepts to help the ministry grow. Of course, not everything we tried has worked, but from the very beginning, I told the leadership team that the one thing we could not change in Celebrate Recovery is the truth that Jesus Christ is the one and only Higher Power.

This leader's guide is a compilation of what has worked at the Celebrate Recovery model at Saddleback. As you read through the book, you will see that in later chapters every aspect of Celebrate Recovery is explained in detail. This introduction, however, is provided to get you started. The ninety-day start-up strategy will help you organize your church's Celebrate Recovery ministry. The seven keys will show you how Saddleback's Celebrate Recovery model grew from forty-five people in 1991 to more than 700 weekly attendees today. And finally, the meeting format and instructions on how to use the materials list will give you a blueprint or structure from which to start and grow your new Celebrate Recovery ministry.

Implementing the 90-Day Start-Up Strategy

This simple yet effective start-up strategy will help you organize and plan your Celebrate Recovery ministry. The churches that have followed this strategy have been able to smoothly and effectively begin helping those in their church and community who are struggling with a hurt, hang-up, or habit. This strategy is broken up into three phases and each phase is designed to help you build a strong foundation to support your ministry both at the beginning and as it grows.

Phase 1: Investigate, Communicate, and Invite (30 Days)

Investigate

Investigate *www.celebraterecovery.com*

- Under the "Group Finder" tab, look for Celebrate Recovery ministries in your local area. Visit as many of these as you can. Although each ministry will have its own unique personality, you will be able to see how the DNA of Celebrate Recovery is kept intact.
- Investigate to find the Celebrate Recovery state representative closest to your location. Your state rep is a valuable resource who will come alongside you and advise you along the way.
- Investigate one-day seminars/Seven Keys to a Successful Ministry

Investigate *www.saddlebackresources.com*

- Investigate all the Celebrate Recovery resources available to you for a successful ministry. It is highly recommended that you initially order the *Celebrate Recovery Program Starter Kit* which encompasses the "how-tos" and "basics" of starting your ministry.

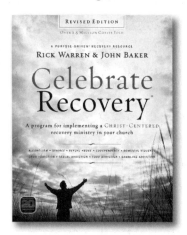

- The kit includes:
    - 1 20-minute DVD, *How to Start a Christ-Centered Recovery Ministry in Your Church*, by Rick Warren and John Baker
    - 1 leader's guide
    - 1 of each of the participant's guides (4 total)
    - 1 CD-ROM with 25 lessons

- 1 CD-ROM with sermon transcripts
- 4-volume audio CD sermon series

- Investigate the *Life's Healing Choices* book. It would be helpful to read it at this time to gain a broad understanding of the Celebrate Recovery principles of recovery.

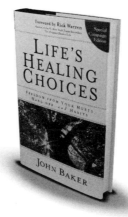

Most importantly, start PRAYING CONTINUOUSLY!

Communicate

Communicate with your state representative.

- Introduce yourself and set a time to meet.

Communicate with your church.

- Set up an appointment to share your vision with your senior pastor and any of those who will be supervising this ministry. On the twenty-minute DVD in the *Celebrate Recovery Program Starter Kit*, Pastor Rick Warren explains the benefits of this program from a pastor's key point of view.
- Use church bulletin announcements, flyers, video, Facebook, Twitter, and your church website to communicate the plans to bring Celebrate Recovery to your church.

Invite

Invite anyone in your church who is interested to join you for an informational meeting.

- Share your plans and begin to recruit support. Christ-centered and/or secular recovery experience is helpful.
- Some people will be potential leaders; others may want to come alongside the ministry in other areas, such as worship or child care.

Phase 2: Train, Plan, Prepare (60 Days)

Train

Familiarize yourself with the *Celebrate Recovery Program Starter Kit* and its components.

Purchase a set of participant's guides and a leader's guide for each volunteer/leader.

Meet on a weekly basis with your initial volunteer/leadership team to provide training and Celebrate Recovery experience. Even though some may have 12 Step experience, you want to ensure that all have experienced aspects of Celebrate Recovery so they may lead others with integrity.

Here is a suggested format for your weekly meetings (2 hours) prior to launching your Celebrate Recovery general meeting night:

Part 1: Planning & Training (1 hour)

- Open with prayer
- Plan: (Refer to next section for topics)
- Train: Training topics from leader's guide might include:
  - Facilitating your general meeting night (see page 50)
  - Open share small group format (see page 54)
  - Small group guidelines (see page 54)
  - Step study small group (see page 57)
  - Celebrate Recovery Newcomers 101 group (see page 59)

Part 2: Step Study Group (1 hour)

- Break up into men's and women's small groups.
- Refer to page 57 for step study small group format.

At the end of the sixty days when you are ready to launch, this initial group will likely have completed Participant's Guide 1 and have started Participant's Guide 2. If possible, leaders should plan on giving two nights per week to the ministry after launching the Celebrate Recovery general meeting night. This will allow the core group to continue to meet together on the second night to complete their step study.

Plan

The heart of the Celebrate Recovery program is found in three different types of groups: the *large group meeting* and the *open share small groups*, which both take place on the general meeting night, and the *step study small groups*, which meet on a separate night. In order to plan for these groups, first determine the day and location of your general meeting night.

Things to consider for your general meeting night:

- Child Care: Determine the ages that will be included. Refer to your family ministries director/pastor for proper procedures for your church.
- Food: Decide if you will be offering fellowship events such as dinner/snacks before the large group meeting or coffee/desserts following the open share small groups.
- Remember that food is an optional element that will help to build community and improve the experience for the whole family, but it is not a requirement. Although child care is not mandatory, it is HIGHLY recommended. Just keep it simple and do what is appropriate for your ministry.

Things to consider for your large group meeting:

- Worship: Determine if the worship component will be through a simple CD player, an iPod with speakers, or a complete band.
- Teaching/Testimony: Decide who will be teaching the twenty-five lessons from the leader's guide along with who will be sharing their written testimony. Consider planning these components on a quarterly basis. See *www.saddlebackresources.com* for available resources ("Testimonies to Go" DVDs, etc.).

Things to consider for your open share small groups:

- Initial Open Share Small Groups: Determine which groups you will offer. A suggestion would be to start with: men's chemically dependent, women's chemically dependent, men's codependent, and women's codependent. You can also start with simply a women's group and a men's group.
- Leaders: Open share group leaders and coleaders should be chosen according to their recovery experience.

Prepare

- Set the date for your first general meeting.
- Contact your state rep to schedule a time for him/her to visit.
- Confirm commitments from those assisting in facilities, worship, child care, and food.
- Finalize assignments for positions in the large group meeting and leader/coleader positions for open share small groups.
- Invite the church. Put information about Celebrate Recovery in the church bulletin and/or set up an information table during church services. Consider creating an informational brochure. You could also use church announcements to show the pastor's support and approval of the program. This will let everyone know that your church is a "safe place" to deal with their "hurts, hang-ups, and habits."
- Invite the outside community. Consider having a "soft launch" or "dress rehearsal" first. This will give you a few meetings to have things running smoothly before the public arrives.
- Open the doors on your launch date—well equipped and ready.
- Have fun!
- PRAY CONTINUOUSLY!

Phase 3: Continuing Growth (Day 91+)

An excellent way to help your Celebrate Recovery ministry grow is to consider having your church use the *Life's Healing Choices* book and *Life's Healing Choices Small Group Study Guide*. This small group study will greatly enhance your congregation's understanding of the scope of Celebrate Recovery's "hurts, hang-ups, and habits."

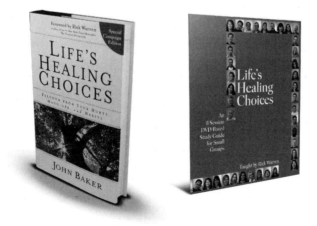

Consider waiting six months or so before offering step study small groups to your Celebrate Recovery participants. This will accomplish two things:

1. Leaders will have time to get through Principle 5, preparing them to be effective step study leaders themselves.
2. Your general meeting night will have a chance to grow and develop.

Consider purchasing the *Celebrate Recovery Advanced Leadership Training Kit*. This resource will be valuable to your ministry to further equip and empower your leaders. The corresponding *Celebrate Recovery Advanced Leadership Training Visual Kit* contains PowerPoint backgrounds and camera-ready artwork for printing of banners, etc.

The kit includes:

- 10 training modules
- 2 DVDs: "3 Doors of Celebrate Recovery," which explains the different group formats, and "Intervention," which explains the "how-tos"
- 2 resource CDs: one with trainers' teaching notes and the other containing the participant handouts, information table sheets, and bulletin inserts for all twenty-five of the Celebrate Recovery lessons
- 2 audio CDs: one containing the "Serenity Prayer" and the second containing the "Recovery Check-Up" lesson

The training modules are excellent tools for you to use during your monthly leaders' meetings. Simply choose a module to cover each month. You may also want to teach certain modules, such as "Module 4—Training New Leaders," on a monthly basis at a different time, as you recruit and introduce more participants into leadership.

As your ministry and leadership grow, consider starting *Celebration Station* and *The Landing*.

- Celebration Station: Celebration Station is created for children ages five to eleven. The beauty of Celebration Station is that it addresses the very same topics adults are learning about in Celebrate Recovery—but in kid-friendly ways. This approach initiates positive, fun, faith-filled conversations between kids and parents that let them practice open communication and sharing in ways they may never have before.

- The Landing: The Landing is a dynamic resource that targets and assists students. Young people can break patterns of unhealthy behavior through the community, teaching, and experiences they'll discover at The Landing. They'll examine the past decisions that led them to where they are today; talk about the patterns and behaviors that keep them trapped; pursue the life-changing truths of freedom found throughout the Bible; and commit to living differently and building healthy relationships with family members, adult leaders, and trusted peers.

- Continue to stay in touch with your state rep. He or she will be able to assist you in the process of getting your program listed on the Celebrate Recovery website.
- Check the Celebrate Recovery website to find one-day seminars and Summit dates.

This start-up strategy is meant to help you prepare, launch, and maintain a healthy Celebrate Recovery ministry. You may need to spend more time in one area than another, and you may not be ready to launch in exactly ninety days. The important thing is that you take advantage of the years of experience of Saddleback Church and thousands of others that have paved the way. Stay connected and don't be afraid to ask questions. You have lots of support!

Seven Keys to Start Your Recovery Ministry and Keep It Growing

There are seven keys to starting a recovery ministry and keeping it growing: **(1) worship, (2) leadership training, (3) senior pastor support, (4) fellowship events, (5) curriculum, (6) new groups, and (7) outreach.**

Think of the seven keys this way. Jesus Christ is the one and only true Higher Power. He is the rock, the foundation, of the Celebrate Recovery program. Proverbs 9:1 (NLT) tells us, "Wisdom has built her spacious house with seven pillars." Each of the seven keys act like a pillar built on the foundation and supported by the foundation—Jesus Christ. The seven keys, in turn, are the pillars that help support your Celebrate Recovery ministry.

Let's begin with what I believe to be the most important key to continued growth in any recovery program: worship.

Worship

Worship has been a central part of Celebrate Recovery since the very first meeting. Every Friday night we begin our large group time with twenty minutes of praise and worship. I believe our worship time is important for the following reasons:

- Worship is a major strength and difference between a Christ-centered and a secular recovery program.

  "And you will sing as on the night you celebrate a holy festival;
  your hearts will rejoice as when people playing pipes go up to the
  mountain of the LORD, to the Rock of Israel." (Isaiah 30:29)

- Worship provides a time for everyone to put aside the busyness and hassles of the world and get in touch with the true Higher Power, Jesus Christ. It allows time for the power of the Holy Spirit to fill all those who attend with a peace and a safety that only He can provide. There will be people present who are hurting so badly that they may be able to express their pain only through silent prayer and worship.
- Worship gives us a vehicle in which to celebrate our recoveries! I suggest keeping the praise songs upbeat to build up, strengthen, and encourage those who attend, and to focus on the joy of God's presence, peace, and power in their recoveries.

I wish everyone could attend the Celebrate Recovery model at Saddleback Church! You would see firsthand the power of worship in recovery; we have upwards of fifteen singers and musicians who weekly minister faithfully to others. It doesn't matter, though, what size your Celebrate Recovery is; a twenty-piece band is not necessary to incorporate worship into your recovery program. When we started Celebrate Recovery in 1991, we had two singers and a three-piece band. Even if you use a CD or simply find someone who can lead while playing a guitar, just be sure to include worship as a key part of your recovery program.

Leadership Training

The second key to growing your recovery ministry is leadership training. Proverbs 23:12 says, "Apply your heart to instruction and your ears to words of knowledge." Pastor Rick Warren has told the Saddleback Church staff over and over, "Once you stop learning, you stop leading."

If I had to choose one word that would describe the leadership training at Celebrate Recovery, it would be *consistent*. We schedule monthly meetings to discuss recovery issues and group dynamics. These leadership meetings include four elements: planning, teaching, sharing, and fellowship time.

Planning time includes assigning the lessons that will be taught by the teaching team for the next month. At this time we also line up the testimonies that will be used to support the particular principle we are working on that month.

In addition, assignments for the Celebrate Recovery information table, Solid Rock Cafe, Bar-B-Que, and other special events are given out at this time. In this planning element of the meeting, group participation is essential.

Teaching time is also very important. The majority of the teaching will be done by the training team and ministry leader. More about these roles will be explained on pages 33 and 36. In addition, Christian counselors have volunteered their time and support to help instruct and support our leaders. They have taught on a variety of topics from "how to handle someone in your group who is suicidal" to "helping the parents in your groups get needed help for their children."

During *sharing time* I encourage the leaders to break into small groups. This gives them an opportunity to share different ideas for handling a conflict in their group, enforcing the five guidelines, or any general tip or strategy that has worked in their group. They also share their experiences, strengths, hopes, and especially their struggles with one another.[2]

We use the *fellowship time* in our leadership meetings to celebrate the Lord's Supper. This is a great time to share what Christ has done in each of our lives and to bond us as a ministry team in purpose and spirit. The meeting concludes with a light dinner or an old-fashioned potluck. Sometimes we include spouses and families.

The leaders sign an annual leadership covenant and they also must meet the following qualifications:

1. They must be a growing Christian, not a new believer.
2. They must have completed all levels of the church's leadership classes.
3. They need to have worked hard on their own recovery and be able to talk comfortably about their own victories and struggles.
4. They have completed a step study using the four Celebrate Recovery participant's guides.
5. They need to have a strong personal support network: family, recovering friends, accountability partners, church leaders, Christian counselor, and so forth.
6. They must agree to attend ongoing monthly Celebrate Recovery leadership training sessions.

2. Because we encourage leaders to always share their hopes and victories with their Friday night groups, they understand that if they have had a tough week and feel that they are unable to lead their Friday night group with encouragement and hope, they can come to me before the meeting and I will find a replacement for them for that evening.

We tell them that we see their admission of a struggle as a strength, not as a weakness. We will meet with them during the upcoming week to encourage them. Usually by the next Friday night they are back leading their group, sharing Christ's hope and power with a new enthusiasm and compassion.

7. They must agree to be alert to the temptation of developing a codependent relationship with members of their group.[3]

Let me offer you a word of caution. If you are trying to run your recovery ministry or your church's pastoral care all by yourself, you are going to burn out. And not only will you burn out as a leader, but eventually your own recovery will begin to suffer.

The way to be an effective Celebrate Recovery leader is to start giving the responsibilities of your leadership away.

Exodus 18:13–21 (TLB) tells us:

The next day Moses sat as usual to hear the people's complaints against each other, from morning to evening. When Moses' father-in-law saw how much time this was taking, he said, "Why are you trying to do all this alone, with people standing here all day long to get your help? … It's not right! You're going to wear yourself out — and if you do, what will happen to the people? Moses, this job is too heavy a burden for you to try to handle all by yourself. Now listen, and let me give you a word of advice … find some capable, godly, honest men [to help you]."

If you want to be a great recovery leader, and if you want to last and have your ministry grow and be more effective in reaching and helping hurting, broken people, I strongly suggest that you consider one important word: T-E-A-M!

At Celebrate Recovery we manage the ministry by the T-E-A-M structure. We have one person responsible for each of the following:

T — training
E — encouraging
A — assimilation
M — ministry leader

This is how we make Celebrate Recovery a truly lay-driven ministry. On pages 33–36 are explanations of each team member's role and responsibilities:

---

3. When you're just starting your Celebrate Recovery program, your leaders will not be able to fulfill these seven qualifications. The important thing is that they agree to complete them as soon as possible.

T = Training Coach

"All Scripture is God-breathed and is useful for teaching, rebuking, correcting and training in righteousness, so that the servant of God may be thoroughly equipped for every good work."
(2 Timothy 3:16–17)

The Training Coach's role is to equip Celebrate Recovery leaders for ministry in an environment that allows each leader to grow in God and confidence. A key responsibility of the trainer is to ensure the DNA of an authentic Celebrate Recovery, which is vital in bringing accountability and credibility to the ministry.

An effective Training Coach:

Conducts *NEW LEADER TRAINING* and Orientation

When you are ready to begin training your new leaders, a helpful tool to consider is the *Advanced Leadership Training Guide* (ALT). The ALT is divided into ten modules and will provide you with all the training materials you need (*www.saddlebackresources.com*). Using the ALT, you are free to be as creative as you want. Take the ALT, pull various sections together, and create your own training topics.

• Training New Leaders	ALT Module 4
• Writing Your Testimony	ALT Module 5
• Training Open Share Group Leaders	ALT Module 6
• Training Step Study Group Leaders	ALT Module 7
• Implementing the Small Group Guidelines	ALT Module 8
• Training Sponsors	ALT Module 9
• Additional Training for Great Leaders	ALT Module 10

Helpful tips for Training Coaches can be found for free on our Celebrate Recovery blog and podcast at *www.celebraterecoveryblog.com*, or you can join us on the Celebrate Recovery Facebook page.

Provides training sessions for *MONTHLY LEADERSHIP MEETINGS*

It is not necessarily the Training Coach's responsibility to conduct all of these sessions but to work in conjunction with the Ministry Leader to determine the needs of the ministry.

Develops and oversees leadership for *SMALL GROUPS*

The Training Coach supports group leaders, being sensitive to any issues specific to a particular group dynamic, or leader and coleader conflicts.

Develops a Training Coach *APPRENTICE*

Look for someone within your existing leadership to train and develop as an apprentice. A good trainer possesses the ability to see the vision and articulate it in a way that everyone can easily understand, training from personal experience. Motivation is caught, not taught.

E = Encourager Coach

"Do not let any unwholesome talk come out of your mouths, but only what is helpful for building others up according to their needs, that it may benefit those who listen." (Ephesians 4:29)

The Encourager Coach's role is to funnel positive energy into Celebrate Recovery leaders so they can handle the struggles and stress that may come from working with people who are hurting. They also serve as a bridge for the participants, who begin to serve through volunteerism on their pathway to becoming leaders themselves.

An effective Encourager Coach:

Provides and oversees the *SHEPHERDING CARE* needs of the groups and ministry leaders

The Encourager Coach speaks life into the leadership of the ministry and helps support the TEAM coaches by building them up, continually encouraging them with the Word of God and through prayer. The Encourager Coach recognizes milestones that have been reached by leaders, volunteers, and participants (as applicable) in their recovery.

Creates *FELLOWSHIP EVENTS* for the leaders and groups

In order to keep the leadership and ministry fun and friendly, the Encourager Coach plans fellowship events, both small and large. These events are not to interfere with your general meeting night, but to be held other days/times during the week. Particularly consider adding a fun teambuilding game at your monthly leaders' meeting.

Encourager Coaches also support the Assimilation Coaches with Outreach fellowship events.

Helpful tips for Encourager Coaches can be found for free on our Celebrate Recovery blog and podcast at *www.celebraterecoveryblog.com*, or you can join us on the Celebrate Recovery Facebook page.

Helps identify *NEW APPRENTICE GROUP LEADERS*

Encourager Coaches should be on the "watch" for individuals who are working the Steps through the participant's guides, and who are really making changes in their lives. This is a good indication.

Identifying new leaders must be intentional. Look for recovery experience. Look for those with a heart for hurting people. Do not compromise on the standards for leadership. To achieve this, consider visiting step study groups that are in the last participant's guide. This is an opportunity to recruit and identify new leaders.

Develops an Encourager Coach *APPRENTICE*

The Encourager Coach develops someone from within Celebrate Recovery to be an apprentice. This role will have both men and women serving the needs of the leadership team.

The Encourager Coach's personality traits and spiritual gifts:

- Natural encourager
- Helping
- Pastoring
- Relational
- Caring
- Good listener
- Understands group life and dynamics
- Spiritually mature
- Passionate
- Loves to pour into other leaders

A = Assimilation Coach

"I will praise the LORD at all times. I will constantly speak his praises. I will boast only in the LORD; let all who are discouraged take heart. Come, let us tell of the LORD's greatness; let us exalt his name together." (Psalm 34:1–3, NLT)

The Assimilation Coach's role is to communicate favorably with the church family and community about Celebrate Recovery. An Assimilation Coach will gain information and knowledge about churches and secular recovery groups in his/her area as well as local Christian counselors and probation departments.

An effective Assimilation Coach:

Is responsible for the *PROMOTION* of Celebrate Recovery to the members, the church, the community, and the world

Members and the Church:

- Create Celebrate Recovery brochures, business cards, and newsletters (*Visual Kit 2* has Celebrate Recovery logo: *www.eyeeffectsworship.com*).
- Utilize your church's bulletin and website.
- Produce a video about your Celebrate Recovery display pictures.
- Encourage your pastor to include Celebrate Recovery testimonies in sermons.
- Use Celebrate Recovery shirts, hats, etc. from *www.shop.celebraterecoverygear.com*.

The Community:

- Use brochures, newsletters, and video.
- Utilize advertising in local newspapers and magazines.
- Network with other ministries in your area.

The World:

- Help another church start Celebrate Recovery. Contact your regional director to help you reach out to other churches.

Helpful tips for Assimilation Coaches can be found for free on our Celebrate Recovery blog and podcast at *www.celebraterecoveryblog.com*, or you can join us on the Celebrate Recovery Facebook page.

Recruits and interviews new *LEADERSHIP CANDIDATES*
The "A" Coach may visit step studies on Step 12 to share the joy of serving as a leader and hand out Celebrate Recovery leader information sheets. (Sample Celebrate Recovery Leader Information Sheet and Interview Questions, Appendix 2)

Use the Leader Information Sheet and Interview Questions to help during the interview process and conclude by signing the Leadership Covenant. (Sample Celebrate Recovery Leadership Covenant, Appendix 1)

Provide other opportunities where anyone can serve. (Examples: Bar-B-Que team, worship team, coffee shop team)

Develops and maintains *GROUP INFORMATION MATERIALS* for groups and information tables
The "A" Coach sets up and replenishes Celebrate Recovery information/resource table, including copies of: the four participant's guides, the *Celebrate Recovery Bible*, the *Celebrate Recovery Journal*, *Life's Healing Choices* books, and group information sheets.

Develops an Assimilation Coach *APPRENTICE*
Pray for God to provide the right person with a heart to get the word out about Celebrate Recovery: a "people" person, outgoing and good at developing relationships; someone with a passion for spreading the word that there is a place to find help from life's hurts, hang-ups, and habits.

M = Ministry Leader

"Follow my example, as I follow the example of Christ." (1 Corinthians 11:1)

The Ministry Leader has many important roles. However, the most important thing any effective Ministry Leader can do is to set the **TONE** in his or her Celebrate Recovery ministry. Let's look at some of the things a Ministry Leader can do to make Celebrate Recovery a great experience for everyone who attends.

An important way a Ministry Leader can set the TONE is **T**eaching by example. The Ministry Leader needs to be someone *in* recovery. While a pastor or staff person may oversee the ministry while not engaging in it, the Ministry Leader should be someone who recognizes the need for personal recovery, working the Celebrate Recovery Principles in his or her own life. That's one way to teach by example. When the Ministry Leader is involved in personal recovery, he or she is more effective in dealing with people who are in the same boat.

Teaching by example includes doing the things he or she is asking others to do. By showing up early to set up chairs, helping prep the ingredients for the Bar-B-Que, and greeting newcomers, the Ministry Leader can show the rest of the TEAM, as well as other leaders, how they should interact on the general meeting night. In short, teach with more than just words.

As Paul told the church in 1 Corinthians 11:1, "Follow my example, as I follow the example of Christ."

Next, the Ministry Leader sets the TONE by **O**penly sharing his or her hurts, hang-ups, and habits. Ministry Leaders should be transparent, not unapproachable or "fixed." So, in teaching the lessons, they should use personal illustrations to show how Celebrate Recovery has and is helping them in their own lives. Yes, Ministry Leaders should be sure to share about how Jesus Christ has changed them, but shouldn't shy away from sharing about the work they still have to do. This means Ministry Leaders should participate in open share and step study groups, and be part of the overall Celebrate Recovery ministry.

Remember, there's no limitation. James 5:16 says, "Therefore confess your sins to each other and pray for each other so that you may be healed." That applies to all of us, from newcomer to Ministry Leader.

Setting the TONE also means to **N**ever forget to keep the *Celebrate* in Celebrate Recovery. Recovery can be hard, especially at the beginning, but Jesus changes things. The Ministry Leader should make sure to help people remember the joy that is possible in Christ when He works in our lives. Pick uplifting, high-energy songs for worship, use jokes (even bad ones) in the lessons, have a smile on your face and ask the leaders and TEAM to do the same. Make sure every testimony has a section dedicated to celebrating what Christ has done.

This will help us do what Paul instructs in Philippians 4:4: "Rejoice in the Lord always. I will say it again: Rejoice!" By remembering to celebrate the changes God will make in our lives, not just focusing on the problems of today, we can give the participants and newcomers hope.

Last, when the Ministry Leader sets the TONE we see that **E**veryone wants to be a part of something great. When the TEAM is in place, the leaders have been trained, and the TONE has been set, people will be drawn to your healthy Celebrate Recovery ministry. When pastors see lives changed, they will get behind Celebrate Recovery and send people in their congregation to it. When people share about what God has done for them, they will attract their friends and family to check it out. In short, by putting the work in, and by setting the TONE, people will flock to Celebrate Recovery.

We see this happening in Acts 2:44 – 47: "All the believers were together and had everything in common. They sold property and possessions to give to anyone who had need. Every day they continued to meet together in the temple courts. They broke bread in their homes and ate together with glad and sincere hearts, praising God and enjoying the favor of all the people. And the Lord added to their number daily those who were being saved."

An effective Ministry Leader:

Is responsible for the entire *RECOVERY MINISTRY*
Selects and schedules *TEACHERS* **and** *TESTIMONIES* **for general meeting**
Oversees all *CELEBRATE RECOVERY MINISTRY* **volunteer teams**
Serves as the *MAIN CONTACT* **with the church staff**

Helpful tips for Ministry Leaders can be found for free on our Celebrate Recovery blog and podcast at *www.celebraterecovery blog.com*, or you can join us on the Celebrate Recovery Facebook page.

Senior Pastor Support

The third key for growth in your recovery ministry is senior pastor support. I can't emphasize the importance of this key enough. In 1993, Pastor Rick took the entire church through an eight-week series called "The Road to Recovery." It was based on the eight recovery principles found in the Beatitudes in Matthew 5. Celebrate Recovery took off!

Ezra 10:4 (TLB) says, "Take courage and tell us how to proceed in setting things straight, and we will fully cooperate." The people at Saddleback did cooperate, and the ministry not only grew but became a part of the church family. Your senior pastor's support of your recovery program makes it acceptable for someone to be in recovery. It is not just "those" people anymore—it's "us"![4]

In addition, your recovery ministry needs to participate in providing a service to the church other than its main purpose. If you want your recovery program to be respected and supported by the church as a whole, it needs to be and act as a regular ministry of the church, not as something separate. Celebrate Recovery needs to participate in all churchwide events. For instance, we provide a food booth at Western Day, a game booth at the Harvest Party, and we sponsor the sock hop at the church's New Year's Eve Party.

Share the recovery testimonies with your senior pastor. Encourage him to support the ministry by pulpit announcements and announcements in the church bulletin.

If you feel you need help in obtaining your senior pastor's or elder board's support, a great tool is the DVD found in the Celebrate Recovery kit. Make an appointment with your senior pastor or elders and watch the DVD together. It is a concise overview of the Celebrate Recovery ministry. They will have an opportunity to hear from the heart of my senior pastor, Rick Warren, about the changed lives that God has taken through the ministry.

Fellowship Events

The fourth key area for growth is fellowship events.

> *"Two are better than one, because they have a good return for their labor:*
> *If either of them falls down, one can help the other up. But pity anyone*

---

4. Dysfunctional families don't talk, don't trust, and don't feel. Safe families do talk, do trust, and do feel! The church is a family as well. It can be a dysfunctional family, in which you are not allowed to feel, to talk openly, or to trust others; or it can be a safe place, a healing place, in which members can express their feelings, talk openly, and trust that others will not judge them. What we don't talk out creatively, we will act out destructively. Your church needs to be a safe place!

who falls and has no one to help them up!... Though one may be overpowered, two can defend themselves. A cord of three strands is not quickly broken." (Ecclesiastes 4:9–10, 12)

It was not that many years ago that those in recovery were viewed by others as lacking the courage to seek help for their life's problems. Some of the early AA meetings were held in church basements, where members would enter by the back door so that no one would see them and identify them as alcoholics. Thank God, those back-door days in the basements are gone. Your recovery program needs to be out in the open. It should be a regular place where people in recovery can join together, fellowship with one another, and share God's answer on how to overcome their struggles by His power.

At Celebrate Recovery we have two main fellowship events, the Bar-B-Que and Solid Rock Cafe (see Appendix 4). The Bar-B-Que starts at 6 p.m. every Friday night throughout the summer. Our menu includes Recovery Dogs, 12-Step Chicken, Serenity Sausages, and Denial Burgers. We have great prices and great fellowship! Solid Rock Cafe follows our open share group time. It is a great place to "unofficially" continue the meeting.

At Celebrate Recovery, the main focus of every fellowship event is to help participants develop healthy relationships that will grow into a support team of sponsors and accountability partners. Both the Bar-B-Que and Solid Rock Cafe are designed to encourage individuals to meet either before or after our Friday night meetings. They provide a forum for the building of accountability teams and sponsorship relationships. (We don't assign sponsors; it is each person's responsibility to find and establish that important and personal relationship.)

Also, these fellowship events are great ways to get everyone involved in 12-Step service. Someone may not meet all the requirements of being a Celebrate Recovery small group leader. However, he or she can start serving and giving back by volunteering to help out at one of the fellowship events. Remember, in God's eyes all service is valued (Matthew 10:42).

Curriculum

The fifth key for a successful recovery program is finding the right curriculum. The number-one question I get asked about starting a recovery ministry is, "What is the best curriculum?"

There is a wide variety of resources from which to choose, but I believe the foundation for an effective recovery ministry curriculum should all be the same: the Bible. God's Word needs to be at the center of your recovery program. And it can't be if it is not the center of your curriculum.

Romans 15:4 tells us, "For everything that was written in the past was written to teach us, so that through the endurance taught in the Scriptures and the encouragement they provide we might have hope." The Big Book of Alcoholics Anonymous contains twelve great promises, but God's Big Book—God's love letter to us—has over seven thousand miraculous promises!

Second, make sure your curriculum can be applied to all groups—all areas of recovery. If it is biblically based, it will! At Celebrate Recovery, we want to try to break the family's cycle of dysfunction at the youngest level—the kids. That's why we have The Landing for teens and Celebration Station for five- to eleven-year-olds. Both programs are based on Celebrate Recovery.

A third thing to look for in choosing a curriculum is its usability: Is the curriculum easy to use? Remember, it's impossible to eat an elephant in one bite, but if you cut it up in small pieces it becomes much easier (though not necessarily any tastier!).

Fourth, the material needs to create movement through the steps. Some books do a great job of teaching *about* the 12 Steps and specific areas of recovery; however, they do not encourage movement *through* the steps. I have seen many individuals get to the 4th Step and get bogged down, dwelling in the mud of their past. Even worse, they judge the program as too hard and stop the recovery process altogether!

The Celebrate Recovery curriculum fills all four of these curriculum requirements: it is built on God's Word; it can be used in all areas of recovery; it is packaged in four easy-to use, bite-size participant's guides; and completing each of the books gives a sense of progress and assurance of movement through the steps and principles.

> Celebrate Recovery® is trademarked. This is for your protection. The following statement is on the value of using the Celebrate Recovery name for your new ministry:
>
> ### The Value of Using the Celebrate Recovery® Name
> Celebrate Recovery® desires to be a network of like-minded, Bible-based, Christ-centered recovery ministries. This growing network crosses denominational and cultural boundaries to help hurting people in our church and community.

There are many benefits of using the Celebrate Recovery® name. Here are just a few:

Connection

Your ministry is part of an international movement to bring Christ-centered, Bible-based recovery to the world. As a genuine Celebrate Recovery ministry you join in a network of thousands of other local Celebrate Recovery ministries reaching people for Christ and helping them break free from their hurts, hang-ups, and habits.

Support

Your ministry has the support and partnership of the Celebrate Recovery National Team, as well as assistance from your state and regional representatives. These entities work to help your ministry succeed.

Resources

Your ministry has access to the materials and resources from Saddleback Church that have proven to be invaluable tools in recovery.

Validation

Your ministry is validated in your church and community by being associated with Celebrate Recovery.

Promotion

Your ministry is listed with the other Celebrate Recovery programs on the official Celebrate Recovery® websites.

It is our desire for each local Celebrate Recovery ministry to have a clear and consistent character that identifies it as a genuine part of the Celebrate Recovery movement, yet maintaining its own creative distinctions of the local ministry and church.

To illustrate, here's an example of what it means to have consistency while allowing for creativity.

A McDonald's restaurant in Boulder, Colorado may have a Western theme and a McDonald's in Orlando, Florida may have a Mickey Mouse theme. Nevertheless, you can be sure when you order a "Big Mac" it will taste the same at both locations. Our desire is that no matter where newcomers or visitors attend a Celebrate Recovery meeting, they will experience the same quality content and program to find God's healing from their hurts, hang-ups, and habits.

The Celebrate Recovery® name is a registered trademark.

In a desire to protect the integrity of the broader ministry, Celebrate Recovery® requires that if you use the Celebrate Recovery® name that the following are an irreducible minimum of your program.

The DNA of an Authentic Celebrate Recovery® Ministry

1. Jesus Christ is the one and only Higher Power. The program is Christ-centered.

2. The Bible and Celebrate Recovery curriculum consisting of the leader's guide, the four participant's guides, and the *Celebrate Recovery Journal* are to be used exclusively. The large group lessons are taught from the leader's guide, keeping at least the acrostic and the Scriptures as the key points in the lessons. This is to keep consistency within groups, allowing teachers to be creative with the introduction and conclusion of each lesson.

   • *Life's Healing Choices* is part of the *only* approved curriculum. You will find this book may be used in many creative ways in your large group, newcomers group, and step study groups. For the five ways you can use *Life's Healing Choices* in your Celebrate Recovery ministry, locate the reference at *www.celebraterecovery.com*.

   • Celebration Station and The Landing are the *only* approved curriculums for kids and youth. They are the only children's and youth curriculums that tie directly with the Celebrate Recovery curriculum for adults.

   • Use of the *Celebrate Recovery Bible* is strongly encouraged due to the fact that it is the only Bible that corresponds directly to the Celebrate Recovery curriculum. The *Celebrate Recovery Bible* has been designed to work with the resources developed and tested in the national and international ministry of Celebrate Recovery.

   • The *Celebrate Recovery Bible* on Kindle, iBooks, and Nook is also approved curriculum.

3. The ministry is "group based." All groups are gender specific and use the group guidelines and format.

4. The Celebrate Recovery "Five Small Group Guidelines" are implemented and followed.

5. We expect each group to be accountable to Christ, their local church, and the model of Celebrate Recovery established at Saddleback Church. They agree to receive help and suggestions from their state representatives and regional directors.

A church or organization may decide to use the Celebrate Recovery® curriculum and mix it with other materials, or other programs, which is certainly up to their discretion. HOWEVER, they are prohibited from using the Celebrate Recovery® name.

All written materials and other items produced for commercial sale using the Celebrate Recovery® name are strictly prohibited.

New Groups

The sixth key for growing your recovery ministry is building new groups. Built around individual needs and recovery issues, new groups act like blood transfusions in your recovery ministry. People gain a sense of excitement and enthusiasm when a new group starts. Second Corinthians 9:12 says, "This service that you perform is not only supplying the needs of the Lord's people but is also overflowing in many expressions of thanks to God."

I would, however, like to offer a word of caution: *Start your recovery ministry slowly.* I guarantee you that you will have masses of people coming to you saying, "Why don't you have a group for this addiction or this compulsion or behavior?" or "Don't you consider _____ as important as your chemically dependent group?" And being the compassionate person that you are, your first instinct will be to say, "We'll start it next week!" Then you go off and try to find someone to lead it.

That's the wrong way to start your recovery program. We started the Celebrate Recovery model with just four groups — chemically dependent men, chemically dependent women, codependent men, and codependent women. From there, I have used the following system for starting new groups.

When someone comes to me and asks why we don't have a group for "XYZ" recovery, I usually respond, "Do you have any experience/recovery in that specific area?" (This experience could be Christ-centered or secular.) And then, "Do you know of anybody that has recovery in that area?" If the response to both of those questions is no, then I ask for the person's name and phone number and keep the information on file so that we can notify the person when that group starts.

Also, we do not start a new group until we have a trained leader and coleader, trained by the leader, in place. Once we have the leaders, we run announcements for the new group in the church bulletin for two weeks. Next, we have the leader and coleader give their testimonies in our Celebrate Recovery large group time. After completing that process, the new group begins meeting.

I can't tell you the number of women who asked me if we had a group for sexual, physical, and emotional abuse. I had to say, "Not yet." It was *two years* before God sent us the right leadership team. I would rather disappoint people by not having a group when they want it than cause someone great harm by having a group without trained and qualified leaders. It was during that time of waiting that God sent me eight very brave ladies. They had all experienced sexual, physical, or emotional abuse. We met every Wednesday morning for ten weeks and rewrote the 12 Steps for women in recovery from sexual, physical, or emotional abuse. You will find them in Appendix 3. Our regular 12 Steps would not have helped individuals recovering from this issue. Today, this is one of our largest and most successful groups.

At Celebrate Recovery we do not have coed groups. Let me share with you the two main reasons:

First, we have found that the level of sharing is not as deep when men and women are in the same group. How can someone struggling with sexual addiction share in a mixed group? It is simply inappropriate for them to share in a mixed group to the level that they need to.

The second reason is to increase the level of safety for the individuals in the group.

Let me give you an example: Let's say a woman shares about how her husband mistreats her. She opens up and shares about the way that she would really like to be treated. And there is a guy in the group who is not there for all the right reasons. After the meeting he starts sharing with her how he is all the things that her husband is not. If your Celebrate Recovery is going to last and grow, it has got to be a safe place. Having same-sex groups helps keep it safe.

Allow me to offer you a suggested pathway for new group growth:

Celebrate Recovery's Suggested Pathway for Growth

Phase 1 (Less than 10 participants)

- Have your large group time together — the worship, teaching, and testimony time. Then break into accountability teams for sharing.
- Develop men's and women's accountability teams for sharing. An example: you may have three men and six women. You can have the three men form an accountability team and the six women form two accountability teams of three persons each.
- As you grow, the goal is to form two same-sex groups — ASAP!

Phase 2 (10 to 20 participants)

- Have your large group time together — the worship, teaching, and testimony time. Then break into your groups for sharing.

- Start separate men's and women's groups. You can begin to break into your recovery specific groups. Let's say that you have ten men and ten women. Five women are all dealing with codependency. You can have them break into their own issue-specific women's codependency group and have the other five women, all with different recovery issues, meet in a mixed-issues women's group. Of the ten men, let's say five are dealing with alcoholism. You can have them break into their own men's chemically dependent group and have the other five men, all with different issues, meet in a mixed-issues men's group.

Phase 3 (20 participants and above)

- Have your large group time together—the worship, teaching, and testimony time. Then break into your groups for sharing.
- Start men's and women's groups for specific addictions and compulsions.
- Suggested beginning groups:
  - Chemically dependent men's
  - Chemically dependent women's
  - Codependent men's
  - Codependent women's
- Over time, all of your other new groups can grow out of these.

Outreach

The last of the seven keys for keeping your recovery ministry healthy and growing is outreach.

Matthew 5:14–16 tells us that we are to be "the light of the world. A town built on a hill cannot be hidden. Neither do people light a lamp and put it under a bowl. Instead they put it on its stand, and it gives light to everyone in the house. In the same way, let your light shine before others, that they may see your good deeds and glorify your Father in heaven."

It's great to have Celebrate Recovery for those who attend your church. So many of our new people come into the church full of the world and all its baggage. Celebrate Recovery provides a safe place for them to begin their journey of stepping out of their denial and into God's grace, as well as helping them to start dealing with their life's hurts, hang-ups, and habits.

While just "being" here is great, it falls short of putting our lamps on a stand and letting our light shine before others.

In this key, we want to look at some of the possible areas for your Celebrate Recovery ministry to consider for outreach. You can actually model Jesus when He said, "I'm here inviting outsiders, not insiders — an invitation to a changed life, changed inside and out" (Luke 5:32, MSG).

So what are some areas of outreach for your recovery ministry to consider?

One way we have been successful is by *starting meetings at local recovery houses*. The ones we have been successful in working with use the Celebrate Recovery curriculum in their recovery houses. Our leaders volunteer to lead their weekly meetings. On Friday nights, they take vans and attend Saddleback's Celebrate Recovery meetings. (Just a note: They started just attending our Friday night Celebrate Recovery meetings, now the vans show up for church on Sunday mornings!)

Also, we have been successful in *bringing Celebrate Recovery to rescue missions*. In December 2000, the Orange County Rescue Mission asked if we could supply leaders to start the Celebrate Recovery program in their women's and men's facilities. We started Celebrate Recovery small group step studies every Wednesday evening.

At first, the residents were decidedly resistant to these "do-gooders" from Saddleback. They felt these church people had no idea about their lives and struggles. They believed that we were there to take them through "just another program." But week after week, share after share, God did His work with His program. Over time, trust and relationships were built.

Today, we have transitioned the running of the mission's Celebrate Recovery program completely over to their staff.

Another outreach opportunity is to *help other churches start recovery ministries*. There are several ways we do this. First, we go to a local church with our Celebrate Recovery band and leadership team. We spend the day giving testimonies and teaching on the third principle: "Consciously choose to commit all my life and will to Christ's care and control." This attracts church members who are already attending secular recovery programs or Christ-centered recovery programs at other churches.

Pastors have often said to me, "We don't have those kinds of problems in my church." When I hear this, I say a short, silent prayer. The truth of the matter is that every church has people in it who are struggling with hurts, hang-ups, and habits. They also have people who have had years of experience with secular 12-Step recovery programs and who could help lead this kind of ministry. They are just waiting until they know it's safe to come forward and serve.

The second way we have helped local churches is by having their leadership attend Celebrate Recovery meetings at Saddleback Church.

A third way of helping other churches is to have a "Testimonies to Go Ministry." At Saddleback, we help provide testimonies to Celebrate Recovery churches that are just getting started. The individuals serving in this Celebrate Recovery ministry will travel and share their story with a new Celebrate Recovery within a two-hour driving radius of Saddleback. This is very important because when a church is just starting the program it may have difficulty in finding two testimonies per month.

I encourage you to share your testimonies with other Celebrate Recovery churches in your area. The issues we are dealing with are much too important to be territorial over—it's a matter of life and death! We need to forget denominational affiliations and all work together!

An additional opportunity for outreach is to send out short-term mission teams. Over the years we have sent Celebrate Recovery teams to over thirty countries. The Celebrate Recovery material has been translated into twenty-three languages. Once you let the light of the Lord shine, it keeps shining.

The fourth suggestion is to *inform local Christian counselors about your program.* At Saddleback we have a list of church-approved Christian counselors and therapists who have been interviewed by two of our staff pastors. This ensures that their counseling is built on God's Word and not on the world. We work very closely with these counselors and they refer many of their clients to Celebrate Recovery.

Yet another suggestion is to *invite guest speakers.* Dr. John Townsend and Dr. Henry Cloud are regular guest speakers at the Celebrate Recovery model. When they speak, our attendance increases by 20 percent. I try to have a guest speaker once per quarter. Not only does this attract new people, it's a refreshing change for the participants of Celebrate.

The sixth outreach opportunity is to encourage your members to *attend secular recovery meetings* and share the one and only true Higher Power, Jesus Christ! We cannot wait for the unsaved to come to us. We need to get out and reach them where they are! Remember, "Let your light shine before others, that they may see your good deeds and glorify your Father in heaven" (Matthew 5:16).

We make Celebrate Recovery hats and shirts available to our participants. We ask them to wear them to their secular meetings. We encourage them to share the "Good News" when someone asks them, "What's Celebrate Recovery?" Items can be found at *www.shop.celebraterecovery.com.*

The last outreach opportunity we will discuss here is to *visit area prisons*. Isaiah 61:1 tells us, "The Spirit of the Sovereign LORD is upon me, because the LORD has appointed me to bring good news to the poor. He has sent me to comfort the brokenhearted and to announce that captives will be released and prisoners will be freed" (NLT).

That verse calls us to minister to the physical, emotional, mental, and, most importantly, spiritual needs of:

- The homeless — "Appointed me to bring good news to the poor"
- Those in crisis — "He has sent me to comfort the brokenhearted"
- The addicted — "And to announce that captives will be released"
- Those in prison — "And prisoners will be freed"

Not only do we need to start Celebrate Recovery ministries in our churches for the congregation and the community, to help those trapped by their pain and their past. But we also need to take Celebrate Recovery into the prisons.

Leticia's story is just one example of what Christ can do through Celebrate Recovery to change the life of someone in prison:

During the years of my incarceration, I attended substance abuse classes, NA and AA meetings. Even though those programs may work for others, they didn't work for me. Finally, I began attending Celebrate Recovery.

The principles used and brought to light through the Scriptures opened my heart and mind and got me on my way to "real" recovery. I say real because it opened my mind to change and gave me hope. The Scriptures and principles showed me that I still needed to admit that I was still in denial about many things, but at the same time the Word gave me courage to "accept the things I cannot change," but to use that time in prison to change the things I can.

Upon my release, I continued applying the principles to life and of course continued reading the Scriptures. They have both helped me to maintain a drug-free life, which in turn helped me obtain employment and become a productive member of society again.

I believe that the forgiveness lesson impacted my life most of all. I finally forgave myself and asked forgiveness from those I had injured during my addiction.

It is my opinion that Celebrate Recovery should be made available in all correctional facilities; not only for the residents, but the staff also. We all have issues, whether we are behind bars or imprisoned in our minds and hearts. Celebrate Recovery and the Word of God will definitely help.

A unique advantage of the Celebrate Recovery program for prisons is that while the inmate is getting recovery inside, the family can get recovery and support from a church in their area that has the Celebrate Recovery program. Also, when the individual is released, he or she can make an immediate connection with and receive support from a local Celebrate Recovery church.

That's the power of Jesus Christ — that's outreach!

Meeting Formats and Materials

This section will provide you with the "nuts and bolts" of starting and running the three types of Celebrate Recovery meetings.

One-Year Large Group Teaching Schedule and Curriculum Plan

First, we will look at the one-year large group teaching schedule and curriculum plan. This plan is designed to cover the twenty-five lessons in the four Celebrate Recovery participant's guides — all of the eight principles and 12 Steps — over a one-year period. A lesson is taught one week and then supported by a testimony or other special service the following week.[5] This schedule is repeated annually.

Participant's Guide 1: *Stepping Out of Denial into God's Grace*

Week	Principle	Large Group Teaching
1		Introduction of Program
2	1	Lesson 1: Denial
3	1	Testimony
4	1	Lesson 2: Powerless
5	1	Testimony
6	2	Lesson 3: Hope
7	2	Testimony
8	2	Special music or outside speaker
9	2	Lesson 4: Sanity
10	2	Testimony
11	3	Lesson 5: Turn
12	3	Testimony
13	3	Lesson 6: Action
14	3	Communion

5. Several testimonies are included in this leader's guide. Use them as examples to guide you as you choose members from your own group to share their stories.

Participant's Guide 2: *Taking an Honest and Spiritual Inventory*

Week	Principle	Large Group Teaching
15	4	Lesson 7: Sponsor
16	4	Testimony
17	4	Lesson 8: Moral
18	4	Testimony
19	4	Lesson 9: Inventory
20	4	Testimony
21	4	Special Music or Outside Speaker
22	4	Lesson 10: Spiritual Inventory (Part 1)
23	4	Testimony
24	4	Lesson 11: Spiritual Inventory (Part 2)

Participant's Guide 3: *Getting Right with God, Yourself, and Others*

Week	Principle	Large Group Teaching
25	4	Lesson 12: Confess
26	4	Testimony
27	4	Lesson 13: Admit
28	4	Testimony
29	5	Lesson 14: Ready
30	5	Testimony
31	5	Lesson 15: Victory
32	5	Testimony
33	6	Lesson 16: Amends
34	6	Testimony
35	6	Lesson 17: Forgiveness
36	6	Testimony
37	6	Lesson 18: Grace
38	6	Testimony
39	6	Special Music and Communion

Participant's Guide 4: *Growing in Christ While Helping Others*

Week	Principle	Large Group Teaching
40	7	Lesson 19: Crossroads
41	7	Testimony
42	7	Lesson 20: Daily Inventory
43	7	Testimony

Since individuals will join the program at different times throughout the year, you need to caution them against trying to catch up with the teaching. For example: If a newcomer enters the program during week 35, when you are teaching on Principle 6, he or she should still begin in Participant's Guide 1, *Stepping Out of Denial into God's Grace*, working on Principle 1. Newcomers need to understand that this is an ongoing program and that they need to work through the principles and join a new step study group. What they are learning in the large group teaching time will be extremely valuable to them when they get to each particular principle. In addition, they should be encouraged to get a sponsor and/or accountability partner as soon as possible.

1. Large Group Meeting Format: Worship and Teaching Time

The large group worship and teaching time at Celebrate Recovery is designed to enable those attending to set aside the busyness and the stresses of the outside world by participating in a twenty-minute time of prayer, praise, and worship. It also includes a time for teaching a lesson from the *Celebrate Recovery Leader's Guide* or a testimony. This time begins to unfold the "safe" environment that is essential to any recovery program. It allows all those present to get in touch with the one and only Higher Power, Jesus Christ.

"Praise the LORD. Praise God in his sanctuary; praise him in his mighty heavens. Praise him for his acts of power; praise him for his surpassing greatness. Praise him with the sounding of the trumpet, praise him with the harp and lyre, praise him with timbrel and dancing, praise him with the strings and pipe, praise him with the clash of cymbals, praise him with resounding cymbals. Let everything that has breath praise the LORD. Praise the LORD." (Psalm 150:1–6)

During the large group time everyone meets together; all the men and women combined.

Following is the agenda for Celebrate Recovery's large group worship and teaching time:

6:30 p.m.	Doors open — greeters in place
7:00 p.m.	Opening song
	Welcome and opening prayer
7:05 p.m.	Song #2
	Song #3
	Song #4
7:20 p.m.	Reading of the eight principles and their corresponding Beatitudes or the 12 Steps and their biblical comparisons
7:25 p.m.	Announcements (Celebrate Recovery news)
7:30 p.m.	Special music
7:35 p.m.	Teaching or testimony
7:55 p.m.	Serenity prayer
	Closing song
8:00 p.m.	Dismissal to small groups

Greeters

Greeters are extremely important both in making a positive first impression on all newcomers and in encouraging regular attendees. In addition to greeting, they also hand out the Celebrate Recovery bulletin for the evening.

The Celebrate Recovery Bulletin

The Celebrate Recovery bulletin contains the following information:

Song sheet (unless words are projected on screen)
Small group meeting room assignments
Solid Rock Cafe/Bar-B-Que information sheets
Small group meeting guidelines
Eight recovery principles
Twelve steps and their biblical comparisons
List of all the open share groups that are meeting that night
List of the open step study small groups that meet during the week
Announcements of upcoming special events
Prayer request sheets

A sample bulletin (jacket and inside pages) as well as examples of some of the above elements can be found in Appendix 4.

Opening Song, Welcome, and Prayer

We attempt to begin each week promptly at 7:00 p.m., and end by 8:00 p.m. This will ensure that you have a full hour for the small group meetings. Choose an opening praise song that is very upbeat and familiar. After the song, someone on the leadership team welcomes everyone, especially newcomers, then prays the opening prayer.

Set of Three Songs

The music continues with songs chosen to go along with the particular principle the group will be working on that evening.

Some examples would be:

Principle 1: "The Power of Your Love"
Principle 2: "I Have a Hope"
Principle 3: "The Potter's Hand"
Principle 4: "Fear Not," "White as Snow"
Principle 5: "Great Redeemer," "Change My Heart, O God"
Principle 6: "God Can Make It Right," "Healing Grace"
Principle 7: "Everyday," "More of You in My Life"
Principle 8: "The Road to Recovery"

This praise and worship time is extremely important!

Reading of the Eight Principles and Their Corresponding Beatitude or the Twelve Steps and Their Biblical Comparisons

Two individuals are selected to read the eight principles or the 12 Steps and their biblical comparisons. The purpose is twofold: (1) to reinforce the biblical foundation for the program, and (2) to allow increased participation for Celebrate Recovery attendees.

One person is asked to read the principle/step and another reads the Bible verse for that principle/step until all eight principles/12 Steps are completed. Example:

First reader: "Principle 1: Realize I'm not God. I admit that I am powerless to control my tendency to do the wrong thing and that my life is unmanageable."

Second reader: "Happy are those who know they are spiritually poor." (Matthew 5:3, GNT)

The opportunity to read is used to reward regular attendees and encourage prospective new coleaders.

Announcements

The purpose of the announcements is to help the newcomers feel welcome and inform them about the special group for newcomers where they can get their questions answered—Newcomers 101. While an important part of the program, announcements can be rather "dry," so we attempt to make them light and fun. The remainder of the time is used to announce upcoming events and introduce the "special music" for the evening.

Special Music

Special music supports the teaching or the testimony for the evening. It is usually a solo performed by one of the Celebrate Recovery singers. In the past we brought outside singers from other groups in the church, but we have found that the group really enjoys supporting "one of their own."

Also, during the special music selection, a collection, or "love offering," can be taken. The money collected could be used to support child care, to pay for special speakers, and to offset regular expenses.

Teaching or Testimony

As mentioned previously, we teach the twenty-five lessons from the *Celebrate Recovery Leader's Guide*. Typically, we follow a teaching week with a testimony week, which supports the teaching of the previous lesson. Appendix 5 is a guide to help you generate healthy testimonies.

Serenity Prayer, Closing Song, and Dismissal to Small Groups

The large group meeting ends with one of the leaders leading the group in the reading of the complete version of Reinhold Neibuhr's Serenity Prayer. The prayer is printed on the inside cover of the bulletin jacket. Then we sing the closing song and everyone is encouraged to quickly go to their small group meetings located throughout the church campus. Meeting locations are also noted in the bulletin. If people have questions, they can stop by the Celebrate Recovery information table or ask one of the Celebrate Recovery leaders. The leaders are easy to spot because they wear a Celebrate Recovery leader's shirt.

Celebrate Recovery's Small Group Formats

2. Open Share Small Group

These small groups meet immediately after the large group concludes. There are separate groups for men and women.

Format

8:00 p.m.	Opening prayer and welcome
	Introductions
	Reading of Celebrate Recovery's small group meeting guidelines
8:05 p.m.	Leader's focus on the principle
8:10 p.m.	Group open sharing
8:50 p.m.	Wrap-up, prayer requests, closing prayer
9:00 p.m.	Invitation to the Solid Rock Cafe

Opening Prayer, Welcome, and Introductions

This time allows the small group to again focus their attention to the Lord and to feel the bond of their small group. It is also another opportunity to softly welcome newcomers.

Reading of Celebrate Recovery's Small Group Meeting Guidelines

Read at every small group meeting, these five simple rules (see box) are designed to keep the group *safe!* If your recovery meetings are not safe, they will fail! It is the responsibility of the group leader and coleader to ensure that these guidelines are followed. To reinforce their importance, the guidelines are also read every four to six weeks during the large group time.

Small Group Guidelines

READ AT EVERY SMALL GROUP MEETING. These five simple rules are designed to keep the group safe! If your recovery meetings are not safe, they will fail! It is the responsibility of the group leader and coleader to ensure that these guidelines are followed. To reinforce their importance, the guidelines are also read every four to six weeks during the large group time.

1. **Keep your sharing focused on your own thoughts and feelings. Limit your sharing to three to five minutes.**

This is a very important guideline. Focusing on one's own thoughts and feelings will keep sharing short, eliminate cross talk, and keep the person sharing from "wandering" to other people's problems or non-group related topics. Please be strict about the three-to-five-minute rule. It is very frustrating for others in the group to miss an opportunity to share because someone else spoke for ten minutes or more. Come up with a signal, if necessary, and announce it at the start of the group. If anyone goes over his or her time, give the "signal" to stop, so no one feels singled out.

2. **There is NO cross talk. Cross talk is when two individuals engage in conversation excluding all others. Each person is free to express his or her feelings without interruptions.**

   Cross talk can also be identified as someone saying, "I can relate to you because . . ." or "I can't relate to you because . . ." comments, asking questions, and so on. We don't have to be legalistic about it, but we must be very careful not to offend anyone. If this guideline is abused, someone may get very hurt and give up on recovery altogether.

3. **We are here to support one another, not "fix" another.**

   We all have wonderful intentions and want to share the wisdom we have gained from being in this awesome program. Many times, however, a person is not in the proper emotional state to hear or understand. The members of your group are going to look to you to protect them and enforce this guideline. Fixing can be described as offering advice to solve a problem someone has shared, offering a Scripture, offering book referrals, or offering counselor referrals.

4. **Anonymity and confidentiality are basic requirements. What is shared in the group stays in the group. The only exception is when people threaten to injure themselves or others.**

   It can be very hurtful to discover that someone's sharing is being discussed outside of the small group time. Most of the people in recovery have never been able to "tell the secret"—they need to be assured that this is the safe place to do it. When making phone calls to members of your group, you must be careful about protecting anonymity when leaving phone messages.

5. **Offensive language has no place in a Christ-centered recovery group.**

   Because many of us grew up hearing and/or using offensive language, this can be a painful trigger to members of our group.

> *NOTE:*
> - *The above explanation of each guideline is given for your understanding. Only the guidelines themselves (bold type) are read in the small group.*
> - *Read the guidelines at every single meeting no matter how long you have been together!*
> - *Continue to read the guidelines even if you have been together six months or a year. In fact, the guidelines become even more important if your group is extremely bonded.*
>
> **Thank your group in advance for honoring these guidelines.**
>
> As your group matures, it is not necessary to elaborate on each guideline; however, if one particular area starts to be a problem, address it at the next meeting by reemphasizing that particular guideline. This might be all it will take to refocus the group. If it continues to be a problem with one particular person, address it with him or her individually.

Leader's Focus on the Principle

The leader spends just a few minutes going over the key points from the evening's lesson, then asks the group to start their sharing about one or two of the questions provided from the lesson's exercise. For example, if the teaching was on lesson one, the leader could ask the group the question from Principle 1 of the *Stepping Out of Denial into God's Grace* Participant's Guide: "What areas of your life do you have power (control) over?"

If there was a testimony that evening, the leader could ask the group to focus on what part of the testimony touched them the most.

Group Discussion and Open Sharing

The participant can choose to share on the focus question or just share whatever is on his or her heart.

Wrap-Up, Prayer Requests, Closing Prayer

Wrapping up the session is the leader's responsibility. It is up to him or her to see that the group has enough time for closure—that the meeting does not just come to an abrupt halt or go on and on and on. Before the session ends, there should also be a time for participants to give specific prayer requests and for the group to close in prayer. If there were any major issues raised in the group, the leader should be sure to get the individual's name for follow-up.

Invitation to the Solid Rock Cafe

The meeting can now continue "unofficially" at the Solid Rock Cafe, a place designed specifically for fellowship. At the cafe, individuals have an opportunity to continue to share with those with whom they feel safe. It is a time for participants to develop accountability partners and sponsorship relationships.

3. Step Study Small Groups

The step study groups are the second type of Celebrate Recovery small groups. They meet a different night of the week from the large group and open share groups meeting. The step study groups actually go through the four Celebrate Recovery participant's guides together. They answer and discuss the questions at the end of each lesson together. They close the group (i.e., no new participants) after they have completed the lessons on the third principle. Step study groups meet together for approximately twelve months. There are separate groups for men and women.

We need to encourage our members to get into a step study group, because this is where they get into the heart of the program and true healing from their lives' hurts, hang-ups, and habits occurs. It is from these groups that your new leaders are born.

Format

7:00 p.m.	Opening prayer and welcome
	Introductions
	Serenity Prayer
	Reading of the eight principles and/or the 12 Steps and their biblical comparisons
	Reading of Celebrate Recovery's small group meeting guidelines
	Leader's focus on the principle or topic
7:15 p.m.	Group discussion of that night's lesson from the participant's guide. Go around the group and let all members have a chance to share their answer to each question. Depending on the size of the step study, it may take two weeks to cover one lesson.
8:50 p.m.	Wrap-up, prayer requests, closing prayer
9:00 p.m.	Closing

The following illustration will help you see the components of each of the three types of Celebrate Recovery groups: large group, open share small group, and the step study small group.

Large Group
- Worship
- Read the steps or principles
- Announcements
- Teach lesson from the *Celebrate Recovery Leader's Guide* or have a testimony
- Serenity Prayer
- No obligation to share
- Mixed group
- Dismiss to open share groups or Newcomers 101
- Information table

Open Share Group
- Recovery issue specific
- Follows large group
- Gender specific
- One-hour meeting
- Share struggles and victories
- Acknowledge sobriety (chips)
- Open to newcomers
- Find a sponsor
- Follow the five small group guidelines

Step Study Group
- Use *Celebrate Recovery* participant's guides
- Answer and discuss questions at the end of each lesson of the guides
- Two-hour meeting
- Mixed recovery OR recovery issue specific
- High level of accountability
- Weekly attendance expected
- Follow the five small group guidelines
- Gender specific

The Celebrate Recovery "Growth Funnel" will help you visualize how the large group meeting ties into the program's two types of small groups: open share small groups and step study small groups. With Jesus Christ as "The Higher Power," this is a winning combination for a "changed life."

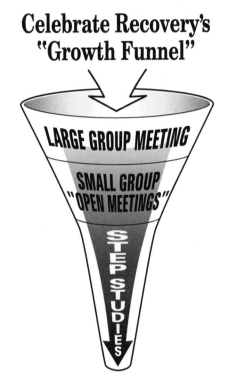

Celebrate Recovery's "Growth Funnel"

LARGE GROUP MEETING

SMALL GROUP "OPEN MEETINGS"

STEP STUDIES

Jesus Christ "The Higher Power" = "a changed life"

Newcomers 101

> *"Praise be to the God and Father of our Lord Jesus Christ, the Father of compassion and the God of all comfort, who comforts us in all our troubles, so that we can comfort those in any trouble with the comfort we ourselves receive from God." (2 Corinthians 1:3–4)*

It is essential to remember that when a person comes to Celebrate Recovery for the first time, he may be overwhelmed with feelings of pain, humiliation, sadness, and hopelessness. The whole concept of recovery may be unfamiliar and a little frightening. Selecting and identifying with an open share group may seem to be an impossible task.

With the newcomers' feelings in mind, the most important thing to remember about leading Newcomers 101 is to project a friendly, open, approachable demeanor. Also, by wearing a Celebrate Recovery leader's shirt, you identify yourself as someone who "has worked the program" and achieved credibility with your church.

In keeping with the format of the regular meeting night of Celebrate Recovery, the Newcomers 101 group will be divided into two parts: a large group meeting and an open share group. **It is imperative to go through the large group time as quickly as possible, twenty minutes at most, in order to move to the open share group time that is so important for the newcomer. The purpose of this sharing time is to help the participant choose the group to attend next week.**

An audiovisual presentation is advisable so the participants can follow along. A welcome slide would be appropriate as the newcomers enter the room.

1. Distribute Solid Rock Coupons

Begin walking around the room and greeting the men and women who are new to the program. Pass out Solid Rock coupons, the coffee time hosted after the meetings, or coupons for the meal your program provides before the meeting. This allows you to connect and "break the ice." Mention that these fellowship events are great opportunities to meet others in the program.

During this time, if there are other leaders present, do not stand in groups talking to one another! Move around, smile, and look approachable. Give the impression that you are looking forward to Newcomers 101. And you are! What a wonderful opportunity to share what Jesus has done in your life!

2. Open in Prayer

Wait until all of the newcomers are settled and then open in prayer. Keep the prayer upbeat. We want to give hope and victory!

3. Welcome Participants; Show a Newcomers' Video

We strongly suggest that your program develop its own newcomers' video. This video should show leaders from different areas of recovery talking about the changes the program has made in their lives. If your senior pastor is willing to be a part of the video, the newcomers know, right from the start, that your program has senior pastor support.

Until you are able to create your own newcomers' video, Saddleback's newcomers' video, called "Words" is available through *www.saddlebackresources.com.*

4. Introduce the Leaders

Leaders can rotate into Newcomers 101 so that they may continue to attend their own meetings. However, they must have strong coleaders to run the groups in their absence. Or leaders may choose to attend Newcomers 101 because their meetings are on another night of the week.

In order to get through all of the information needing to be covered during the large group part of the evening, the introductions need to be very concise—one to two minutes maximum. The emphasis should focus on the important difference between Celebrate Recovery and a secular program: that we believe in the one and only true Higher Power, Jesus Christ. We also want to make it clear that our lives have changed as a result of this program.

An example of an introduction for this group is: "Hi, my name is _____ and I'm a believer who struggles with codependency. After attending this program, my marriage was reconciled, and I love to give back to this ministry." In this example, newcomers learn the name of the leader; that she is a Christian who struggles with codependency; and that she feels she has changed enough to give back to the program. The underlying message is upbeat and gives hope to newcomers.

These introductions help the newcomers to relax, without the fear of having to speak in front of the entire group while also being able to relate to the leaders.

5. Very Briefly State the Goal of Newcomers 101

Summarize briefly the goal of Newcomers 101. For example, you might say, "The goal of Newcomers 101 is to explain how Celebrate Recovery works and to help you find a group to attend next week. The Newcomers group is a one-time attendance group only."

Explain that the large group will be divided into a men's group and a women's group during the second half of the evening—just like the open share groups that are meeting throughout the church.

Again, we want to help the newcomers feel comfortable in our program. So for that evening only, you can explain that questions will be welcomed after the open share group sharing. However, questions are not a part of the regular open share groups.

6. Announce Time and Place for Celebration Station and The Landing

Announcing the provision of programs for elementary school, junior high, and high school students emphasizes that the entire family can find healing in one program. This will open up your Celebrate Recovery to more people.

7. Explain the Different Components of the Program

Very briefly mention that the tools of Celebrate Recovery are the *Celebrate Recovery Bible*, the four participant's guides, and the *Celebrate Recovery Journal*. *Life's Healing Choices* is the recommended book to better understand the eight recovery principles and be encouraged by the sixteen great testimonies. (PowerPoint slides showing these tools are recommended for familiarity.)

Although the step study groups are an important part of Celebrate Recovery, it might be too confusing to explain at this point. A long explanation about sponsors and accountability partners might also take up too much time. A question time has been provided at the end of the open share group. If time permits, at the end of this group, information about the step study groups, accountability partners, and sponsors could be covered.

In conclusion, finish with a quick review: "The dinner or Bar-B-Que meets at 6:00 p.m., at 7:00 we meet for our large group time, and at 8:00 we break up into our smaller open share groups. After our groups, at 9:00, we go to Solid Rock Cafe for coffee and dessert. At the dinner and coffee, you can make new friends and start to form accountability partners and sponsors which you will learn about in our large group meetings."

8. Next Read the Five Small Group Guidelines

Mention that these guidelines are to protect the participants of Celebrate Recovery and to provide a safe place for sharing. (Refer to page 54.)

1. Keep your sharing focused on your own thoughts and feelings. Limit your sharing to three to five minutes.
2. There is no cross talk. Cross talk is when two individuals engage in conversation excluding all others. Each person is free to express their feelings without interruptions. (Tell these newcomers that for tonight only, we will be breaking the cross talking guideline when we accept questions at the end of the sharing. At future meetings, this guideline will be obeyed. Otherwise, we will abide by the rest of the guidelines.)
3. We are here to support one another. We are not here to "fix" another.

4. Anonymity and confidentiality are basic requirements. What is shared in the group stays in the group. The only exception is when someone threatens to injure themselves or others.
5. Offensive language and graphic descriptions have no place in a Christ-centered recovery group.

9. Divide into Men's and Women's Groups

Couples who have come together might be uncomfortable splitting up. Gently explain that this division makes the program a safe place for people to share.

Tell the open share group that you will be abiding by the five small group guidelines. Let newcomers know your signal for "wrapping up" their sharing.

Encourage newcomers to give their name, to name a specific recovery group if they can identify with one already, or to say what brought them to Celebrate Recovery for the first time.

Give them the opportunity to pass if they are not ready to share.

Explain some of the basics: "We say 'Hi' and the person's name after they have introduced themselves in order to get better acquainted, and we clap as an affirmation after someone has shared."

After the group has completed their sharing, open up for questions, again emphasizing that this will not happen in their regular open share groups. If there are no questions, and time permits, you can explain accountability partners, sponsors, and/or step studies.

Encourage attendance for several weeks before deciding to try a different group. It may be that the regular attenders have been absent, or because of denial, the group may feel uncomfortable. If, after several weeks, the group still feels uncomfortable, suggest trying another group. Leaders will not be offended.

If there is any time remaining, you might encourage the group to talk informally. They might want to walk to the Solid Rock Cafe together or arrange to return together to Celebrate Recovery the following week.

Those who decided to pass in their sharing can meet with the leader one-on-one while the rest of the group talks informally. However, if persons do not want to share, we need to let them know that we understand how difficult it is to share for the first time. Encourage them to go to the open share group the following week, emphasizing that they are not required to share until they are ready.

10. Close in Prayer

11. Remind Them of Your Availability

Let the group know that you are always available to answer any questions they may have in the future.

The Information Table and Materials

The information table is a key part of helping the newcomer feel welcome. The location of the information table is very important. After the newcomer has been greeted, the information table should be their next experience. They do not have to go to it upon their arrival, but it is important that they know its location.

The table should be staffed by at least one man and one woman. We do this to be sensitive to those in attendance. A woman with abuse issues, for example, would find it difficult to seek information from a man. Also, it is important to have an information table leader who is responsible for staffing the table, maintaining fresh handouts, and for administrating curriculum and Bible sales.

Handouts should be colorful and have some uniformity. The following are some examples of the handouts we use at the information table at Saddleback:

Welcome Newcomers (Appendix 6)
8 Recovery Principles Based on the Beatitudes
Celebrate Recovery's 12 Steps and their biblical comparisons
12 Steps for Sexual, Physical, and Emotional Abuse (Appendix 3)
Things We Are, Things We Are Not (Appendix 7)
Codependency Description (Appendix 8)
Chemical Addiction Description (Appendix 9)
Freedom from Anger
Sexual Addiction Men's Group

How This Leader's Guide Is Organized

As stated earlier, this leader's guide is designed to cover the twenty-five lessons found in the four *Celebrate Recovery* participant's guides—all of the eight principles. Each lesson has been written so that you can either read it in its entirety or "cut and paste" in your own illustrations. Just follow the basic format. Be sure to include the recovery acrostic and Bible verses for each lesson. May God bless you and your ministry as you lead others on their road to recovery.

PRINCIPLE 1

Realize I'm not God. I admit that I am powerless to control my tendency to do the wrong thing and that my life is unmanageable.

"Happy are those who know they are spiritually poor." (Matthew 5:3)

DENIAL

Principle 1: Realize I'm not God. I admit that I am powerless to control my tendency to do the wrong thing and that my life is unmanageable.

"Happy are those who know they are spiritually poor." (Matthew 5:3)

Step 1: We admitted we were powerless over our addictions and compulsive behaviors, that our lives had become unmanageable.

"For I know that good itself does not dwell in me, that is, in my sinful nature. For I have the desire to do what is good, but I cannot carry it out." (Romans 7:18)

Introduction

Tonight we begin a journey together, a journey on the road of recovery. This journey begins with Principle 1, where we admit that we are powerless to control our tendency to do the wrong thing and that our lives have become unmanageable, out of control. But before we begin this exciting journey together, we need to ask ourselves two questions:

- Am I going to let my past failures prevent me from taking this journey?
- Am I afraid to change? Or, what are my fears of the future?

Failures from the Past

Let's look at Hebrews 12:1 (TLB):

Since we have such a huge crowd of men of faith watching us from the grandstands, let us strip off anything that slows us down or holds us back, and especially those sins that wrap themselves so tightly around our feet and trip us up; and let us run with patience the particular race that God has set before us.

There are two things I would like to point out in this verse. First, God has a particular race, a unique plan, for each of us. A plan for good, not a life full of dependencies, addictions, and obsessions.

The second thing is that *we need to be willing* to get rid of all the unnecessary baggage, the past failures, in our lives that keep us stuck. Again, it says, "Let us strip off anything that slows us down or holds us back, and especially those sins that wrap themselves so tightly around our feet and trip us up."

For many of us, our past hurts, hang-ups, and habits hold us back, trip us up! Many of us are stuck in bitterness over what someone has done to us. We continue to hold on to the hurt and we refuse to forgive the ones who had hurt us.

You may have been hurt deeply. Perhaps you were abused as a child, or maybe you were or are in a marriage where your spouse committed adultery.

I want you to know that I hurt for you. I'm truly sorry for you, sorry that you had to go through that hurt. But holding on to that hurt and not being willing to forgive the person who hurt you in the past is allowing them to continue to hurt you today, in the present.

Working this Christ-centered recovery program will, with God's power, allow you to find the courage and strength to forgive them. Now don't get all stressed out. You don't have to forgive them tonight! But as you travel your road to recovery, God will help you find the willingness to forgive them and be free of their hold on your life.

Some of you are bound by guilt. You keep beating yourself up over some past failure. You're trapped, stuck in your guilt. You think that no one anywhere is as bad as you are, that no one could love the *real* you, and that no one could ever forgive you for the terrible things that you have done.

You're wrong. God can. That's why Jesus went to the cross, for our sins. He knows everything you've ever done and everything you've ever experienced. And there are many here tonight that have faced similar failures and hurts in their life and have accepted Christ's forgiveness. They are here to encourage and support you.

The apostle Paul had a lot to regret about his past. He even participated in Stephen's murder. Yet in Philippians 3:13 (TLB) he tells us, "No, dear brothers, I am still not all I should be but I am bringing all my energies to bear on this one thing: Forgetting the past and looking forward to what lies ahead."

Here's the bottom line if you want to be free from your past hurts, hang-ups, and habits: You need to deal with your past bitterness and guilt once and for all. You need to do as Isaiah 43:18 tells us, "Forget the former things; do not dwell on the past." That doesn't mean *ignore* the past. You need to *learn* from your past, offer forgiveness, make amends, and then release it. Only then can you be free from your guilt, grudges, and grief!

Let's face it, we have all stumbled over a hurt, hang-up, or habit. But the race isn't over yet. God isn't interested in how we started, but how we finish the race.

Fears for the Future

You may worry about your future and be afraid to change. We all worry about things that we do not have any control over and do not have the power to change. And we all know worrying is a lack of trust in God.

The truth is, we can say without any doubt or fear, "The Lord is my Helper and I am not afraid of anything that mere man can do to me" (Hebrews 13:6, TLB).

You may have been in your hurt, habit, or hang-up for so long that it has become your identity. You may be thinking, "What will happen if I really give recovery a chance? Will I change? If I give up my old hurts, hang-ups, and habits, what will I become? Who will I be?"

You may have been abusing alcohol, prescription drugs, or food. You're afraid of what you will do without your substance of choice.

You may have been enabling someone in a dysfunctional relationship for years. Perhaps you wonder, "What if I change and my alcoholic husband gets mad at me?"

God doesn't want you to stay frozen in an unhealthy relationship or a bad habit. He wants you to do your part in becoming healthy.

Even if our past was extremely painful, however, we may still resist change and the freedom that can be found in really working this program. Because of our fear of the unknown or because of our despair, we just close our minds because we think that we don't deserve any better.

As you work the principles and steps, remember 1 John 4:18 (NCV): "Where God's love is, there is no fear, because God's perfect love drives out fear."

You are not here by mistake tonight. This room is full of changed lives. It is my prayer for each of you that you will not let your past failures or your fear of your future stop you from giving Celebrate Recovery a real try.

Are you wearing a mask of denial tonight? Before you can make any progress in your recovery, you need to face your denial. As soon as you remove your mask, your recovery begins—or begins again! It doesn't matter if you're new in recovery or have been in recovery, working the steps for years. Denial can rear its ugly head and return at any time! You may trade addictions or get into a new relationship that's unhealthy for you in a different way than the previous one. So this lesson is for all of us.

We have a saying around here: "Denial isn't just a river in Egypt." But what is it?

What Is Denial?

Denial has been defined as "a false system of beliefs that are not based on reality" and "a self-protecting behavior that keeps us from honestly facing the truth."

As kids we all learned various coping skills. They came in handy when we didn't get the attention we wanted from our parents and others or to block our pain and our fears.

For a time these coping systems worked. But as the years progressed they confused and clouded our view of the truth of our lives.

As we grew, our perception of ourselves and our expectations of all those around us also grew. But because we retained our childish methods of coping, our perceptions of reality became increasingly more unrealistic and distorted.

Our coping skills grew into denial, and most of our relationships ended up broken or less fulfilling than they could have been.

Did you ever deny that your parents had problems? Did you ever deny that you had problems? The truth is, we can all answer yes to these questions to some extent. But, for some of us, that denial turned to shame and guilt.

Denial is the "pink elephant" sitting in the middle of the living room. No one in the family talks about it or acknowledges it in any way. Do any of the following comments sound familiar to you?

- "Can't we stop talking about it? Talking only makes it worse."
- "Billy, if we *don't* talk about it, it will go away."
- "Honey, let's pretend that it didn't really happen."
- "If I tell her that it hurts me when she says that, I'm afraid she will leave me."
- "He really doesn't drink that much."
- "It really doesn't hurt when he does that; I'm fine!"
- "Paul drinks more than I do."
- "Joan has been married three times; I've only been married twice."
- "I eat because you make me so mad!"
- "If you didn't nag me all the time, I wouldn't . . ."

- "Look honey, I have a tough job; I work hard. I need a few drinks to relax. It doesn't mean that I have a problem."

Folks, that's DENIAL.

As I said earlier, before we can take the first step of our recovery, we must first face and admit our denial. God says in Jeremiah 6:14 (TLB), "You can't heal a wound by saying it's not there!"

Effects of Denial

Okay, let's look at tonight's acrostic:

DENIAL
Disables our feelings
Energy lost
Negates growth
Isolates us from God
Alienates us from our relationships
Lengthens the pain

The *D* in denial stands for DISABLES our feelings. Hiding our feelings, living in denial, freezes our emotions and binds us. Understanding and feeling our feelings is where we find freedom.

Second Peter 2:19 (GNT) tells us: "They promise them freedom, while they themselves are slaves of destructive habits—for we are slaves of anything that has conquered us."

For me, the basic test of freedom is not what I'm free to do, it's what I'm free not to do! I'm free not to take that drink.

We find freedom to feel our true feelings when we find Christ and step out of denial.

The next letter in denial is *E*, which stands for ENERGY lost.

A major side-effect of denial is anxiety. Anxiety causes us to waste precious energy dealing with past hurts and failures and the fear of the future. As you go though this program you will learn that it is only in the present that positive change can occur. Worrying about the past and dreading the future make us unable to live and enjoy God's plans for us in the present.

We let our fears and our worries paralyze us, but the only lasting way we can be free from them is by giving them to God. Psalm 146:7 (TLB) says, "He frees the prisoners, . . . he lifts the burdens from those bent down beneath their loads."

If you will transfer the energy required to maintain your denial into learning God's truth, a healthy love for others and yourself will occur. As you depend more and more on your Higher Power, Jesus Christ, you will see the light of truth and reality.

Let's move on to the *N* in denial.

Denial NEGATES growth.

We are as sick as our secrets and, again, we cannot grow in recovery until we are ready to step out of our denial into the truth. God is waiting to take your hand and bring you out. The Bible says, "They cried to the Lord in their troubles, and he rescued them! He led them from the darkness and shadow of death and snapped their chains" (Psalm 107:13–14, TLB).

As you travel the road of your recovery you will come to understand that God never wastes a hurt; God will never waste your darkness. But He can't use it unless you step out of your denial into the light of His truth.

Denial also ISOLATES us from God.

Adam and Eve are a great example of how secrets and denial separate us from true fellowship with God. After they sinned, their secret separated them from God. Genesis 3:7 tells us that Adam and Eve hid from God because they felt naked and ashamed.

Of course, good old Adam tried to rationalize. He said to God, "The woman you put here with me — she gave me some fruit from the tree" (Genesis 3:12). First he tried to blame God, saying, "The woman you put here with me ..." Then he tried to blame it on Eve: "*She* gave me some fruit."

Remember, God's light shines on the truth. Our denial keeps us in the dark. "God is light; in him there is no darkness at all. If we claim to have fellowship with him and yet walk in the darkness, we lie and do not live out the truth. But if we walk in the light, as he is in the light, we have fellowship with one another, and the blood of Jesus, his Son, purifies us from all sin" (1 John 1:5–7).

Our denial not only isolates us from God, it ALIENATES us from our relationships.

Denial tells us we are getting away with it. We think no one knows, but they do. But while denial may shield us from the hurt, it also keeps us from helping ourselves or the people we love the most. We don't dare reveal our true selves to others for fear of what they will think or say if they knew the real us. We must protect ourselves — our secrets — at any cost. So we isolate ourselves and thereby minimize the risk of exposure and possible rejection from others. But at what price? The eventual loss of all our important relationships.

What's the answer? Listen to Ephesians 4:25 (TLB). "Stop lying to each other; tell the truth, for we are parts of each other and when we lie to each other we are hurting ourselves."

Remember it is always better to tell the ugly truth rather than a beautiful lie. Finally, denial LENGTHENS the pain.

We have the false belief that denial protects us from our pain. In reality, denial allows our pain to fester and grow and to turn into shame and guilt. Denial extends your hurt. It multiplies your problems.

Truth, like surgery, may hurt for a while, but it cures. God promises us in Jeremiah 30:17 (TLB), "I will give you back your health again and heal your wounds."

Wrap-Up

Tonight I encourage you to *step out* of your denial! Walking out of your denial is not easy. Taking off that mask is hard. Everything about you shouts, "Don't do it! It's not safe!" But it is safe. It's safe at Celebrate Recovery. Here you have people who care about you and who love you for who you are — people who will stand beside you as truth becomes a way of life.

Jesus tells us, "Know the truth, and the truth will set you free" (John 8:32). Step out of your denial so you can step into Jesus' unconditional love and grace and begin your healing journey of recovery.

POWERLESS

———— ⌒ ————

Principle 1: Realize I'm not God. I admit that I am powerless to control my tendency to do the wrong thing and that my life is unmanageable.

"Happy are those who know they are spiritually poor." (Matthew 5:3)

Step 1: We admitted we were powerless over our addictions and compulsive behaviors, that our lives had become unmanageable.

"For I know that good itself does not dwell in me, that is, in my sinful nature. For I have the desire to do what is good, but I cannot carry it out." (Romans 7:18)

———— ⌒ ————

Introduction

In Principle 1, we realize we're not God. We admit we are powerless to control our tendency to do the wrong thing and that our lives have become unmanageable. As soon as we take this step and admit that we are powerless, we start to change. We see that our old ways of trying to control our hurts, hang-ups, and habits didn't work. They were buried by our denial and held on to with our false power.

Tonight we are going to focus on four actions: two things we have to *stop* doing and two things we need to *start* doing in our recoveries. We need to take these four actions to complete Principle 1.

Four Actions

In Lesson 1 we talked about the first action we need to take.

1. Stop denying the pain.

We said that our denial had at least six negative effects: It disables our feelings, wastes our energy, negates our growth, isolates us from God, alienates us from our relationships, and lengthens our pain.

You are ready to accept Principle 1 when your pain is greater than your fear. In Psalm 6:2–3 (TLB) David talks about a time when he came to the end of his emotional and physical resources: "Pity me, O Lord, for I am weak. Heal me, for my body is sick, and I am upset and disturbed. My mind is filled with apprehension and with gloom." When David's pain finally surpassed his fear, he was able to face his denial and feel the reality of his pain. In the same way, if you want to be rid of your pain, you must face it and go through it.

The second action we need to take is to:

2. Stop playing God.

You are either going to serve God or self. You can't do both! Matthew 6:24 (GNT) says, "You cannot be a slave of two masters; you will hate one and love the other; you will be loyal to one and despise the other."

Another term for serving "ourselves" is serving the "flesh." Flesh is the Bible's word for our unperfected human nature, our sin nature.

I love this illustration: If you leave the *h* off the end of flesh and reverse the remaining letters, you spell the word *self.* Flesh is the self-life. It is what we are when we are left to our own devices.

When our "self" is out of control, all attempts at control — of self or others — fail. In fact, our attempt to control ourselves and others is what got us into trouble in the first place. God needs to be the one in control.

There are two jobs: God's and mine! We have been trying to do God's job, and we can't!

On the flip side, He *won't* do our job. We need to do the footwork! We need to admit that we are not God and that our lives are unmanageable without Him. Then, when we have finally emptied ourselves, God will have room to come in and begin His healing work.

Let's go on now to the third action we need to take:

3. Start admitting our powerlessness.

The lust of power is not rooted in our strengths but our weaknesses. We need to realize our human weaknesses and quit trying to do it by ourselves. We need to admit that we are powerless and turn our lives over to God. Jesus knew how difficult this is. He said, "With man this is impossible, but with God all things are possible" (Matthew 19:26).

When we keep doing things that we don't want to do and when we fail to do the things we've decided we need to do, we begin to see that we do not, in fact, have the power to change that we thought we had. Life is coming into focus more clearly than ever before.

The last action we need to take is to:

4. Start admitting that our lives have become unmanageable.

The only reason we consider that there's something wrong, or that we need to talk to somebody, or that we need to take this step is because we finally are able to admit that some area—or all areas—of our lives have become unmanageable!

It is with this admission that you finally realize you are out of control and are powerless to do anything on your own. When I got to this part of my recovery I shared David's feelings that he expressed in Psalm 40:12 (TLB): "Problems far too big for me to solve are piled higher than my head. Meanwhile my sins, too many to count, have all caught up with me and I am ashamed to look up."

Does that sound familiar? Only when your pain is greater than your fear will you be ready to honestly take the first step, admitting that you are powerless and your life is unmanageable.

Tonight our acrostic will help us to focus in on the first half of Principle 1: powerless.

Powerless

Our acrostic tonight demonstrates what happens when we admit we are POWERLESS. We begin to give up the following "serenity robbers":

Pride
Only ifs
Worry
Escape
Resentment
Loneliness
Emptiness
Selfishness
Separation

The first letter in tonight's acrostic is *P*. We start to see that we no longer are trapped by our PRIDE: "Pride ends in a fall, while humility brings honor" (Proverbs 29:23, TLB).

Ignorance + power + pride = a deadly mixture

Our false pride undermines our faith and it cuts us off from God and others. When God's presence is welcome, there is no room for pride because He makes us aware of our true self.

Next we begin to lose the ONLY ifs. That's the *O* in Powerless.

Have you ever had a case of the "only ifs"?

Only if they hadn't walked out.

Only if I had stopped drinking.

Only if this. Only if that.

How reluctantly the mind consents to reality. But when we admit that we are powerless, we start walking in the truth, rather than living in the fantasy land of rationalization.

Luke 12:2–3 (GNT) tells us: "Whatever is covered up will be uncovered, and every secret will be made known. So then, whatever you have said in the dark will be heard in broad daylight."

The next letter in powerless is the *W*, which stands for WORRYING. And don't tell me that worrying doesn't do any good; I know better. The things I worry about never happen!

All worrying is a form of not trusting God enough! Instead of worrying about things that we cannot possibly do, we need to focus on what God can do. Keep a copy of the Serenity Prayer in your pocket and your heart to remind you.

By working this program and completing the steps, you can find that trust, that relationship, with the one and only Higher Power, Jesus Christ, so that the worrying begins to go away.

Matthew 6:34 (TLB) tells us, "Don't be anxious about tomorrow. God will take care of your tomorrow too. Live one day at a time."

The next thing that happens when we admit we are powerless is that we quit trying to ESCAPE. That's the *E*.

Before we admitted we were powerless, we tried to escape and hide from our hurts, habits, and hang-ups by getting involved in unhealthy relationships, by abusing drugs such as alcohol, by eating or not eating, and so forth.

Trying to escape pain drains us of precious energy. When we take this first step, however, God opens *true* escape routes to show His power and grace. "For light is capable of 'showing up' everything for what it really is. It is even possible (after all, it happened to you!) for light to turn the thing it shines upon into light also" (Ephesians 5:13–14, PH).

The *R* in powerless stands for RESENTMENTS.

If they are suppressed and allowed to fester, resentments can act like emotional cancer.

Paul tells us in Ephesians 4:26–27: "'In your anger do not sin': Do not let the sun go down while you are still angry, and do not give the devil a foothold."

As you continue to work the principles, you will come to understand that in letting go of your resentments, by offering your forgiveness to those who have hurt you, you are not just freeing the person who harmed you, you are freeing you!

But if we try to maintain our false power, we become isolated and alone. That's the *L* in powerless: LONELINESS.

When you admit that you are powerless and start to face reality, you will find that you do not have to be alone.

Do you know that loneliness is a choice? In recovery and in Christ, you never have to walk alone again.

Do you know that caring for the lonely can cure loneliness? Get involved! Get involved in the church or in your neighborhood or here at Celebrate Recovery! If you become a regular here, I guarantee that you won't be lonely.

"Continue to love each other with true brotherly love. Don't forget to be kind to strangers, for some who have done this have entertained angels without realizing it!" (Hebrews 13:1–2, TLB).

When you admit you are powerless you also give up another *E*, the EMPTINESS.

When you finally admit that you are truly powerless by yourself, that empty feeling deep inside—that cold wind that blows through you—will go away.

Jesus said, "My purpose is to give life in all its fullness" (John 10:10, TLB). So let Him fill the emptiness inside. Tell Him how you feel. He cares!

Next you will notice that you are becoming less self-centered.

The first *S* stands for SELFISHNESS.

I have known people who have come into recovery thinking that the Lord's Prayer was "Our Father who art in heaven … Give me … give me … give me!" Luke 17:33 (TLB) tells us, "Whoever clings to his life shall lose it, and whoever loses his life shall save it." Simply said, selfishness is at the heart of most problems between people.

The last thing that we give up when we admit that we are powerless is SEPARATION.

Some people talk about "finding" God—as if He could ever be lost.

Separation from God can feel real, but it is never permanent. Remember, He seeks the lost. When we can't find God, we need to ask ourselves, "Who moved?" I'll give you a hint. It wasn't God!

For I am convinced that nothing can ever separate us from his love. Death can't, and life can't. The angels won't, and all the powers of hell itself cannot keep God's love away.... Nothing will ever be able to separate us from the love of God demonstrated by our Lord Jesus Christ when he died for us (Romans 8:38–39, TLB).

Wrap-Up

The power to change only comes from God's grace.

Are you ready to truly begin your journey of recovery? Are you ready to stop denying the pain? Are you ready to stop playing God? Are you ready to start admitting your powerlessness? To start admitting that your life has become unmanageable? If you are, share it with your group tonight.

I encourage you to start working and living this program in earnest. If we admit we are powerless, we need a power greater than ourselves to restore us. That power is your Higher Power—Jesus Christ!

Let's close in prayer.

Dear God, Your Word tells me that I can't heal my hurts, hang-ups, and habits by just saying that they are not there. Help me! Parts of my life, or all of my life, are out of control. I now know that I cannot "fix" myself. It seems the harder that I try to do the right thing the more I struggle. Lord, I want to step out of my denial into the truth. I pray for You to show me the way. In Your Son's name, Amen.

PRINCIPLE 1 TESTIMONY

My name is Greg, and I am a grateful believer in Jesus Christ who struggles with drug addiction.

For the first thirty-eight years of my life, I did everything possible to run from my fears, insecurities, and worries. I chose to follow the ways of the world and not live the life Christ wanted me to. I was the guy who drove intoxicated but never got a DUI. I was the guy who used way too much drugs and alcohol but never had an overdose. I was the guy who participated in many illegal activities but never got arrested. Having used alcohol and drugs for over twenty-four years, my luck seemed to be running out, and my life was beginning to catch up with me. Fueled by my denial and the attitude that I was untouchable, I continued with the insanity of my addictions.

I was the firstborn son to my two loving parents. We lived in a picture-perfect new development in Westminster, California.

When I was four years old, our family was blessed with the birth of my baby brother. He was born with a narrow valve and two holes in his heart.

At eighteen months old, he went in for open heart surgery. The surgery was a success and the doctors assured my parents that he would be fine. As my brother grew older, my mom began to notice that he was not developing at the normal rate. When he was three, it was confirmed that my brother was severely developmentally disabled.

My early years with my brother were amazing. We played and enjoyed each other like brothers do. At this time, I did not realize that my brother was different. The older we got, the more and more I noticed our relationship was changing. Instead of being brothers, I was more like a third parent to him. My brother's mental capacity was that of a five-year-old, and he really would never exceed that. A lot of the time, I felt like I was an only child with nobody to talk to. I spent a lot of time occupying myself with games and activities. I loved and will always love my brother, but the reality of not being able to connect with him emotionally was tough. I felt confused and alone.

Life in our household felt quite chaotic. I remember many nights as a kid when I would be down in the family room and my parents would be fighting and yelling at each other. I would put pillows over my ears or turn up the TV to block out the chaos. It made me feel alone.

One of the ways I would occupy my time as a kid was by playing sports. Whatever season was in, I would play. I was the kid who would play outside until the street lights came on or until my parents would yell for me.

As my brother grew older, I watched as his behaviors made it more stressful and difficult for my parents to take care of him. They had to spend an excessive amount of time with him, and I didn't want to bother them with my problems. Honestly, I was afraid to approach them because I thought they were too busy with my brother.

This is when I decided to do things on my own. I decided to start living for myself *and* my brother, and be the best son for both my parents. I wanted to help my parents forget about the troubles of my brother. This put a lot of pressure on me to excel. I dreamed that I would one day become a professional athlete, which would allow me to take care of my brother for the rest of his life.

Having a severely mentally disabled brother made me feel so different from other kids. Some of the friends I hung out with would ask questions about my brother. There were even times when some of them would make fun of him. I was very protective of my brother and would get into fights with whoever said mean or negative things about him.

In junior high, I started to act out. I was the star athlete but was struggling in school. So in my attempt to keep pressure off of my parents, I began cheating on tests, forging notes, and lying about everything.

At the end of my eighth grade year, I was introduced to alcohol. I liked the way that the alcohol made me feel or not feel. My fears and insecurities seemed to go away when I was drunk, and I felt more at ease around my friends and, for the first time, felt like I fit in.

In high school, I was labeled the jock and was expected to do great things. I felt a great deal of pressure and did not like the attention that it brought me. I just wanted to be like everybody else, so I started hanging out with all sorts of kids. I would hang out with the jocks, surfers, student government kids, and partiers. I became a chameleon and wanted to be accepted by everyone. Unfortunately, I did not know who I was or who I wanted to be.

I began living a double life. I would try to keep this image of a good kid during the school days and would party hard on the weekends. I was out of control on the weekends. Everybody wanted to party with me, and I never had any limits of how much I drank or when NOT to drive. I thought I was indestructible and could not be stopped.

My senior year, I developed as one of the best basketball players in southern California and even received a full scholarship to play Division 1 basketball. This brought me one step closer to my childhood dream of becoming a professional athlete. My double life continued and I began to occasionally use marijuana. This drug made me feel very uneasy and uncomfortable. But, of course, if somebody had any, I would partake just to be cool and fit in.

Leaving for college was an exciting time for me. I thought I was going to be the superstar on the basketball team and have the freedom to do whatever I wanted. I would practice three or four hours a day, maybe go to some of my classes, and party at night. After my first semester, my GPA was 1.7 and I was put on academic probation.

My basketball career did not start like I had planned. During the fifth game, I hurt my knee and was out for the rest of the season.

I fell into a depression as my basketball season was cut short. I remember going into the head coach's office. He explained to me that he did not know if I "fit into" this program. I was hurt and confused. He told me that I could work off my scholarship in the locker room by cleaning up after the basketball team. I felt like a complete disgrace and failure.

It was Christmas break and I was all alone. I decided to end my life. I went to my dorm room and took a bottle of pills and drank a lot of beer. I felt like I had let everybody down in my family, and did not want to live anymore. I believe God (who I knew nothing about) was with me that night. It was not my time, and instead of dying, I got really sick and had one horrible hangover.

I would attend three more colleges to play basketball, go to school sometimes, and continue to party a lot. Something I am not proud of is that I played college basketball at every level: Division 1, 2, 3, and junior college. Not a lot of stability in my life.

After college, I got a job in my father's industry. This industry was perfect for me; everybody worked hard and partied hard after hours.

For the next four years, I lived in Newport Beach. I wanted to fit in with the hip crowds down in the peninsula so I started to experiment with drugs. I participated in underground raves and the club scene and used ecstasy, acid, and other types of drugs. When I saw one of my roommates going out of control, I told myself I needed to slow down.

One night while hanging out in a bar in Hermosa Beach, I met this wonderful woman. She was not like any girl I had ever met. I enjoyed talking to her and knew deep down she was the perfect match for me. She was beautiful, funny, hardworking, mature, and a loving Christian woman. All the qualities that she possessed were what I was not. It was hard to believe she did not want me at first, and this is where I began the manipulation and lies to persuade her to like me. I would tell her everything she wanted to hear. Church was very important to her so I told her that I was a Christian. I even started attending church with her on Sundays. I knew deep down inside, she was the perfect person for my life. Unfortunately for her, she did not know that I was fake, a liar, and the person she should NOT be with.

It was easy for me to keep the truth from her as her schedule was filled with school and work. I would hang out with her a couple of days during the week and party with my friends on the weekends.

After about a year of dating, we got engaged and six months later were married. I thought at the age of thirty, it was time for me to grow up, settle down, and start a family. I honestly thought that if I got married, I would change.

I would like to say our marriage was the fairy tale, but it was far from it. At our beautiful wedding, I would leave her alone to hang out and party with my friends. Even our wedding night, which was supposed to be this special time, was not to happen. I was too intoxicated.

We were trying to live the American dream. We each had great jobs and we bought our first home in Rancho Santa Margarita and had two dogs. On the outside, everybody thought we were the perfect couple. They had no idea that we were struggling and drifting apart.

My wife started to have panic attacks and became very depressed. I was confused and frustrated about how to help her. Thoughts were coming in my head that I was going to have to take care of her like I had to take care of my brother. Since I felt I failed with taking care of my brother, I was afraid I would do the same thing to my wife.

During this time, I began to hang out more and more with a group of my partying friends. I continued to run away from my stress by numbing out on alcohol. I started opening up to these friends about the pressures in my life. The bad thing was, I was spending less time with my wife, and we were drifting further and further apart.

On August 21, 2005, we were blessed with the birth of our daughter. I thought that her birth would make life easier and, hopefully, straighten me out. When I held this little girl, I wanted to give her everything she deserved. On the outside, we looked like the happy family. But I was not happy, and soon I would find a new way to help me ease the stress in my life.

At age thirty-five, while playing poker at a friend's house, I was introduced to cocaine. I remember telling myself, *Nobody my age gets hooked on drugs.* That was a lie. For the next three years of my life, I would put this demon into my body.

My double life was continuing as I chose to add my drug addiction into the equation. It took a lot of work and lying to hide this secret. I would work from 6 a.m. till noon and meet up with my drug buddies until it was time to go home. To finance my habit, I would cash my expense checks from work. I was stealing from my family.

One of my biggest regrets is that I would pick up my daughter from pre-school while I was under the influence. I was placing my daughter in harm's way. There were even times when my wife would work late, and I would be using drugs in the kitchen while my daughter was in the family room watching TV. At the time, I thought I was only hurting myself. I had no idea I was affecting my wife and child.

Unfortunately, life was getting very difficult, the economy was changing, and we were heading into a recession. For me to be successful, I would have to work even harder to succeed, but my addiction would not allow me to.

Our marriage had gotten so bad that we were on the verge of a separation. Our finances were out of control and we lost our home. My wife insisted that we see a marriage counselor, and I agreed to go. I took no ownership of my part in our relationship, and at times I would even go to the therapy high. The constant lying was getting heavier and heavier to maintain. I felt like I was on the verge of having a breakdown from living this double life.

I tried and had two months of sobriety (white knuckling it) by myself, cutting my ties from my drug friends, and trying to get my life back to normal.

Who was I kidding? I could not handle my life for thirty-eight years, and now I was going to stop using drugs by myself?

The time came when I had an opportunity to use again and I did. The bad, or you could say good thing, was my wife found drugs and confronted me. I sat with her in her car and she persistently asked me what was going on. Then something came over me, and I knew I could not lie anymore. I broke down to her and told her I was addicted to cocaine. The feeling of getting this off my chest was a huge step for me and for my relationship with my wife.

The next step was for me to get help. Sitting down with our marriage counselor, we discussed a plan. Our counselor told me of this place called Celebrate Recovery that is a Christian-based recovery program. Deep down I knew I needed help, but I had no personal relationship with Christ and was not sure if this was the place for me.

I was terrified the first time I went to Celebrate Recovery. I was not like these people (denial), and I was petrified somebody would recognize me as one of those "sick" people. I sat in the back, singing a little bit and looking around. That night a woman who was a drug addict gave her testimony. As I was staring at her, I realized my worst fears. Her son was in the same class as my daughter. I attended several more weeks, hiding from this lady, making sure she did not see me.

I would like to say that I never saw the blonde lady again, but one day my wife asked me to go to our daughter's field trip. And guess who was there? Yep, the blonde lady. Something inside of me was pushing me to talk to her. How do you approach somebody and say, "Hey, are you that drug addict who gave her testimony?" I did my best not to sound creepy and asked her if she went to church on Friday nights. From there, I opened up about myself and told her about my problems with drugs. We talked for thirty minutes and she told me that I needed to meet her husband.

My wife and I decided we needed to go to Celebrate Recovery as a family since she was struggling with her life as well. We started attending Celebrate Recovery together and from the first night we knew we found a home. This is when I met my sponsor. The first time I heard him talk, I knew I needed this guy in my life. He has been a huge impact on my life. I finally had that person who I could sit down with, pour out my junk, and not feel judged.

Principle 1 says, "Realize I'm not God; I admit that I am powerless to control my tendency to do the wrong thing and that my life is unmanageable." "Happy are those who know they are spiritually poor" (Matthew 5:3).

A few months later, I was driving to lunch when I saw all these cars turning into a church. For some reason I felt I needed to go to this service. As I walked up alone to this strange church, I was informed that this was Good Friday. I sat in the church with hundreds of people and learned about the death of Jesus Christ. I was floored by this service and at that moment, I accepted Jesus Christ in my life and nailed my sin (drug addiction) to the cross. I remember sitting down by myself crying and realizing it was God who led me to church that day to start my relationship with Christ.

Principle 3 says, "Consciously choose to commit all my life and will to Christ's care and control." "Happy are the meek, for they will inherit the earth" (Matthew 5:5).

It began with submitting my life to Christ and as I continued attending Celebrate Recovery I learned even more tools to help me on my road of recovery. I created a bucket list of goals I wanted and needed to accomplish in my life. I wanted to attend two meetings a week (check). I wanted to get into a step study — this is where the rubber meets the road (check). I wanted a sponsor and accountability team (check). I wanted to become a member of Saddleback Church and take classes 101 to 401 (check — all four with my wife). And finally I wanted to get baptized (check). For once in my life I had goals and I accomplished them.

After being eight months sober, life was getting better. But there was something deep inside that was eating me up. One night at Celebrate Recovery I felt like God was speaking directly to me. The focus question for the night was "What one thing are you holding on to, that you are afraid to let go of?" I had a secret that I thought I was going to die with. That night I broke down to my small group: in the past I had twice been unfaithful to my wife.

I knew I needed to sit down with my wife and finally tell her the truth. I knew she would be hurt and I feared that she would leave me. I sat with her that night and told her everything. I was trusting in God and knew in order for our relationship to work, I had to be honest. I remember a long pause and she looked at me and said, "I forgive you." She told me that she had been seeing a real transformation in me and this was why she was able to forgive me. She truly is an amazing woman. After everything I have done to her with the lies, drug use, and now cheating, there was NO way I was going to turn back.

Since I have been attending Celebrate Recovery, my life has changed dramatically for the better. I needed a program that would not only get me sober, but also a place where I was going to become a better husband, father, friend, brother ... person. First and foremost, I needed to find Christ. For thirty-eight years, I was not a Christian. Finding Jesus Christ was the way I was going to get sober and stay sober.

I struggle with opening up and expressing my thoughts and feelings. Through this program, I have met men who have similar struggles, but who I can freely open up to without feeling ashamed or embarrassed. I have developed meaningful relationships with my sponsor, accountability partners, and other godly men who are there for me. Celebrate Recovery gave me and my family a place where people love us for who we really are.

I came to Celebrate Recovery as a drug addict, but through the process of attending the meetings, small groups, and step study I learned that I struggle with anger, lust, and basically life in general. I am a grateful addict because my addiction led me down the path to Christ and set me up to become a healthy person and deal with the demons that I pushed down for so many years.

I now give back to the program that gave me so much. I help lead the men's chemically addicted group on Thursday nights in San Clemente and am a coleader on Friday nights at The Landing (tenth- and eleventh-grade students) in Lake Forest. I also have the privilege of sponsoring men, and I can see the Lord work miracles in their lives as He did in mine.

First and foremost I owe this to my Lord and Savior Jesus Christ. I would also like to thank my beautiful wife for not giving up on me and being there through our ups and downs. I could not have done this without them.

I know that I am a work in progress and have only scratched the surface, which is why I keep coming back. I have a passion to be of service for the next person who is struggling with life. I want to give that struggling person a hope that Celebrate Recovery works.

When I introduced myself, I told you I was in recovery for drug addiction. When I was writing my testimony, I realized that I used alcohol a lot during my life. I now choose to never drink alcohol again, because I do not want to go back to how my life was. The greatest part is, my daughter will never see her father ever put a drink or a drug in his body!

My life verse is 2 Corinthians 5:17: *"When someone becomes a Christian, he becomes a new person inside. He is not the same anymore. A new life has begun."*

Thank you for letting me share.

PRINCIPLE 2

Earnestly believe that God exists, that I matter to Him, and that He has the power to help me recover.

"Happy are those who mourn, for they shall be comforted." (Matthew 5:4)

HOPE

Principle 2: Earnestly believe that God exists, that I matter to Him, and that He has the power to help me recover.

"Happy are those who mourn, for they shall be comforted."
(Matthew 5:4)

Step 2: We came to believe that a power greater than ourselves could restore us to sanity.

"For it is God who works in you to will and to act in order
to fulfill his good purpose." (Philippians 2:13)

Introduction

In Principle 2 we earnestly believe that God exists, that we matter to Him, and that He has the power to help us recover. Hebrews 11:6 tells us, "Anyone who comes to [God] must believe that he exists and that he rewards those who earnestly seek him." Psalm 62:5 says, "Yes, my soul, find rest in God; my hope comes from him."

In the first principle, we admitted we were *powerless*. It is through this admission of our powerlessness that we are able to *believe* and *receive* God's power to help us recover. We do need to be careful, though, not to just cover the bottomless pit of our hurts, hang-ups, and habits with layers of denial or try some quick-fix. Instead, we need to keep those hurts exposed to the light so that through God's power they can truly heal.

It's in the second principle that we come to believe God exists, that we are important to Him, and that we are able to find the one true Higher Power, Jesus Christ! We come to understand that God wants to fill our lives with His love, His joy, and His presence.

One of my very favorite parables is in Luke 15, the story of the prodigal son. Though the story is about a father's love for his lost son, it is really a picture of God the Father's love for you. God's love is looking for you, no matter how lost you feel. God's searching love can find you, no matter how many times you may have fallen into sin. God's hands of mercy are reaching out to pick you up and to love and forgive you.

Ladies and gentlemen, that's where you will find hope, and that's why I call Principle 2 the "hope" principle.

Hope

Let's look at what the word HOPE means in Principle 2:

Higher Power
Openness to change
Power to change
Expect to change

H stands for HIGHER Power. Our Higher Power is the one and only true Higher Power and He has a name: Jesus Christ!

In the past you may have believed in Jesus' existence and you may have even attended church. But what you will find in Principle 2 is a personal relationship with Christ. You will see that Jesus desires a hands-on, day-to-day, moment-to-moment relationship with us. For He can do for us what we have never been able to do for ourselves. Romans 11:36 (TLB) says, "Everything comes from God alone. Everything lives by his power."

Many people today believe their doubts and doubt their beliefs! Have you ever seen an idea? Have you ever seen love? Have you ever seen faith? Of course not. You may have seen *acts* of faith and love, but the real things — the lasting things — in the world are the invisible spiritual realities.

This leads us to the first four words of the second step: "We came to believe . . ." Saying that we "came to believe" in anything describes a process. Belief is a result of consideration, doubt, reasoning, and concluding.

In 2 Corinthians 12:9 (PH), Jesus tells us, "My grace is enough for you: for where there is weakness, my power is shown the more completely."

The next letter in hope is *O*, which stands for OPENNESS to change.

What is the process that leads to solid belief, which leads you to change your life? Let's look at the first four words in Step 2 again: "We came to believe . . ."

- "We came . . ." We took the first step when we attended our first recovery meeting!
- "We came to . . ." We stopped denying our hurts, hang-ups, and habits!

- "We came to believe . . ." We started to believe and receive God's power to help us recover.

Hope is openness to change. Sometimes we are afraid to change, even if our past was painful. We resist change because of our fear of the unknown, or, in our despair, we think we don't deserve anything better.

Here's the good news: Hope opens doors where despair closes them! Hope discovers what can be done instead of grumbling about what can't be done. Throughout your life you will continue to encounter hurts and trials that you are powerless to change, but with God's help you can be open to allow those circumstances and situations to change you—to make you better— not bitter.

Ephesians 4:23 (TLB) gives us a challenge to that end: "Now your attitudes and thoughts must all be constantly changing for the better. . . . You must be a new and different person."

How will you do that? The letter *P* tells us about POWER to change.

In the past, we may have wanted to change and were unable to do so; we could not free ourselves from our hurts, hang-ups, or habits. In Principle 2, we understand that God's power can change us and our situation. Philippians 4:13 (TLB) confirms it: "For I can do everything God asks me to with the help of Christ who gives me the strength and power."

Power to change comes from God's grace. You see, hope draws its power from a deep trust in God, like that of the psalmist, who wrote, "Lead me; teach me; for you are the God who gives me salvation. I have no hope except in you" (Psalm 25:5, TLB).

In Principle 2, we begin to understand that God's power can change us and our situation. And once we tap into that power, right actions—Christlike actions—will follow naturally as by-products of working the principles and following the one and only Higher Power, Jesus Christ.

The last letter in hope is *E*: EXPECT to change.

Remember you are only at the second principle. Don't quit before the miracle happens! With God's help, the changes that you have longed for are just *steps* away. Philippians 1:6 (TLB) expresses my heart: "I am sure that God who began the good work within you will keep right on helping you grow in his grace until his task within you is finally finished on that day when Jesus Christ returns."

You know, you can't do anything unless you get started, so how much faith do you need to get started?

Matthew 17:20 tells us, "If you have faith as small as a mustard seed, you can say to this mountain, 'Move from here to there,' and it will move. Nothing will be impossible for you."

It's reassuring to know that you do not need large amounts of faith to begin the recovery process. You need only a small amount, "as small as a mustard seed," to effect change, to begin to move your mountains of hurts, hang-ups, and habits.

Wrap-Up

Eternal life does not begin with death; it begins with faith! Hebrews 11:1 tells us what faith is: "Faith is confidence in what we hope for and assurance about what we do not see." Faith—even faith the size of a mustard seed so small you can hardly see it—is the avenue to salvation. You can't find salvation through intellectual understanding, gifts of money, good works, or attending church. No! The way to find salvation, is described in Romans 10:9: "If you declare with your mouth, 'Jesus is Lord,' and believe in your heart that God raised him from the dead, you will be saved."

Yes, all you need is just a little faith. If you will put the faith you have in Jesus, your life will be changed! You will find hope in the only Higher Power, Jesus Christ. His Spirit will come with supernatural power into your heart. It can happen to you! It happened to me!

Tonight I encourage you to take this step of hope. It will give you the courage to reach out and hold Christ's hand and face the present with confidence and the future with realistic expectancy.

Simply put, my life without Christ is a hopeless end; with Him it is an endless hope.

SANITY

Principle 2: Earnestly believe that God exists, that I matter to Him, and that He has the power to help me recover.

"Happy are those who mourn, for they shall be comforted."
(Matthew 5:4)

Step 2: We came to believe that a power greater than ourselves could restore us to sanity.

"For it is God who works in you to will and to act in order to fulfill his good purpose." (Philippians 2:13)

Introduction

We spent our first month on Principle 1. We finally were able to face our denial and admit that we are powerless to control our tendency to do the wrong thing and that our lives had become unmanageable—out of control!

Now what do we need to do? How and where do we get the control? The answer is to take the second step on our journey of recovery.

The second step tells us that we have come to believe that a power greater than ourselves could restore us to sanity. "Wait a minute!" you're saying. "I spent an entire month hearing that to begin my recovery I had to face and admit my denial. Now you're telling me that I must be crazy? That I need to be restored to sanity? Give me a break!"

No, Step 2 isn't saying that you're crazy. Let me try to explain what the word *sanity* means in this step.

As a result of admitting our powerlessness in Principle 1, we can move from chaos to hope in Principle 2. We talked about that in our last teaching session. Hope comes when we believe that a power greater than ourselves, our Higher Power, Jesus Christ, can and will restore us! Jesus can provide that power where we were powerless over our addictions and compulsive behaviors. He alone can restore order and meaning to our lives. He alone can restore us to sanity.

Sanity

Insanity has been defined as "doing the same thing over and over again, expecting a different result each time."

Sanity has been defined as "wholeness of mind; making decisions based on the truth."

Jesus is the only Higher Power who offers the truth, the power, the way, and the life.

The following acrostic, using the word *sanity*, shows some of the gifts we receive when we believe that our true Higher Power, Jesus Christ, has the power and will restore us to SANITY!

Strength
Acceptance
New Life
Integrity
Trust
Your Higher Power

The first letter is *S*, which stands for STRENGTH.

When we accept Jesus as our Higher Power, we receive strength to face the fears that, in the past, have caused us to fight, flee, or freeze. Now we can say, "God is our refuge and strength, an ever-present help in trouble. Therefore we will not fear" (Psalm 46:1–2) and "My mind and my body may grow weak, but God is my strength; he is all I ever need" (Psalm 73:26, GNT).

Relying on our own power, our own strength is what got us here in the first place. We believed we didn't need God's help, strength, or power. It's almost like we were disconnected from our true power source—God! Choosing to allow my life to finally run on God's power—not my own limited power, weakness, helplessness, or sense of inferiority—has turned out to be my greatest strength. God came in where my helplessness began. And He will do the same for you!

The next letter, *A*, stands for ACCEPTANCE.

Romans 15:7 (GNT) says, "Accept one another, then, for the glory of God, as Christ has accepted you."

When we take Step 2, we learn to have realistic expectations of ourselves and others. We learn not to relate to others in the same old way, expecting a different response or result than they have given us time and time again.

We begin to find the sanity we have been searching for. We remember to pray and ask God "to give us the courage to change the things we can and to accept the things we cannot change."

As our faith grows and we get to know our Higher Power better, it becomes easier for us to accept others as they really are, *not as we would have them be!*

With acceptance, however, comes responsibility. We stop placing all the blame on others for our past actions and hurts.

The next letter, *N*, stands for NEW life.

In the pit of our hurts, habits, and hang-ups, we were at our very bottom. We know the feelings expressed in 2 Corinthians 1:8–9 (TLB): "We were really crushed and overwhelmed, and feared we would never live through it. We felt we were doomed to die and saw how powerless we were to help ourselves; but that was good, for then we put everything into the hands of God."

The verse goes on to say, "God … alone could save us … and we expect him to do it again and again."

The penalty for our sins was paid in full by Jesus on the cross. The hope of a new life is freedom from our bondage! "When someone becomes a Christian he becomes a brand new person inside. He is not the same any more. A new life has begun!" (2 Corinthians 5:17, TLB).

The next benefit of this step is the *I* in sanity: INTEGRITY.

We gain integrity as we begin to follow through on our promises. Others start trusting what we say. The apostle John placed great value on integrity: "Nothing gives me greater joy than to hear that my children are following the way of truth" (3 John 4, NCV).

Remember, a half-truth is a whole lie, and a lie is the result of weakness and fear. Truth fears nothing—nothing but concealment! The truth often hurts. But it's the lie that leaves the scars.

A man or woman of integrity and courage is not afraid to tell the truth. And that courage comes from a power greater than ourselves—Jesus Christ, the way, the TRUTH, and the life.

The *T* in sanity stands for TRUST.

As we work Step 2, we begin to trust in our relationships with others and our Higher Power. "It is dangerous to be concerned with what others think of you, but if you trust the Lord, you are safe" (Proverbs 29:25, GNT).

As we "let go and let God" and admit that our lives are unmanageable and we are powerless to do anything about it, we learn to trust ourselves and others. We begin to make real friends in recovery, in our groups, at the Solid Rock Cafe, and in church. These are not the mere acquaintances and the fair-weather friends we knew while we were active in our addictions and compulsions.

In recovery you can find real friends, brothers and sisters in Christ, to walk beside you on your journey through the principles—friends whom you can trust, with whom you can share, with whom you can grow in Christ.

The last letter in our acrostic this evening is *Y*: YOUR Higher Power, Jesus Christ, loves you just the way you are! "While we were still sinners, Christ died for us" (Romans 5:8).

No matter what comes your way, together you and God can handle it! "And God is faithful; he will not let you be tempted beyond what you can bear. But when you are tempted, he will also provide a way out" (1 Corinthians 10:13). "Praise be to the Lord, to God our Savior, who daily bears our burdens" (Psalm 68:19).

When we accept Jesus Christ as our Higher Power and Savior, we are not only guaranteed eternal life, but we also have God's protection in time of trials. Nahum 1:7 says, "The LORD is good, a refuge in times of trouble. He cares for those who trust in him."

Wrap-Up

Recovery is a daily program, and we need a power greater than ourselves—a Higher Power who will provide us with the strength, acceptance, new life, integrity, and trust to allow us to make sane decisions based on His truth!

And if you complete the next principle, Principle 3, your future will be blessed and secure! Matthew 6:34 (TLB) says, "So don't be anxious about tomorrow. God will take care of your tomorrow too. Live one day at a time."

Let's close in prayer.

Dear God, I have tried to "fix" and "control" my life's hurts, hang-ups, or habits all by myself. I admit that, by myself, I am powerless to change. I need to begin to believe and receive Your power to help me recover. You loved me enough to send Your Son to the cross to die for my sins. Help me be open to the hope that I can only find in Him. Please help me to start living my life one day at a time. In Jesus' name I pray, Amen.

PRINCIPLE 2 TESTIMONY

My name is Jamie, and I am a grateful believer in Jesus Christ who struggles with anger.

As a little girl I had many dreams of becoming successful and living happily ever after until reality stepped in. Growing up, there were many lies that

I believed about myself. One of the most deeply rooted lies for me was that I would never amount to anything. I was convinced that these lies were true by my circumstances, wrong choices, and the abusive relationships that surrounded me.

My dysfunction started at a young age, beginning with my parents' abusive relationship. My father was an abusive man, who had his own addictions, and who would habitually lose self-control. This caused me to hide in my closet and tremble with fear. I would hear them yelling and screaming in the next room; my dad yelling with anger and my mother screaming in fear. I didn't understand why they would behave this way. While hiding in my closet, I often comforted myself by saying that everything would be okay.

My mother eventually packed us up and left my father. As much as I wanted it to be okay, it only got worse. My mom became angry and an addict and all that came with it. She was no longer my protector, but became the person who continued to drill into my mind that I was good for nothing.

For many years, I dealt with verbal abuse that would break me down to nothing as well as physical abuse that would constantly make me fearful and on guard. I became hyper-vigilant and, through all of the circumstances, I eventually became addicted to anger, drugs, alcohol, and promiscuity. I really wanted a way of escape.

My mom was either working, at happy hour, or at night clubs. I didn't have any supervision as a child, so my free time was free rein. Usually what I did with my time was drink and use drugs with my "friends."

I had friends who were various ages and I found that I was good at manipulating people into getting what I wanted. So good that I met a guy friend who would often lend me his car. I was sixteen and he was thirty. My days consisted of using this vehicle to joy-ride, gather all my friends, and consume as much alcohol or marijuana as we could. Eventually, this guy friend realized he was not getting what he wanted. He turned the tables around and reported that I stole his car and pressed charges against me.

So, at sixteen, I started the downward spiral of incarceration. I now had constant supervision: a probation officer. I was in and out of juvenile facilities thereafter. This spiral included giving dirty urine samples, positive for drugs or alcohol; stealing from department stores; failing to comply, more like refusing to comply, with probation rules and home supervision monitors; along with other juvenile delinquent activities. While in this lifestyle, alcohol and marijuana played a big role in my decisions. I believe it was a way out of my abusive home because the actions I would commit were always so mindless. I didn't receive any guidance from my mother or family. The things I learned from them were how to hold my liquor and how to smoke from a pipe. I was very self-destructive and I hated my life. Eventually I became more addicted. I felt empty.

All these addictive habits meshed into my first marriage at nineteen. This relationship would become a combination of the lies that were told to me and that I believed were true. My marriage was full of so much verbal and physical abuse that it caused my anger to breed and further develop. It manifested to the extent that I felt such a sense of powerlessness, torment, and bondage that I did what I knew best. I became even angrier. All these circumstances created a world of complete chaos for me. I made many more poor choices, one after another, not realizing that the consequences of my choices would make me and my situations worse.

I was hospitalized for depression and suicide attempts. I had many counselors, but I did not find one to be helpful. I was so codependent in my marriage that I gave in to having multiple abortions to appease my husband. I couldn't see through all my issues anymore. From pent-up emotional abuse, feelings of inadequacy, and the sense that I was trapped in my circumstances, something terrible was bound to happen. I was a walking time bomb, until I eventually went over the deep end.

I was doped up on psych meds, extremely depressed, and had just found out my husband was in an affair for quite some time. We were together for ten years. I had put all my hope into this one person who I thought loved me unconditionally. As he was drinking, my husband told me I would never leave him. Even worse, deep down inside, I knew that I would never have the power to do so.

One day, I decided that I *was* going leave him. As I was pleading with him to give me the car keys, he continued to heckle and belittle me. In the midst of all the chaos, confusion, and pain, I so desperately wanted to escape my situation that I picked up a knife and stabbed him in his leg. Our three-year-old son was sitting right next to him. In terror I picked up my son and ran to the neighbor's house, called my aunt, and told her she needed to come and take my son.

While I was gone, my husband's family came running into the apartment and immediately called 911. The street was flooded with police, onlookers, and emergency personnel. I told my son that I would have to leave him and I kissed him good-bye. I returned to my apartment complex, flagged down a policeman, and told him who I was and what I did. I was handcuffed and once again taken into police custody for questioning. I was stripped down and all my clothes were taken for evidence.

In my mind, I was hoping that my husband would not press charges against me. After all, this was our lifestyle. We drank and then we argued. That's the way it was. While being questioned, the investigator asked me, "Do you want to know how your husband is doing?" I responded to the officer, "Of course I do." I clearly remember like it was yesterday. Then he said, "Your husband is dead and you're being charged with first-degree murder."

I was in complete shock; it was almost as if I were in a Lifetime Channel movie. I was told that the stab wound punctured a main artery, causing my husband to bleed to death. My bail was set at one million dollars and I was looking at a sentence of twenty-five years to life in prison; one sentence I felt I did deserve—and one I knew I was going to get. This was my bottom. *"For troubles without number surround me; my sins have overtaken me, and I cannot see. They are more than the hairs of my head, and my heart fails within me" (Psalm 40:12).*

That night in 2003, I needed to have some type of rescue from my guilt of taking someone's life, especially someone I loved. In that moment, ending my life was what I thought would be the best escape route.

Before I did so this time, I prayed. I remember crying out and saying words I never thought would come out of my mouth, "God, if You're real, I NEED YOU." Not realizing that these little words would have so much power, that same night my world was flipped upside down. *"You will seek me and find me when you seek me with all your heart" (Jeremiah 29:13).*

At that moment, the correctional officer let me out of my jail cell and said I had a visit from my lawyer. My lawyer told me I was being escorted by police officers to go see my husband before they buried him. The impossible was done in my circumstance in a way I never would have imagined. My husband's mother unexpectedly pleaded with the warden to let me see my husband before they buried him and the warden agreed. God was truly at work here.

Principle 2 says, "Earnestly believe that God exists, that I matter to him, and that He has the power to help me recover." "Happy are those who mourn, for they shall be comforted" (Matthew 5:4).

I truly recognized that, when I called out to God, He heard me. I wanted to be restored. I was given a Bible and cracked it opened and read. I was in lockdown for twenty-three hours of the day. Hours would pass and I would still be reading. I wanted more of this amazing power and peace that I was experiencing. Throughout that week, I slowly started feeling the weight of my guilt being released and feeling a peace that I couldn't explain. Even sitting in a solitary jail cell, looking at prison for the rest of my life, and being away from my child, I still had peace. In my whole life of seeking fulfillment with things that never stayed, and lasted for only but a moment, I recognized real satisfaction and it was only in seeking my Lord, Jesus Christ.

I did not get the twenty-five-years-to-life sentence. I believe it was God's way of proving Himself to me that I could trust Him. Realizing that I had a son at home, I no longer was condemning myself to accepting life in prison. I did negotiate my sentence with God, the REAL judge. It started with praying about not receiving a life term, then to not being able to do the eleven years the district attorney offered. I went boldly before the throne, requesting that I get no more than five years. My sentence was three years and eight months.

I was not instantly changed. I still had addictive habits going into prison. Through Jesus, I was able to overcome many adversities while incarcerated. There were many struggles—from homosexuality to drugs and alcohol, all of which is readily available in prison—but there was a greater power working in me. Doors were opened for me to step into Bible studies where I met genuine Christian friends who wanted to be changed. I ministered to all my roommates who came and went throughout the years. I was later asked to work in the chapel as an usher and help with the outside guests who came in to speak to us.

The founders of Celebrate Recovery, John and Cheryl Baker, came to the Valley State Prison for Women where I was incarcerated. They trained about forty women on how to lead a Celebrate Recovery step study group while in prison. This was an honor, because my anger that brought me to prison was the topic of the recovery group I led for other inmates. I learned to control my anger by practicing to step back from the situation and meditate on Scriptures on self-control. There were many opportunities for my anger to get out of control. But using the Christ-centered 12 Steps and the biblical comparisons were the perfect outline to use to work through my struggles. Surprisingly, while in prison, I was able to obtain fulfillment, love, companionship, and self-control through the power of Jesus Christ.

My desires started to change and it became clearer what to do with my life. The closer I drew to God through prayer and learning of Him through His Word, the closer He drew to me with comfort, peace, and real friendships. I was also able to see my child often.

I later realized how God was trying to get my attention. Prior to getting arrested, I went to a church service and responded to an altar call. I asked God to come into my life. I remember feeling so broken that day. The following Sunday my husband's sister asked if we were going to church again, she enjoyed it so much, but I told her, "No, I feel better now." That was the day

I got arrested. Before, I only called on God in trouble and forgot about Him when I thought things were going my way. *"But God chose the foolish things of the world to shame the wise; God chose the weak things of the world to shame the strong. God chose the lowly things of this world and the despised things—and the things that are not—to nullify the things that are, so that no one may boast before him"* (1 Corinthians 1:27–29).

"The Spirit of the Sovereign LORD is on me, because the LORD has anointed me to proclaim good news to the poor. He has sent me to bind up the broken-hearted, to proclaim freedom for the captives and release from darkness for the prisoners" (Isaiah 61:1).

As I was getting closer to release, I was filled with so much anticipation on what God was going to do with my life. I knew stepping out of those gates that my life was new, because it was already transforming into something new while I was incarcerated. God compelled me to make new and different choices that allowed my recovery to be successful.

I've now been home for four and a half years and discharged from parole supervision. God has transformed many things in my life since spending time in prison. I have a great job where God is using my gifts, and I have experienced and embraced job stability. It feels great to have an employer who trusts me with the keys to the business. My relationships with my parents are growing and being healed. I am experiencing the blessing of being a mother to my son. I was given a second chance at marriage with a godly man. My husband and I have done missionary work and lead Bible studies together. We are members of a church in the San Francisco area and participate in our Celebrate Recovery program. I have been privileged to help with the Angel Tree Project, which gives Christmas gifts to children whose parents are incarcerated. I have been cleared to go into the San Francisco jails to minister to hurting men and women in post-abortion recovery.

In prison, while studying my Bible, I would just start daydreaming and pretending that I was speaking to crowds about how God saved me. I would ask God, "Can You use the most painful circumstances in my life, and if so, how?" He said this is how: "Stand and be My voice!"

In 2010, I shared my testimony in front of three thousand people at the Celebrate Recovery Summit! I have even been invited to share my testimony at the same prison where I served my sentence!

God is using me in ways that I could never have imagined.

Thank you for letting me share.

PRINCIPLE 3

Consciously choose to commit all my life and will to Christ's care and control.

"Happy are the meek." (Matthew 5:5)

TURN

Principle 3: Consciously choose to commit all my life and will to Christ's care and control.

"Happy are the meek." (Matthew 5:5)

Step 3: We made a decision to turn our lives and our wills over to the care of God.

"Therefore, I urge you, brothers and sisters, in view of God's mercy, to offer your bodies as a living sacrifice, holy and pleasing to God —this is your true and proper worship."
(Romans 12:1)

Introduction

Principle 3 states that we choose to commit our *lives* and *wills* to Christ's care. Step 3 in AA's 12 Steps says, "turn our *wills* and *lives*." I think Bill W., founder of Alcoholics Anonymous, got this step turned around. I believe that we must first commit and surrender our lives to the true Higher Power, Jesus Christ, and then we are able to turn over our wills to Him. Would you all agree with that?

When you choose to live this principle, you consciously choose to commit all your life and will to Christ's care and control. How do you do that? How do you turn your life and will over to your Higher Power, Jesus Christ?

Turn

Let's look at tonight's acrostic for the answer to that question.

Trust
Understand
Repent
New life

This step ends with new life, but you must first take three actions before that life can be yours. You must trust, understand, and repent.

First let's talk about TRUST.

Have you ever been behind a semitruck on a two-lane mountain road? Last summer Cheryl and I were taking Highway 1 toward Northern California. We were in the mountains and the scenery was beautiful. At one point, we approached a very steep incline and there must have been ten cars ahead of us. All of us were stuck behind a very slow-moving eighteen-wheeler.

The truck chugged very slowly up the hill. All of a sudden, the driver stuck his arm out of the window and motioned the cars to go around him. By his arm movement, he was telling us it was safe, there was no oncoming traffic ahead, and we could pass him. One by one, the drivers of the cars trusted their own and their families' lives to a total stranger, as they moved out and in *blind trust* went around the slow truck.

All of a sudden, it hit me! Not the truck. No, I realized that we trust our lives to complete strangers every day. We trust that oncoming cars will stop at intersections. We trust that the hamburgers we eat at fast-food restaurants won't make us sick.

Why then is it so hard for us to trust our lives to the care of God, whose eye is always upon us? I don't know about you, but I would rather walk with God in the darkest valley than walk alone, or with a stranger, in the light.

In Principle 3, you make the one-time *decision* to turn your life over to the care of God. It's your choice, not chance, that determines your destiny. And that decision only requires trust, putting your faith into action!

But what is faith? Faith is *not* a sense, sight, or reason. Faith is simply taking God at His word! And God's Word tells us in Romans 10:9 (GNT): "If you confess that Jesus is Lord and believe that God raised him from death, you will be saved."

For some people that's just way too simple. They want to make salvation much more difficult. But it isn't! Our salvation, thank God, depends on God's love for us, not our love for Him.

After you have decided to trust, the next step is to UNDERSTAND. Relying solely on our own understanding got most of us into recovery in the first place! After you make the decision to ask Jesus into your life, you need to begin to seek His will for your life in all your decisions. You need to get to know and understand Him and what He wants for your life.

Proverbs 3:5–6 says, "Trust in the LORD with all your heart and lean not on your own understanding; in all your ways submit to him, and he will make your paths straight."

You see, our understanding is earthbound. It's human to the core. Limited. Finite. We operate in a dimension totally unlike that of our Lord. He knows no such limitations. We see now; God sees forever!

You know something really strange? It has taken me all my life to understand that it is not necessary for me to understand everything.

First Corinthians 13:9–13 (GNT) tells us, "For our gifts of knowledge … are only partial; but when what is perfect comes, then what is partial will disappear.… What we see now is like a dim image in a mirror; then we shall see face-to-face. What I know now is only partial; then it will be complete, as complete as God's knowledge of me."

Someday we will see Jesus face to face. The fog of interpretation will be lifted, and our understanding will be perfected.

Praise God that we do not need a perfect understanding of Him to ask Jesus into our lives as our Lord and Savior. Why? Because God does not lead you year by year. Not even day by day. God directs your way step by step.

The third letter in our acrostic, *R*, stands for REPENT.

Some people repent of their sins by thanking the Lord that they aren't half as bad as their neighbors. That's not true repentance! Repentance is how you begin to enjoy the freedom of your loving relationship with God. True repentance affects our whole person and changes our entire view of life. Repentance is to take God's point of view on our lives instead of our own.

To truly repent you need to do two things: First, turn away from your sins; second, turn toward God. The Bible has much to say about repentence:

Turn from your sins and act on this glorious news! (Mark 1:15, TLB)

Repent! Turn away from all your offenses; then sin will not be your downfall. Rid yourselves of all the offenses you have committed, and get a new heart and a new spirit. (Ezekiel 18:30–31)

Don't let the world around you squeeze you into its own mould, but let God re-mould your minds from within, so that you may prove in practice that the plan of God for you is good, meets all his demands and moves towards the goal of true maturity." (Romans 12:2, PH)

It seems that most people repent of their sins more from a fear of punishment than from a real change of heart. But repentance is not self-loathing; it is God-loving. God isn't looking forward to punishing you! He is eagerly anticipating with open arms your turning toward Him. Then when you have chosen to turn from your sin toward Him, He will joyously give to you what the last letter in tonight's acrostic stands for: NEW life.

The new life that you will receive is the result of taking the three actions that we just covered: trusting, understanding, and repenting.

As a pastor, I have heard some pretty glum definitions of life. These are just a few:

"Life is a hereditary disease."

"Life is a sentence that we have to serve for being born."

"Life is a predicament that precedes death."

"Life's a tough proposition; and the first hundred years are the hardest."

Those are depressing words that you may feel are true if your life doesn't include Jesus Christ. After you ask Jesus into your heart, you will have a new life! You will no longer be bound to your old sinful nature. You will receive a new loving nature dwelling within you from Christ.

God has declared you "not guilty," and you no longer have to live under the power of sin! Romans 3:22 (TLB) says it well: "Now God says he will accept and acquit us—declare us 'not guilty'—if we trust Jesus Christ to take away our sins."

Second Corinthians 5:17 (GNT) says: "Anyone who is joined in Christ is a new being; the old is gone, the new has come."

In what ways does the "new life" demonstrate itself in us?

The "old you" said,	**The "new you" says,**
Save your life!	You must lose your life to keep it (Mark 8:35).
Get, get, get!	Give, and it will be given to you (Luke 6:38).
Lead, at all costs.	Serve (John 13:12).
Lie; the truth only complicates things.	Speak the truth in love (Ephesians 4:15).
Hate your enemy.	Love your enemy (Matthew 5:44).

Let's wrap this up now.

Wrap-Up

Again, the "turn" in Principle 3 includes three very important actions that lead to a new life in Christ: trusting, understanding, repenting.

The good news is, turning your life over to Christ is a once-in-a-lifetime commitment. Once you accept Christ in your life, it's a done deal. Ephesians 1:13 says your salvation is "sealed." You can't lose it! It's guaranteed by the Holy Spirit.

The rest of the principle, however, turning your *will* over to Him, requires daily recommitment! You can begin by going to your Bible regularly, opening it prayerfully, reading it expectantly, and living it joyfully!

If you haven't asked Jesus Christ to be your Higher Power, the Lord and Savior of your life, I encourage you to do so this evening. What are you waiting for? Pray this prayer.

Dear God, I have tried to do it all by myself on my own power, and I have failed. Today I want to turn my life over to You. I ask You to be my Lord and my Savior. You are the one and only Higher Power! I ask that You help me think less about me and my will. I want to daily turn my will over to You, to daily seek Your direction and wisdom for my life. Please continue to help me overcome my hurts, hang-ups, and habits, that victory over them may help others as they see Your power at work in changing my life. Help me to do Your will always. In Jesus' name I pray, Amen.

ACTION

Principle 3: Consciously choose to commit all my life and will to Christ's care and control.

"Happy are the meek." (Matthew 5:5)

Step 3: We made a decision to turn our lives and our wills over to the care of God.

*"Therefore, I urge you, brothers and sisters, in view of God's mercy,
to offer your bodies as a living sacrifice, holy and pleasing to God
—this is your true and proper worship." (Romans 12:1)*

Introduction

When we get to Principle 3, we have worked, with God's help, the first two principles to the best of our ability. We admitted our lives were out of control and unmanageable, and we came to believe that God could restore us.

But even after taking the first two steps we can still be stuck in the *cycle of failure* that keeps us bound by guilt, anger, fear, and depression.

Tonight we are going to see how to get "unstuck."

How do we get past those old familiar negative barriers of pride, fear, guilt, worry, and doubt—those barriers that keep us from taking this step? The answer is *action!*

Principle 3 is all about ACTION. It states: "Consciously choose to commit ..." Making a choice requires action.

Almost everyone knows the difference between right and wrong, but most people don't like making decisions. We just follow the crowd because it's easier than making the decision to do what we know is right. We procrastinate making commitments that will allow change to occur from the pain of our hurts, hang-ups, and habits.

Do you know that some people think that deciding whether or not to discard their old toothbrush is a major decision? Others are so indecisive that their favorite color is plaid!

But seriously, do you know that not to decide is to decide?

Do you know putting off the decision to accept Jesus Christ as your Higher Power, Lord, and Savior really is making the decision *not to accept Him*?

Principle 3 is like opening the door: All you need is the willingness to make the decision. Christ will do the rest!

He said, "Here I am! I stand at the door and knock. If anyone hears my voice and opens the door, I will come in and eat with that person, and they with me" (Revelation 3:20).

Action

Let's look at tonight's acrostic: ACTION.

Accept
Commit
Turn it over
It's only the beginning
One day at a time
Next step

The first letter, *A*, stands for **AC**CEPT Jesus Christ as your Higher Power and Savior!

Make the once-in-a-lifetime *decision* to ask Jesus into your heart. Make the decision to establish that personal relationship with your Higher Power that He so desires. Now is the time to choose to commit your life. God is saying make it today! Satan says do it tomorrow.

In Romans 10:9 (GNT) God's Word tells us, "If you confess that Jesus is Lord and believe that God raised him from death, you will be saved."

It's only after you make this decision that you can begin to COMMIT to start asking for and following *His* will! That's the *C* of the word action.

I would venture that all of us here tonight have tried to run our lives on our own power and will and found it to be less than successful. In Principle 3, we change our definition of willpower. Willpower becomes the willingness to accept God's power to guide your life. We come to see that there is no room for God if we are full of ourselves.

We need to pray the prayer the psalmist prayed when he said, "Teach me to do your will, for you are my God; may your good Spirit lead me on level ground" (Psalm 143:10).

The letter *T* in action stands for TURN it over.

"Let go and let God." You have heard that phase many times in recovery. It doesn't say just let go of some things to God. It doesn't say just let go of, turn over, only the *big* things.

Proverbs 3:6 (TLB) tells us, "In *everything* you do, put God first, and he will direct you and crown your efforts with success."

"In *everything* you do." Not just the big things, not just the little things. Everything! You see, Jesus Christ just doesn't want a relationship with part of you. He desires a relationship with *all* of you.

What burdens are you carrying tonight that you want to turn over to Jesus? He says, "Come to me and I will give you rest—all of you who work so hard beneath a heavy yoke. Wear my yoke—for it fits perfectly—and let me teach you; for I am gentle and humble, and you shall find rest for your souls; for I give you only light burdens" (Matthew 11:28–30, TLB).

The next letter in ACTION is *I*. IT'S only the beginning.

In the third principle we make the initial decision to accept Christ as our personal Savior. Then we can make the commitment to seek and follow God's will. The new life that begins with this decision is followed by a life-long process of growing as a Christian.

Philippians 1:6 (TLB) puts it this way: "God who began the good work within you will keep right on helping you grow in his grace until his task within you is finally finished."

I like to compare the third principle to buying a new house. First you make the decision to buy the new house. But that's only the beginning. There are still more steps that you need to take before you actually can move into the house. You need to go to the bank and apply for a loan. You need to get an appraisal. You need to complete the escrow. You need to contact the moving company. You need to contact the utility companies—all before you are ready to move in.

Recovery is not a three-principle program! Principle 3 is only the exciting beginning of a new life—a life we live in a new way: ONE day at a time.

The letter *O* in ACTION stands for ONE day at a time.

Our recoveries happen one day at a time. If we remain stuck in the yesterday or constantly worry about tomorrow, we will waste the precious time of the present. And it is only in the present that change and growth can occur. We can't change yesterday and we can only pray for tomorrow. Jesus gave us instructions for living this philosophy: "Don't be anxious about tomorrow. God will take care of your tomorrow too. Live one day at a time" (Matthew 6:34, TLB).

Believe me, if I could go back and change the past, I would do many things differently. I would choose to spare my family the pain and the hurt that my sin-addiction to alcohol caused. But I can't change even one thing that happened in my past. And neither can you.

And on the other side of the coin, I can't live somewhere way off in the future, always worrying if "this or that" is going to happen. And neither can you. I leave that up to God.

But I can and do live in today! And I can, with Jesus Christ's guidance and direction, make a difference in the way I live today. And so can you. You can make a difference one day at a time.

Wrap-Up

This finally brings us to the last letter in our acrostic. *N* stands for NEXT step.

The next step is to ask Jesus into your life to be your Higher Power. How? It's very simple.

Pastor Rick Warren has developed an easy way for you to establish a "spiritual B.A.S.E." for your life. Ask yourself the following four questions, and if you answer yes to all of them, pray the prayer that follows. That's it. That's all you have to do!

Do I

- **B**elieve Jesus Christ died on the cross for me and showed He was God by coming back to life? (1 Corinthians 15:2–4)
- **A**ccept God's free forgiveness for my sins? (Romans 3:22)
- **S**witch to God's plan for my life? (Mark 1:16–18; Romans 12:2)
- **E**xpress my desire for Christ to be the director of my life? (Romans 10:9)

If you are ready to take this step, in a minute, we will pray together. If you have already taken this step, use this prayer to recommit to continue to seek and follow God's will.

Dear God, there are some here this evening that need to make the decision to commit their lives into Your hands, to ask You into their hearts as their Lord and Savior. Give them the courage to silently do so right now in this moment. It is the most important decision that they will ever make.

Pray with me. I'll say a phrase and you repeat it in your heart.

Dear God, I believe You sent Your Son, Jesus, to die for my sins so I can be forgiven. I'm sorry for my sins, and I want to live the rest of my life the way You want me to. Please put Your Spirit in my life to direct me, Amen.

If you made the decision to invite Christ into your life, let someone know. I would love to talk to you after our fellowship time.

PRINCIPLE 3 TESTIMONY

My name is Jacki, and I am a grateful believer in Jesus Christ who struggles with sexual addiction.

I was born and raised in a typical middle-class family, in a small town, in the high desert of Southern California. I am the youngest of five children. My dad was the breadwinner of the family and my mom worked inside the home as a full-time wife and mother. I have a lot of great memories of my childhood. My dad would always make us laugh by telling us captivating stories of lizards drag racing across the dry lake bed, or how Santa Claus once stole his toys on Christmas Eve. We'd have neighborhood football games in the street in front of our house until well into the night. And then there was my mom, who'd pile a bunch of us into the station wagon and take us on some of the wildest adventures. Those were good times.

Some memories of my childhood are not as enjoyable. When I was six years old, two teenage neighbor boys began molesting my sisters and me. As we'd ride our bikes or roller-skate up and down the sidewalk, the two of them would lure us into their garage and begin touching us inappropriately. After the second or third incident, I told my parents. Without hesitation, my dad promptly marched down to their house and confronted the boys and their parents. They were never a problem again. For reasons I couldn't comprehend, I had the courage to tell my parents about the situation with the neighbor boys, but I was too frightened to tell them about the abuse that was happening within our family. My eldest brother was molesting me as well. It became a fairly common thing; my parents would leave the house and my brother would abuse me. I don't remember when it started or why it finally stopped. I never felt like I could tell my mom and dad.

We were a very "emotionally dysfunctional" family. On the one hand, there was my mom, who taught us to find humor in virtually everything. Then there was my dad, who taught us "never to air our dirty laundry," or let anyone see us hurt. Instead, we'd focus on something that would make us laugh; that way we could avoid feeling pain and there'd be no need to cry.

I don't recall the last time I told my parents I loved them, or hearing either one of them saying it to me. Love was always one of those "understood" things. I can remember as a small child, kissing my parents good night, and hurrying off to bed. In contrast though, I don't recall embracing either one of them. It just wasn't something we did. I knew that they loved me, and I thought that was enough.

I had my first encounter with pornography when I was seven years old. I was playing with my dad's tools in the garage and found some adult magazines under his bench. I was intrigued by the images I saw. As I got a little older, I'd go to the local drugstore and sneak an adult magazine to the back of the store so I could look at the pictures without anyone knowing. Even at such a young age, I was discrete so that no one would find out my secrets.

I started attending church with a friend of mine when I was fifteen. After about a year, I prayed to receive Christ as my personal Lord and Savior. My relationship with the Lord really began to grow while I was in high school. When I graduated from that Christian school, I naively thought that I'd be "exempt" from the typical challenges of young adulthood. Several years later, my mom was diagnosed with a neurological disease. I had a very difficult time coping with the idea of watching this disease rob my mom of her independence. I felt utterly helpless. I didn't know how to express feelings of pain or fear, so I turned to alcohol and began drinking in an attempt to eradicate the pain.

As my addictive lifestyle was beginning to take shape, I accepted an information security position at work. My new job would be to monitor the networks and to investigate cases of personnel accessing pornography over the corporate networks. For more than eight years, from eight to five, my job was to go through each and every downloaded image and evaluate the content.

I also had a second job as a bartender at a local restaurant. After some time, I began dating some of my customers. In the beginning, I told myself that I would just go for the casual dinner and that would be it. But eventually, I ignored the boundary I had set for myself and began taking customers home.

When I wasn't working, I'd be at home drinking or surfing websites on the Internet. I'd spend between four and five hours per night, visiting the online dating services, adult chat rooms, and the telephone to act out with people all over the country. While all of this was going on, I continued keeping up the variety of appearances that had sustained me throughout the years.

At work, I was the professional. To my family, I was strong and responsible. To my church, I was a devoted Christian who never missed a Sunday. I had everyone fooled, including myself. I honestly believed that I could stop acting out any time I wanted.

I set many "boundaries," telling myself that I would do "this" but definitely not "that." I crossed every one of those boundaries and eventually entered a whole new realm of acting out. I began having sexual relationships with women. I had become so disconnected from reality that it didn't matter who the person was, where they came from, if a spouse was involved, or even if the person was healthy. Reality as I knew it was gone.

As things appeared to be spiraling out of control, I began to realize that I needed help, but I didn't know where to turn. A short while later, a pastor from out of town came to my church. Ironically, that night he preached on the "woman at the well." At first I thought that was simply a peculiar coincidence, that is, until his wife was called up to the pulpit and mentioned she was a Christian family therapist. I felt as though God had just dropped these two people out of the sky for me. Once the new pastor and his wife, Susan, moved to town, I began seeking counseling. From the beginning, I was honest about where I was at in my life and what I was doing. After a year or so, it became clear that my counselor and I saw my self-created dilemma differently. I knew I had "issues," but I was absolutely convinced that I could stop whenever I wanted to. My counselor, on the other hand, had the audacity to ask me if I thought I could be sexually addicted. Without hesitation, my response was, "Are you out of your mind? That's ridiculous!" Even though I was seeking counseling, I made the decision to walk away from the church.

I drank more than ever and was having countless encounters with people I didn't even know. The guilt of this lifestyle was becoming unbearable, but I finally realized that maybe my counselor was right. I was struggling with sexual addiction. Several months went by, and I started attending church again, but my relationship with the Lord was nonexistent. I couldn't accept that Christ could still love me. It was clear that my sin not only interrupted my fellowship with God, but it distorted my vision of Him as well. The truth of Scripture applied to everyone else but not me.

In the midst of this period of discovery in my life, the Celebrate Recovery ministry started at my home church. I attended a few times, but I did not feel safe. I live in a rural area and feared the gossip that often comes from a small town. I just could not take that risk. Before too long, I gave up on the possibility of recovery.

So, I continued to act out and got to a place where the fear of stopping was much greater than the fear of being "found out." I just didn't care anymore. The addiction in my life had taken me on a journey that I never thought was possible. I am reminded of the Scripture reference found in *Deuteronomy 30:4, "Even though you are at the ends of the earth, the* LORD *your God will go and find you and bring you back again."* I knew that it would take something huge for me to change.

Then on my birthday weekend, three years ago, the bottom seemed to fall out of my world into a cloud of deceit and lies. I was devastated by the person I was involved with. Over the years, I had isolated myself from nearly all of my Christian friends. I couldn't bring myself to call anyone and explain my circumstances. I began feeling this heart-wrenching pain, so I locked myself in my house for three days straight, closed the blinds, and did nothing but drink alcohol and watch pornography. I honestly didn't care if I lived or died. I had finally reached my bottom.

A few days later I met with my counselor, and she suggested I drive down to Saddleback Church and attend Celebrate Recovery. It took a few more weeks, but I reluctantly agreed to check it out. This was no small feat for me, for you see, I still live in that same small town, 180 miles away. Despite the three-and-a-half-hour commute, I knew that I had exhausted all of my other options. I had finally come to the realization that I couldn't stop acting out on my own. I knew I needed help, and I had to go to any length to get it.

My first visit to Saddleback Church, Celebrate Recovery was nothing short of terrifying. It was scary to sit in a room with a bunch of people that I didn't know. I vividly remember sitting there and listening to the small group leader read the definition of women's sexual addiction, and thinking, *That sounds exactly like me.* When the realization finally sank in, part of me wanted to crawl under the chair and hide. The only thing that brought me solace was listening to the women in the group share, knowing they understood what was going on in my head and heart, and realizing I wasn't alone. Even though I didn't share that night, I knew that I had come to the right place. But that, in itself, was a scary admission for me. As I pulled out of the parking lot that night, I remember saying to myself that I would never come back.

While I was driving home the next morning, I had a lot of time to think about the night before, and I couldn't help but reflect on my life and what had brought me to Saddleback Church in the first place. The life that I had been leading was nothing but a Pandora's box of lies. Over the next few weeks, I thought a lot about my trip to Celebrate Recovery and decided that I would return.

On my second or third visit, I picked up a *Celebrate Recovery Bible* and a set of Celebrate Recovery participant's guides.

As I began working through the lessons in the participant's guides, I remember feeling as though it was such a futile effort. Every time it seemed as though I was gaining a "foothold" in my recovery, inevitably an ex-affair partner would knock on the door, a tempting email would arrive in the inbox, or a voice from the past would call me on the phone. For several months, I'd find myself at home alone in the evenings or late into the night, wanting so badly to act out. I felt as though my own home wasn't safe for me to be in. But I did feel safe with the godly women I had met at Celebrate Recovery. I found it relatively easy to pick up the phone and let one of my accountability partners know that I was struggling. The one thing I couldn't do was pray. I couldn't bear the thought of looking God in the eye and telling Him where I had been. For years I had filled my head with images and now that was all my eyes could see. It didn't matter what time of day or night it was, or who I was with, all I saw was this filth of my past. It was as though I was being mentally tortured by my thought life. It was these very thoughts that kept me from experiencing any healing in the first part of my recovery.

Principle 3 says, "Consciously choose to commit all my life and will to Christ's care and control." "Happy are the meek" (Matthew 5:5).

It was at this point that I knew I had to make a choice: I could choose life, or I could choose death. I chose life. I made the decision to turn my life and will over to the care of God. I finally accepted that He really does love me. Despite my past failures, He did just as He promised; He met me where I was and offered abundant forgiveness and grace. *"He saved us, not because of the good things we did, but because of his mercy. He washed away our sins and gave us a new life through the Holy Spirit" (Titus 3:5).*

When I walked through those doors three and a half years ago, I never dreamed that the next few years of my life would be so eventful. This journey has certainly provided its share of ups and downs. Yet the Lord always reminds me of something extremely important: *"For I know the plans I have for you, they are plans for good and not for disaster" (Jeremiah 29:11).*

Over the past year, I've found myself being wheeled through the doors of an operating room on more than one occasion. Each time, I was forced to reflect on my entire life, but more importantly, on how the Lord had used such incredible dysfunction in my life to bring me into a Christ-centered recovery program that would reinstate in my heart and mind the all-important, never-ending truths of Scripture. Celebrate Recovery brought me to a place where the longing to be pure and right with the Lord became so much bigger than my weak and selfish desires. Had I never gone through the pain of my past failures, I don't believe that I would've come to a place that I was secure enough to trust the Lord for my physical and spiritual health, but more importantly, for my future, whatever that may look like.

Over these past three and a half years, my biweekly trips to Saddleback Church have become an integral part of my recovery. And in recent months, I've taken the Celebrate Recovery model back to my home church and worked with the ministry leaders to revitalize the program, creating a safe environment where people from my own community can come and experience genuine recovery for themselves. I've started the very first women's step study group, which meets in my living room on Thursday evenings. Recently, I felt led to start Newcomers 101 and have found it to be an exciting opportunity to share about this ministry and how it has quite literally transformed my life.

Last month, I celebrated three years of sobriety. I couldn't possibly have reached this milestone without each of the incredibly brave women in my open share group, who are so dedicated to working their programs and sharing every Friday night. It is because of each one of them, in their individual significant ways, that I can share my recovery story.

I can most assuredly say that I wouldn't be here if it weren't for Tina and Marnie. For over three years now, I've been their shadow, quietly walking behind and observing the miracle of recovery in action. They have often opened their homes to me, which have made my trips to Saddleback logistically simpler. They both fill many roles in my life—as sponsors, accountability partners, nurses, friends—but most importantly, they have become my family away from home.

Thank you for letting me share.

PRINCIPLE 4

Openly examine and confess my faults to myself, to God, and to someone I trust.

"Happy are the pure in heart." (Matthew 5:8)

SPONSOR

Principle 4: Openly examine and confess my faults to myself, to God, and to someone I trust.

"Happy are the pure in heart." (Matthew 5:8)

Step 4: We made a searching and fearless moral inventory of ourselves.

"Let us examine our ways and test them, and let us return to the Lord."
(Lamentations 3:40)

Introduction

Last month, we talked about the importance of having a personal relationship with Jesus Christ, which you found when you made the decision to turn your life and your will over to the care of God.

Now you will see that the road to recovery is not meant to be traveled alone. You will find that you actually need three relationships. Most important is a relationship with Jesus Christ. In addition, you need the relationship of your recovery group or a church family. Last, you need the relationship of a sponsor and/or accountability partner. Identifying a sponsor and/or accountability partner is especially important before you begin Principles 4 through 6, in which you work on getting right with God, yourself, and others.

Principle 4 is all about getting rid of our "truth decay," about coming clean! Proverbs 15:14 tells us, "A wise person is hungry for truth, while the fool feeds on trash." Are you ready to feed on the truth about your life? Well then, it's time to take out the trash!

That trash can get pretty heavy at times, so I don't want you to handle it alone. You need a genuine mentor, coach, or, in recovery terms, a sponsor and/or an accountability partner. Some of you may still be unconvinced that you really need another person to walk alongside of you on your road to recovery, so tonight we are going to answer the five following questions:

1. Why do I need a sponsor and/or an accountability partner?
2. What are the qualities of a sponsor?
3. What does a sponsor do?
4. How do I find a sponsor and/or an accountability partner?
5. What is the difference between a sponsor and an accountability partner?

Why Do I Need a Sponsor and/or an Accountability Partner?

There are three reasons why you need a sponsor and/or an accountability partner.

Having a Sponsor or Accountability Partner Is Biblical

Ecclesiastes 4:9 – 12 (GNT) tells us, "Two are better off than one, because together they can work more effectively. If one of them falls down, the other can help him up. But if someone is alone . . . there is no one to help him. . . . Two people can resist an attack that would defeat one person alone."

Proverbs 27:17 tells us, "As iron sharpens iron, so one person sharpens another." The phrase "one another" is used in the New Testament over fifty times!

Having a Sponsor or Accountability Partner Is a Key Part of Your Recovery Program

Do you know that your recovery program has four key elements to success? If your program includes each of these areas, you are well on your way to the solution, to wholeness.

The first key is maintaining your honest view of reality as you work each step. I have yet to see this program fail for someone who could be completely honest with himself or herself. I have, however, seen some give up on their recoveries because they could not step out of their denial into God's truth. Having someone help to keep you honest is a real plus in successfully working the steps.

The second key element is making your attendance at your recovery group meetings a priority in your schedule. This doesn't include taking the summer off or not going to a meeting because it's raining outside. Don't get me wrong, it's great to take a vacation, but after the two weeks are up, come back to your meetings. Remember, your hurts, hang-ups, and habits don't take vacations. You need to make Friday nights here at Celebrate Recovery and other meeting nights that you attend a priority. A sponsor and/or an accountability partner can encourage you to attend your meetings.

The third element is maintaining your spiritual program with Jesus Christ through prayer, meditation, and study of His Word. We are going to focus more on this in Principle 7, but you don't have to wait until you get there to develop your relationship with Christ. Your sponsor can pray for you and help to keep you centered on God's Word.

The last key element to a successful program is getting involved in service. Once you have completed Principle 8, you will be able to serve as a sponsor. Until that time, however, there are plenty of other service opportunities to get you started.

You know, service is nothing but love in work clothes, and there are plenty of opportunities to "suit up" for at Celebrate Recovery. We need help with the Bar-B-Que, with Solid Rock Cafe, passing out bulletins, and much more. If you want to get involved, see me, give me a call, or speak to your small group leader. Your sponsor can also suggest ways for you to serve.

Without exception, everyone here needs a sponsor and/or an accountability partner.

Having a Sponsor and/or an Accountability Partner Is the Best Guard Against Relapse

By providing feedback to keep you on track, a sponsor and/or an accountability partner can see your old dysfunctional, self-defeating patterns beginning to surface and point them out to you quickly. He or she can confront you with truth and love without placing shame or guilt.

Ecclesiastes 7:5 (TLB) tells us that "It is better to be criticized by a wise man than to be praised by a fool!" The trouble with most of us is that we would rather be ruined by praise than saved by criticism.

What Are the Qualities of a Sponsor?

"Though good advice lies deep within a counselor's heart, the wise man will draw it out" (Proverbs 20:5, TLB).

When you are selecting a sponsor, look for the following qualities:

1. **Does his walk match his talk? Is he living the eight principles?** I have known many people who have the 12-Step "lingo" down pat. But their lifestyle doesn't match their talk. Be certain that the person that you choose as a sponsor is someone whose life example is worthy of imitation.

2. **Does she have a growing relationship with Jesus Christ?** Do you see the character of Christ developing in her?

3. **Does he express the desire to help others on the road to recovery?** There is a difference between helping others and trying to fix others. We all need to be careful to guard the sponsorship relationship from becoming unhealthy and codependent.

4. **Does she show compassion, care, and hope but not pity?** You don't need someone to feel sorry for you, but you do need someone to be sensitive to your pain. As Pastor Rick (Warren) says, "People don't care about how much you know until they know about how much you care!"

5. **Is he a good listener?** Do you sense that he honestly cares about what you have to say?

6. **Is she strong enough to confront your denial or procrastination?** Does she care enough about you and your recovery to challenge you?

7. **Does he offer suggestions?** Sometimes we need help in seeing options or alternatives that we are unable to find on our own. A good sponsor can take an objective view and offer suggestions. He should not give orders!

8. **Can she share her own current struggles with others?** Is she willing to open up and be vulnerable and transparent? I don't know about you, but I don't want a sponsor who says that he has worked the principles. I want a sponsor who is living and working the principles every day!

What Is the Role of a Sponsor?

Let me give you six things that your sponsor can do:

1. **She can be there to discuss issues in detail that are too personal or would take too much time in a meeting.** This is especially true with Principle 4. You don't share your complete inventory in a group setting.

   "I'm the lowest form of life on the earth" is a phrase often repeated by those doing their inventory. Others deny, rationalize, and blame: "Okay, I admit I did such and such, but it's not as if I killed anybody"; "Sure, I did a, b, and c, but my spouse did d through z; compared to my spouse, I'm a saint"; "All right, I admit it, but I never would have done it if my boss wasn't such a jerk."

   The sponsor can be there to share his or her own experiences and to offer strength and hope: "You think you feel like a bum! Let me tell you how I felt when I did my inventory!" The sponsor's role is to model Christ's grace, forgiveness, and to give a sense of perspective.

2. **He is available in times of crisis or potential relapse.** I have always told the newcomers that I have sponsored, "Call me before you take

that first drink. You can still take it after we talk, if you decide to. But please call first!" Remember Ecclesiastes 4:12 (GNT): "Two people can resist an attack that would defeat one person alone."

3. **She serves as a sounding board by providing an objective point of view.** This is especially true in Principle 6. When you are dealing with the sensitive area of making amends and offering forgiveness, you need a good sounding board.

4. **He is there to encourage you to work the principles at your own speed.** It is not his job to work the principles for you! He can coach your progress, confront you when you're stuck, and slow you down when you're working too fast.

5. **Most important, she attempts to model the lifestyle that results from working the eight principles.** It's difficult to inspire others to accomplish what you haven't been willing to try yourself. A good sponsor lives the principles.

6. **A sponsor can resign or be fired.** Sponsorship is not a lifetime position.

How Do I Find a Sponsor and/or an Accountability Partner?

The responsibility of finding a sponsor and/or an accountability partner is yours, but let me give you a few final guidelines to help you in your search.

1. **First and foremost, the person MUST be of the same sex as you.** NO EXCEPTIONS. I don't think I need to expand this one.

2. **Can you relate to this person's story?** If you are choosing someone to be your sponsor, does he or she meet the qualities of a good sponsor that we just covered?

3. **Come to the Bar-B-Que and the Solid Rock Cafe.** Invest some time in fellowship and get to know others in your group. That's the main reason we have these fellowship events.

4. **If you ask someone to be your sponsor and/or an accountability partner, and that person says no, do not take it as a personal rejection.** Remember that their own recovery has to come first. I know a lot of you have asked your small group leader to be your sponsor. They all sponsor others, and the responsibility of leadership is great. If they turn you down, it's not personal. Their plate is simply too full! If someone turns you down, ask someone else! You can even ask for a "temporary" sponsor and/or an accountability partner. Remember, these are not lifetime commitments.

5. **Most important, ask God to lead you to the sponsor and/or an accountability partner of His choosing.** He knows you and everyone in this room. He has someone in mind already for you. All you need to do is ask!

What Is the Difference between a Sponsor and an Accountability Partner?

A sponsor is someone who has completed the four Celebrate Recovery participant's guides and has worked through the eight principles and the 12 Steps. He or she meets the six requirements that we talked about in the "Role of a Sponsor." The main goal of this relationship is to choose someone to guide you through the program.

An accountability partner is someone you ask to hold you accountable for certain areas of your recovery or issues, such as meeting attendance, journaling, and so forth. This person can be at the same level of recovery as you are, unlike a sponsor, who should have completed the eight principles or 12 Steps. The main goal of this relationship is to encourage one another. You can even form an accountability team of three or four.

The accountability partner or group acts as the "team," whereas the sponsor's role is that of a "coach."

You can start forming accountability teams in your small groups tonight. When you share, just ask if anyone is interested. Let God work and see what happens. I can guarantee this, though: nothing will happen if you don't ask.

Start looking for and building your support team tonight!

Let's close in prayer.

Dear God, thank You for this group of people who are here to break out of the hurts, habits, and hang-ups that have kept them bound. Thank You for the leaders You have provided. Thank You that You love us all, no matter where we are in our recoveries. Show me the person You have prepared to be my sponsor. Help us to establish an honest and loving relationship that honors You and helps both me and my sponsor grow stronger in You. In Jesus' name I pray, Amen.

MORAL

Principle 4: Openly examine and confess my faults to myself, to God, and to someone I trust.

"Happy are the pure in heart." (Matthew 5:8)

Step 4: We made a searching and fearless moral inventory of ourselves.

"Let us examine our ways and test them, and let us return to the LORD."
(Lamentations 3:40)

Introduction

Tonight we are going to really dig in and begin the growth process of recovery. Now, even though Principle 4 may bring some growing pains with it, tonight we are going to look at ways to maximize the growth and minimize the pain.

I wish I could say that you can escape the pain of your past altogether by going around it or jumping over it. But the only way I know to get rid of the pain of your past is to go through it. It has been said that "we need to use our past as a springboard, not a sofa—a guidepost, not a hitching post."

I know some people who spend their lives rationalizing the past, complaining about the present, and fearing the future. They, of course, are not moving forward on the road to recovery. By coming tonight, however, you have chosen to continue going forward. And if you choose to embark on the adventure of self-discovery that begins with Principle 4 and continues through Principle 5, I can guarantee you that growth will occur.

Principle 4 begins the process of "coming clean." Pastor Rick Warren calls this "truth decay." It is here that we openly examine and confess our faults to ourselves, to God, and another person we trust. We chip away and clean out all the decay of the past that has built up over the years and has kept us from really seeing the truth about our past and present situations.

A Moral Inventory

You may be wondering, "How do I do this thing called a moral inventory?"

That word *moral* scares some people. It scared me when I first worked this step in AA. Really, the word *moral* simply means honest!

In this step, you need to list, or inventory, all the significant events—good and bad—in your life. You need to be as honest as you can be to allow God to show you your part in each event and how that affected you and others.

Tonight's acrostic will explain the five things you need to do to make a MORAL inventory.

Make time
Open
Rely
Analyze
List

First you need to MAKE time. Schedule an appointment with yourself. Set aside a day or a weekend and get alone with God! God tells us in Job 33:33 (TLB): "Listen to me. Keep silence and I will teach you wisdom!"

The next letter in moral, *O*, stands for OPEN.

Remember when, as a child, you would visit the doctor, and he would say, "Open wide!" in that funny sing-song voice? Well, you need to "open wide" your heart and mind to allow the feelings that the pain of the past has blocked or caused you to deny. Denial may have protected you from your feelings and repressed your pain for a while. But now it has also blocked and prevented your recovery from your hurts, hang-ups, and habits. You need to "open wide" to see the real truth.

Once you have seen the truth, you need to express it. Here's what Job had to say about being open: "Let me express my anguish. Let me be free to speak out of the bitterness of my soul" (7:11, TLB). Perhaps the following questions will help to "wake up" your feelings and get you started on your inventory!

Ask yourself, *What do I feel guilty about?* The first thing that came to your mind is what you need to address first in your inventory.

Do you know and understand the God-given purpose of guilt? God uses guilt to correct us through His Spirit when we are wrong. That's called conviction. And conviction hurts!

Now don't confuse conviction with condemnation. Romans 8:1 tells us, "There is now no condemnation for those who are in Christ Jesus." Once we have made the decision to ask Jesus into our hearts, once we confess our wrongs, accept Christ's perfect forgiveness, and turn from our sins, as far as God is concerned, guilt's purpose—to make us feel bad about what we did in the past—is finished. But we like to hold on to it and beat ourselves over the head—repeatedly—with it!

That's condemnation. But it's not from God, it's from ourselves. Principle 4 will help you let go of your guilt, once and for all.

The next question you need to ask is *What do I resent?*

Resentment results from burying our hurts. If resentments are then suppressed, left to decay, they cause anger, frustration, and depression. What we don't talk out creatively, we act out destructively.

Another big question that you need to openly ask during this step is *What are my fears?*

Personally, I have a fear of going to the dentist. But even though it may hurt while I'm in the chair, when he's done driving the decay away, I feel a lot better.

Fear prevents us from expressing ourselves honestly and taking an honest moral inventory. Joshua 1:9 (GNT) tells us, "Do not be afraid or discouraged, for I, the Lord your God, am with you wherever you go."

Next on the list of hard questions to ask yourself: *Am I trapped in self-pity, alibis, and/or dishonest thinking?* Remember, the truth does not change; your feelings do!

These questions are only the beginning of your inventory, but don't get discouraged. The next letter offers a reminder that you don't have to face this task alone.

The next letter is *R*, which stands for RELY.

Rely on Jesus to give you the courage and strength this step requires. Here's a suggestion: When your knees are knocking, it might help to kneel on them.

Isaiah 40:29 tells us that Jesus "gives strength to the weary and increases the power of the weak." You *can* do this with His help.

Before we go any further, I want to remind you that the principles and steps are in order for a reason (other than to create a nifty acrostic!). You need to complete Principle 3—turning your life and your will over to God— before you can successfully work Principle 4.

Once you know the love and power of the one and only Higher Power, Jesus Christ, there is no longer any need to fear this principle. Psalm 31:23–24 (TLB) tells us: "Oh, love the Lord, all of you who are his people; for the Lord protects those who are loyal to him.... So cheer up! Take courage if you are depending on the Lord." And remember, courage is not the absence of fear but the conquering of it.

Now you are ready to ANALYZE your past honestly.

To do a "searching and fearless" inventory, you must step out of your denial, because we cannot put our faults behind us until we face them. You must look through your denial of the past into the truth of the present—your true feelings, motives, thoughts, and, as Obi-Wan Kenobi says in the *Star Wars* movie, your "dark side."

Proverbs 20:27 (GNT) says, "The Lord gave us mind and conscience; we cannot hide from ourselves." Believe me, I know! I tried! My grandma used to tell me, "Johnny, it's not enough to be as honest as the day is long. You should behave yourself at night too!"

Some of you heard the word *analyze* and got fired up, because you love to pick apart the details of a situation and look at events from all angles. Others of you have broken out into a cold sweat at the thought of analyzing anything! For those of you whose hearts are pounding and whose palms are clammy, listen closely as we talk about the *L* in moral: LIST.

Your inventory is basically a written list of the events of your past—both good and bad. (Balance is important.) Seeing your past in print brings you face to face with the reality of your character defects. Your inventory becomes a black-and-white discovery of who you truly are way down deep.

But if you just look at all the *bad* things of your past, you will distort your inventory and open yourself to unnecessary pain. Lamentations 3:40 tells us, "Let us examine our ways and test them." The verse doesn't say, "just examine your bad, negative ways." You need to honestly focus on the "pros" and the "cons" of your past!

I know people who have neglected to balance their inventory and have gotten stuck in their recoveries. Or even worse, they judged the program to be too hard and too painful and stopped their journey of recovery altogether—and they slipped back to their old hurts, hang-ups, and habits of the past.

An important word of caution: Do not begin this step without a sponsor or a strong accountability partner! You need someone you trust to help keep you balanced during this step, not to do the work for you. Nobody can do that except you. But you need encouragement from someone who will support your progress and share your pain. That's what this program is all about.

Wrap-Up

At the information table, you will find some blank Principle 4 worksheets. In a few weeks, we will be talking about how to put them to use in helping you work this key step.

I encourage you to get Participant's Guide 2 tonight if you have completed Principle 3.

Start working Principle 4. What are you waiting for? Start working this program in earnest.

If you are new to recovery or this is your first recovery meeting, we are glad that you are here. Pick up the first participant's guide, *Stepping Out of Denial into God's Grace*, and start this amazing journey with Jesus Christ. A healing journey that will lead you to freedom and truth. And by listening during the next two months, when you are ready to begin Principle 4, you will have a head start. You will also have a great understanding of the importance of Principle 4.

Let's pray.

Dear God, You know our past, all the good and the bad things that we've done. In this principle, we ask that You give us the strength and the courage to list them so that we can "come clean" and face them and the truth. Please help us reach out to others whom You have placed along our "road to recovery." Thank You for providing them to help us keep balanced as we do our inventories. In Christ's name I pray, Amen.

INVENTORY

Principle 4: Openly examine and confess my faults to myself, to God, and to someone I trust.

"Happy are the pure in heart." (Matthew 5:8)

Step 4: We made a searching and fearless moral inventory of ourselves.

*"Let us examine our ways and test them, and let us return to the LORD."
(Lamentations 3:40)*

Introduction

Tonight we are going to look at how to start your inventory, so get ready to write. Yes, that's right. Your inventory needs to be on paper. Writing (or typing) will help you organize your thoughts and focus on recalling events that you may have repressed. Remember you are not going through this alone. You are developing your support team to guide you; but even more importantly you are growing in your relationship with Jesus Christ!

Inventory

Ephesians 4:31 tells us, "Get rid of all bitterness, rage and anger, brawling and slander, along with every form of malice."

The five-column inventory sheets in Participant's Guide 2 were developed to help you with this task. Let's take a look at each of the columns.

If your inventory is anything like mine, it will take you more than one page to write it out. You have permission to copy the "Celebrate Recovery Principle 4 Inventory Worksheets" on pages 30 and 31, from the Celebrate Recovery Participant's Guide 2, *Taking an Honest and Spiritual Inventory*.

Column 1: "The Person"

In this column, you list the person or object you resent or fear. Go as far back as you can. Remember that resentment is mostly unexpressed anger and fear.

The good news is that as you work completely through Principle 4, you will see that your resentments fade as the light of your faith in Jesus Christ is allowed to shine on them!

Remember to list *all* the people and things that you are holding resentment against.

Column 2: "The Cause"

It has been said that "hurt people hurt people." In this column you are going to list the specific actions that someone did to hurt you. What did the person do to cause you resentment and/or fear? An example would be the alcoholic father who was emotionally unavailable for you as you were growing up. Another example would be the parent who attempted to control and dominate your life. This reflective look can be very painful, but that's why having a sponsor or an accountability team is essential. These people will be there to walk with you through the pain. Of course, Jesus will be with you too. God promises in Isaiah 41:10 (TLB): "Fear not, for I am with you. Do not be dismayed. I am your God. I will strengthen you; I will help you; I will uphold you with my victorious right hand."

Column 3: "The Effect"

In this column write down how that specific hurtful action affected your life both in the past and in the present.

Column 4: "The Damage"

Which of your basic instincts were injured?

- Social — Have you suffered from broken relationships, slander, or gossip?
- Security — Has your physical safety been threatened? Have you faced financial loss?
- Sexual — Have you been a victim in abusive relationships? Has intimacy or trust been damaged or broken?

No matter how you have been hurt, no matter how lost you may feel, God wants to comfort you and restore you. Remember Ezekiel 34:16 (GNT): "I will look for those that are lost, bring back those that wander off, bandage those that are hurt, and heal those that are sick."

Column 5: "My Part"

Lamentations 3:40 states: "Let us examine our ways and test them, and let us return to the LORD." It doesn't say, let us examine *their* ways. You did that already in the first four columns. Now you need to honestly determine the part of the resentment (or any other sin or injury) that *you* are responsible for. Ask God to show you *your* part in a broken or damaged marriage or relationship, a distant child or parent, or maybe a job loss. In addition, in this column list all the people whom you have hurt and how you hurt them.

(You will use column 5 later in Principle 6 when you work on becoming willing to make your amends.)

Psalm 139:23–24 (GNT) tells us: "Examine me, O God, and know my mind; test me, and discover my thoughts. Find out if there is any evil in me and guide me in the everlasting way."

Please note: If you have been in an abusive relationship, especially as a small child, you can find great freedom in this part of the inventory. You see that you had **NO** part, **NO** responsibility for the cause of the resentment. By simply writing the words **"NONE"** or **"NOT GUILTY"** in column 5, you can begin to be free from the misplaced shame and guilt you have carried with you.

Celebrate Recovery has rewritten Step 4 for those who have been sexually or physically abused:

> Made a searching and fearless moral inventory of ourselves, realizing all wrongs can be forgiven. Renounce the lie that the abuse was our fault.

Wrap-Up

There are five tools to help you prepare your inventory:

1. Memorize Isaiah 1:18 (TLB): "Come, let's talk this over!" says the Lord; "no matter how deep the stain of your sins, I can take it out and make you as clean as freshly fallen snow. Even if you are stained as red as crimson, I can make you white as wool!"
2. Read the "balancing the scale verses" on page 29 of Participant's Guide 2!
3. Keep your inventory balanced. List both the good and the bad!

   This is very important! As God reveals the good things that you have done in the past, or are doing in the present, list them on the reverse side of your copies of the "Celebrate Recovery Principle 4 Inventory Worksheet."

4. Continue to develop your support team.
5. Pray continuously.

Don't wait to start your inventory. Don't let any obstacle stand in your way. If you don't have a sponsor or accountability partner yet, talk to someone tonight! If you need a participant's guide, pick one up at the information table. Set a time and place and get busy! You *can* do it!

SPIRITUAL INVENTORY PART 1

Principle 4: Openly examine and confess my faults to myself, to God, and to someone I trust.

"Happy are the pure in heart." (Matthew 5:8)

Step 4: We made a searching and fearless moral inventory of ourselves.

"Let us examine our ways and test them, and let us return to the LORD."
(Lamentations 3:40)

Introduction

Tonight we begin the first of two lessons in which we will look at our spiritual inventory, using the "Spiritual Evaluation" Pastor Rick Warren developed for this step.[6]

Principle 4 begins the process of coming clean, where you openly examine and confess your faults to yourself, to God, and to another person you trust.

Most of us don't like to look within ourselves for the same reason we don't like to open a letter that we know has bad news. But remember what we talked about in Lesson 9: You need to keep your evaluation, your inventory, balanced. It needs to include both the good and the bad within you. Let's look at what a spiritual inventory, or evaluation, is all about!

God's Word tells us, "Search me, O God, and know my heart; test my thoughts. Point out anything you find in me that makes you sad, and lead me along the path of everlasting life" (Psalm 139:23–24, TLB).

---

6. The eight areas of the spiritual inventory were written by Pastor Rick Warren. With his permission, I have added my teaching notes and comments.

Do you know everyone has three different "characters"?

1. The character we exhibit.
2. The character we *think* we have.
3. The character we *truly* have.

No doubt each one has good qualities and bad. Tonight we are going to look at some of the bad, some of our character shortcomings and sins that can block us from receiving all the joy that God has intended. We will work on four areas of our character tonight and four more at our next session. This exercise will help you get started on your inventory as you search your heart!

Relationships with Others

In Matthew 6:12 – 14 (TLB) Jesus tells us to pray, "Forgive us our sins, just as we have forgiven those who have sinned against us. Don't bring us into temptation, but deliver us from the Evil One." Ask yourself the following questions regarding your relationships with others:

1. Who has hurt you?

2. Against whom have you been holding a grudge?

It doesn't take a doctor to tell you that it is better to remove a grudge than to nurse it. No matter how long you nurse a grudge, it won't get better. Writing the grudge down on your inventory is the first step in getting rid of it.

3. Against whom are you still seeking revenge?

Did you know that seeking revenge is like biting a dog just because the dog bit you? It really doesn't help you or the dog!

4. Are you jealous of someone?

In Song of Songs 8:6 jealousy is said to be as unyielding as the grave. It burns like blazing fire!

5. Have you tried to justify your bad attitude by saying it is "their fault"?

I have found that when I'm searching for someone to blame, it's better for me to look in the mirror rather than through binoculars. Hosea 4:4 (NLT) tells us, "Don't point your finger at someone else and try to pass the blame."

The people that you name in these areas will go in column 1 of your "Celebrate Recovery Principle 4 Inventory Worksheet" in Participant's Guide 2.

6. Who have you hurt?

How did you hurt them? You may have hurt them unintentionally. Maybe it was intentional.

7. Who have you been critical of or gossiped about?

It isn't that difficult to make a mountain out of a molehill. Just add a little dirt on it. That's what gossip is—just a little dirt!

I find it amazing that a tongue four inches long can destroy a man six feet tall. That's why James 1:26 tells us to "keep a tight rein on [our] tongues."

The people that you name in these areas will go in column 5 of your "Celebrate Recovery Principle 4 Inventory Worksheet."

Next, let's look at what's important to you.

Priorities in Your Life

We do what is important to us. Others see our priorities by our actions, not our words. Personally, I'd rather see a sermon than hear one any day.

What are the priorities in your life?

Matthew 6:33 (TLB) tells us what will happen if we make God our number-one priority: "He will give ... to you if you give him first place in your life and live as he wants you to."

1. After making the decision to turn your life and your will over to God, in what areas of your life are you still not putting God first?

What closet are you not letting Him enter and clean out?

2. What in your past is interfering with your doing God's will?

Your ambition? Is it driven by serving God or is it driven by envy?

Your pleasures? If your pleasure has been found in the world, Proverbs 21:17 warns, "He who loves pleasure will become poor." Is your pleasure now found in Jesus Christ? Psalm 16:11 (NCV) tells us, "You will teach me how to live a holy life. Being with you will fill me with joy; at your right hand I will find pleasure forever."

3. What have been your priorities in your job? Friendships? Personal goals?

Were they just self-centered, self-serving? Selfishness turns life into a burden. Unselfishness turns burdens into life.

4. Who did your priorities affect?

You know, you will never get so rich that you can afford to lose a true friend.

5. What was good about your priorities?

6. What was wrong about them?

The next area of our spiritual inventory is to examine our attitudes.

141 / Lesson 10: Spiritual Inventory Part 1

Your Attitude

Ephesians 4:31 (GNT) says, "Get rid of all bitterness, passion, and anger. No more shouting or insults, no more hateful feelings of any sort."

1. Do you always try to have an "attitude of gratitude" or do you find yourself always complaining about your circumstances?

When you feel dog tired at night, do you ever think that it might be because you growled all day?

2. In what areas of your life are you ungrateful?

If we can't be grateful for the bad things in our lives that we have received, we can at least be thankful for what we have escaped.

And the one thing we can all be grateful for is found in 1 Corinthians 15:57: "But thanks be to God! He gives us the victory through our Lord Jesus Christ."

3. Have you gotten angry and easily blown up at people?

4. Have you been sarcastic?

Do you know that sarcasm can be a form of verbal abuse?

5. What in your past is still causing you fear or anxiety?

As we have said before, your fear imprisons you; your faith liberates you. Fear paralyzes; faith empowers! Fear disheartens; faith encourages! Fear sickens; faith heals! Faith in Jesus Christ will allow you to face your past fears, and with faith you can be free of fear's chains. First John 4:18 says, "There is no fear in love. But perfect love drives out fear, because fear has to do with punishment. The one who fears is not made perfect in love."

The last area we are going to talk about tonight is your integrity.

Your Integrity

Colossians 3:9 (NCV) tells us, "Do not lie to each other. You have left your old sinful life and the things you did before."

1. In what past dealing were you dishonest?

An honest man alters his ideas to fit the truth. A dishonest man alters the truth to fit his ideas.

2. Have you stolen things?

I told you that your inventory wasn't going to be easy.

3. Have you exaggerated yourself to make yourself look better?

Did you know that there are no degrees of "honest"? Either you are or you aren't!

4. In what areas of your past have you used false humility?

Did you know that humility is never gained by seeking it? To think we have it is sure proof that we don't.

5. Have you pretended to live one way in front of your Christian friends and another way at home or at work?

Are you a "Sunday Christian" or a seven-day, full-time follower of Jesus Christ? Do you try to practice the eight principles seven days a week or just here at Celebrate Recovery on Friday nights?

Wrap-Up

Well, that's enough to work on for one week, but next week we'll dig in again and look at part two of our spiritual inventory. We'll explore our old ways of thinking—our minds; the ways we have treated or mistreated God's temple—our bodies; how we did or didn't walk by faith in the past; our important past relations with our family and church.

As you start to work on your spiritual inventory, remember two things. First, in Isaiah 1:18 (TLB) God says, "No matter how deep the stain of your sins, I can take it out and make you as clean as freshly fallen snow." Second—I can't say it enough—keep your inventory balanced. List the positive new relationships that you have, the areas of your life that you have been able to turn over to God, how your attitude has improved since you have been in recovery, the ways you have been able to step out of your denial into God's truth.

Let's close in prayer.

Father God, thank You for each person here tonight. Thank You for giving them the courage to begin this difficult step of making an inventory. Give them the desire and strength they need to proceed. Encourage them and light their way with Your truth. In the strong name of Jesus I pray, Amen.

SPIRITUAL INVENTORY PART 2

Principle 4: Openly examine and confess my faults to myself, to God, and to someone I trust.

"Happy are the pure in heart." (Matthew 5:8)

Step 4: We made a searching and fearless moral inventory of ourselves.

"Let us examine our ways and test them, and let us return to the LORD."
(Lamentations 3:40)

Introduction

Tonight we are looking at the second part of our spiritual inventory, where we pray, "Search me, O God, and know my heart; test my thoughts. Point out anything you find in me that makes you sad, and lead me along the path of everlasting life" (Psalm 139:23–24, TLB).

Last week, we discussed in part one of our spiritual inventories four areas of our lives. We asked ourselves some hard questions.

We looked at our relationships to others, our priorities, our attitudes, and our integrity. We talked about how our past actions in each of these areas had a negative or a positive effect on our lives and the lives of others.

Tonight, we are going to finish our spiritual inventory. We will look for some of our additional shortcomings or sins that can prevent God from working effectively in our lives and our recoveries.

Evaluating each area will help you complete your inventory.

Your Mind

Did you know that the most difficult thing to open is a closed mind?

Romans 12:2 gives us clear direction regarding our minds: "Do not conform to the pattern of this world, but be transformed by the renewing of your mind. Then you will be able to test and approve what God's will is—his good, pleasing and perfect will."

Some questions to ask yourself in this area:

1. How have you guarded your mind in the past? What did you deny?

Once again you need to see and examine how your coping skills—your denial—may have protected you from pain and hurt in the past. It may have done so, however, by preventing you from living in and dealing with reality.

Do you know that two thoughts cannot occupy your mind at the same time? It is your choice as to whether your thoughts will be constructive or destructive, positive or negative.

2. Have you filled your mind with hurtful and unhealthy movies, Internet sites, television programs, magazines, or books?

Your ears and your eyes are doors and windows to your soul. So, remember "garbage in, garbage out."

Straight living cannot come out of crooked thinking. It just is not going to happen.

Remember Proverbs 15:14 (NLT): "A wise person is hungry for truth, while the fool feeds on trash."

3. Have you failed to concentrate on the positive truths of the Bible?

I believe that three of the greatest sins today are indifference to, neglect of, and disrespect for the Word of God. Have you set aside a daily quiet time to get into God's instruction manual for your life?

Next, let's look at how we have treated our bodies. Did you know that with proper care the human body will last a lifetime?

Your Body

"Haven't you yet learned that your body is the home of the Holy Spirit God gave you, and that he lives within you? Your own body does not belong to you. For God has bought you with a great price. So use every part of your body to give glory back to God, because he owns it" (1 Corinthians 6:19–20, TLB).

1. In what ways have you mistreated your body?

Have you abused alcohol, drugs, food, or sex? This was, and still is, a tough one for me. In the depth of my alcoholism my weight dropped down to 160 pounds (my normal weight is 220 pounds). I almost died. I kept getting my suit pants taken in, and finally, the tailor explained to me that he couldn't take them in any more—the back pockets were touching. I asked God to help me get my strength and weight back. He truly blessed me. Boy, did He bless me! Now, it's time for moderation in my eating.

It is through our bodies or flesh that Satan works, but thank God that the believer's body is the temple of the Holy Spirit. God freely gives us the grace of His Spirit. He values us so much that He chose to place His Spirit within us. We need to have as much respect for ourselves as our Creator does for us.

2. What activities or habits caused harm to your physical health?

Remember, it was the God of creation who made you. Look at Psalm 139:13–14, 16: "For you created my inmost being; you knit me together in my mother's womb. I praise you because I am fearfully and wonderfully made; your works are wonderful, I know that full well.... Your eyes saw my unformed body; all the days ordained for me were written in your book before one of them came to be."

Many people say that they have the right to do whatever they want to their own bodies. Although they think that this is freedom, they really become enslaved to their own desires, which ultimately cause them great harm.

Your Family

In the Old Testament, Israel's leader, Joshua, made a bold statement regarding his household: "If you are unwilling to obey the Lord, then decide today whom you will obey.... But as for me and my family, we will serve the Lord" (Joshua 24:15, TLB).

1. Have you mistreated anyone in your family? How?

Perhaps you have physically or emotionally mistreated your family. Emotional abuse doesn't have to take the form of raging, yelling, or screaming. Tearing down a child's or spouse's self-esteem and being emotionally unavailable to them are both ways you may have harmed your loved ones.

God designed families to be our safety from life's storms. As much as it depends on you, you need to provide a haven for your family. If that isn't possible and you yourself don't feel safe there, let Celebrate Recovery be your family.

2. Against whom in your family do you have a resentment?

This can be a difficult area in which to admit your true feelings. It's easier to admit the resentments you have against a stranger or someone at work than someone in your own family. Denial can be a pretty thick fog to break through here. But you need to do it if you are going to successfully complete your inventory.

3. To whom do you owe amends?

You identify them now and work on becoming willing to deal with amends in Principle 6. All you are really looking for is your part in a damaged relationship.

4. What is the family secret that you have been denying?

What is the "pink elephant" in the middle of your family's living room that no one talks about? That's the family secret! Remember Jeremiah 6:14 (TLB): "You can't heal a wound by saying it's not there."

Your Church

One of the main reasons I started Celebrate Recovery was that I found most members of secular 12-Step groups knew the Lord's Prayer much better than they knew the Lord.

"Let us not neglect our church meetings, as some people do, but encourage and warn each other, especially now that the day of his coming back again is drawing near" (Hebrews 10:25, TLB).

1. Have you been faithful to your church in the past?

Your church is like a bank: the more you put into it, the more interest you gain in it.

2. Have you been critical instead of active?

If you don't like something in your church, get involved so you can help change it or at least understand it better. Turn your grumbling into service!

3. Have you discouraged your family's support of their church?

If you aren't ready to get involved in your church, that's your decision. But don't stop the rest of your family from experiencing the joys and support of a church family!

Wrap-Up

We've made it all the way through the eight different areas to help you begin and complete your inventory.

Once again, listen to Isaiah 1:18 (TLB). Memorize it! God says, "No matter how deep the stain of your sins, I can take it out and make you as clean as freshly fallen snow."

A couple of reminders as we close:

- Use the "Balancing the Scales" verses found in Participant's Guide 2.
- Keep your inventory balanced. List strengths and weaknesses.
- Find an accountability partner or a sponsor. I cannot say this enough: The road to recovery is not a journey to be made alone!

God bless you as you courageously face and own your past. He will see you through!

CONFESS

Principle 4: Openly examine and confess my faults to myself, to God, and to someone I trust.

"Happy are the pure in heart." (Matthew 5:8)

Step 5: We admitted to God, to ourselves, and to another human being the exact nature of our wrongs.

"Therefore confess your sins to each other and pray for each other so that you may be healed." (James 5:16)

Introduction

The following illustration is part of a message I heard at Willow Creek Church, and it is undoubtedly the best illustration that I have found to represent this principle.

Does the name Jessica McClure trip any memory bells in your mind? She was the eighteen-month-old girl from Midland, Texas, who fell in a deep, abandoned well-pipe several years ago. About four hundred people took part in her fifty-eight-hour rescue attempt, which was spurred on by her cries of anguish that could be clearly heard at ground level through the pipe.

Now, I found it fascinating that, at one point, a critical decision was made. The rescuers decided that the rescue would have two phases: Phase one was to simply get somebody down there, next to her, as soon as possible; phase two was actually extracting her from the well.

Phase one was driven by the knowledge that people tend to do and think strange things when they are trapped alone in a dark scary place for long periods of time. They get disorientated and their fears get blown out of proportion. Their minds play tricks on them. Sometimes they start doing self-destructive things. Sometimes they just give up! So the rescue experts decided that they needed to get a person down there to be with her as soon as possible. Then they would turn their attention on how they were going to get her out of the well. The plan worked, and eventually Jessica was rescued.

Now, how does the rescue of Jessica McClure relate to Step 5?

When people like us get serious about recovery, about spiritual growth, when we go on the 12-Step spiritual adventure, when we take that first step, we admit that we have some problems that make our lives unmanageable. When we turn to God and say, "God, I need help with those problems," then we might feel as though we are free falling. In a sense we are. We are out of control in a way. We can no longer live the way we are so used to living. The old ways just don't work anymore.

To complicate matters, on the way down, you find that the problem that you admitted in Step 1 is really being driven by a whole collection of character defects, which have been growing five feet under the surface of your life. And you have to identify those defects. You have to inventory them, as we have talked about for the last two months. You have to list them, admit them, and own them. You need to take responsibility for your pride, anger, envy, lust, greed, gluttony, and sloth. You know, "the big seven."

So, during the last couple of months, if you worked Step 4 honestly and thoroughly, you might be feeling as if *you* are trapped at the bottom of a deep, dark well. If you stay there long enough you can become disoriented and wonder why you took this recovery journey to begin with. You might feel like you want to bail out at this point.

You might start making statements like these: "You know that I am a royally messed up man." "The truth about me is that I'm a royally messed up woman." "No one's collection of sins and character defects is as bad as mine." "If anyone ever found out the truth about me, they would never have anything to do with me for the rest of their life."

Some of you get to that point and you say, "Why don't I just bail out of this program? Why don't I just go back to projecting an image of adequacy to everybody and not deal with all this unsettling truth about myself?"

It's at this critical point in the process that we need to get another human being to come alongside of us in that well as soon as possible. You need to get someone next to you before you give up and get back into denial. In a way, the 5th Step says that you can only grow so far alone; then you reach the point that continued growth and healing is going to require assistance from someone else.

We are right at that critical juncture tonight. We are at the point where we are being asked to come clean by telling another human being the truth about who we really are. But how?

Confess

The first step is to CONFESS my wrongs. Tonight's acrostic will show you just how to do that.

Confess your shortcomings, resentments, and sins
Obey God's direction
No more guilt
Face the truth
Ease the pain
Stop the blame
Start accepting God

The *C* in confess is CONFESS your shortcomings, resentments, and sins. God wants us to *come clean* and admit that wrong is wrong, that we're "guilty as charged." We need to "own up" to the sins we discovered in our inventory.

For the person who confesses, shame is over and realities have begun. Proverbs 28:13 tells us, "Whoever conceals their sins does not prosper, but the one who confesses and renounces them finds mercy." Confession is necessary for fellowship. Our sins have built a barrier between us and God.

The *O* in confess stands for OBEY God's direction.

Confession means that we agree with God regarding our sins. Confession restores our fellowship.

Principle 4 sums up how to obey God's direction in confessing our sins. First, we confessed (admitted) our faults to ourselves, to God, and to someone we trust. "'As surely as I am the living God, says the Lord, everyone will kneel before me, and everyone will confess that I am God.' Every one of us, then, will have to give an account to God" (Romans 14:11 – 12, GNT).

Then we do what we are instructed to do in James 5:16: "Confess your sins to each other and pray for each other so that you may be healed."

The next letter is *N*: No more guilt.

This principle can restore our confidence, our relationships, and allow us to move on from our "rear-view mirror" way of living that kept us looking back and second-guessing ourselves and others.

In Romans 8:1 (GNT) we are assured that "There is no condemnation now for those who live in union with Christ Jesus." The verdict is in! "All have sinned; . . . yet God declares us 'not guilty' . . . if we trust in Jesus Christ, who freely takes away our sins" (Romans 3:23 – 24, TLB).

So that's the "C-O-N" of confess. The "con" is over! We have followed God's directions on how to confess our wrongs.

After we "fess" up, we will have four positive changes in our lives. The first is that we will be able to FACE the truth. It has been said that "man occasionally stumbles over the truth, but most of the time he will pick himself up and continue on." Recovery doesn't work like that. Recovery *requires* honesty! Jesus said, "I am the light of the world. Whoever follows me will never walk in darkness, but will have the light of life" (John 8:12).

Have you ever noticed that a person who speaks the truth is always at ease? The next positive change that confession brings is to EASE the pain.

We are only as sick as our secrets! When we share our deepest secrets, we begin to divide the pain and the shame. A healthy self-worth develops that is no longer based on the world's standards but on the truth of Jesus Christ!

Pain is inevitable for all of us, but misery is optional. Psalm 32:3–5 (TLB) says, "There was a time when I wouldn't admit what a sinner I was. But my dishonesty made me miserable and filled my days with frustration.... My strength evaporated like water on a sunny day until I finally admitted all my sins to you and stopped trying to hide them. I said to myself, 'I will confess them to the Lord.' And you forgave me! All my guilt is gone."

The first *S* in confess reminds us that we can now STOP the blame.

It has been said that people who can smile when something goes wrong probably just thought of somebody they can blame it on. But the truth is, we cannot find peace and serenity if we continue to blame ourselves or others. Our secrets have isolated us from each other long enough! They have prevented intimacy in all of our important relationships.

Jesus tells us in Matthew 7:3 (PH): "Why do you look at the speck of sawdust in your brother's eye and fail to notice the plank in your own? How can you say to your brother, 'Let me get the speck out of your eye,' when there is a plank in your own?... Take the plank out of your own eye first, and then you can see clearly enough to remove your brother's speck of dust."

Finally, the last *S* shows us that it is time to START accepting God's forgiveness. Once we accept God's forgiveness we are able to look others in the eye. We see ourselves and our actions in a new light. We are ready to find the humility to exchange our shortcomings in Principle 5.

"For God was in Christ, restoring the world to himself, no longer counting men's sins against them but blotting them out" (2 Corinthians 5:19, TLB).

If you asked me to sum up the benefits of Principle 4 in one sentence, it would be this: In confession we open our lives to the healing, reconciling, restoring, uplifting grace of Jesus Christ who loves us in spite of ourselves.

First John 1:9 (NCV) reminds us that "if we confess our sins, he will forgive our sins, because we can trust God to do what is right. He will cleanse us from all the wrongs we have done."

Wrap-Up

Maybe you came tonight a little fearful of having to think about sharing your inventory. I hope you have been encouraged, and I trust you have been able to see the benefits of this task before you. Next time we will discuss the how-tos of finding a person with whom you can share your inventory. Let's close in prayer.

Dear God, thank You for Your promise that if we confess, You will hear us and cleanse us, easing our pain and guilt. Thank You that You always do what is right. In Jesus' name, Amen.

ADMIT

Principle 4: Openly examine and confess my faults to myself, to God, and to someone I trust.

"Happy are the pure in heart." *(Matthew 5:8)*

Step 5: We admitted to God, to ourselves, and to another human being the exact nature of our wrongs.

"Therefore confess your sins to each other and pray for each other so that you may be healed." *(James 5:16)*

Introduction

This week we are going to focus on confessing (admitting) our sins, all the dark secrets of our past, to another person.

We have all heard that the wages of sin is death, but you may not have heard that the wages of sin are never frozen or that they are never subject to income taxes. One of the main reasons for that is because most of the wages of sin go unreported! And, by the way, if the wages of sin is death, shouldn't you quit before payday?

Why Admit My Wrongs?

All joking aside, this part of Principle 4 is often difficult for people. I am often asked, "Why do I have to admit my wrongs to another?"

Many of us have been keeping secrets almost all of our lives. Every day those secrets take a toll on us. The toll we pay is loss of self-respect and energy as well as bondage to old codependent habits. Admitting—out loud—those secrets strips them of their power. They lose much of their hold on us when they are spoken.

Still, we are afraid to reveal our secrets to another person, even someone we trust. We somehow feel as if we have everything to lose and nothing to gain. I want you to hear the truth tonight. Do you know what we *really* have to lose by telling our secrets and sins to another?

1. We lose our sense of isolation. Somebody is going to come down into that well we talked about two weeks ago and be alongside us. Our sense of aloneness will begin to vanish.

2. We will begin to lose our unwillingness to forgive. When people accept and forgive us, we start to see that we can forgive others.

3. We will lose our inflated, false pride. As we see and accept who we are, we begin to gain true humility, which involves seeing ourselves as we really are and seeing God as He really is.

4. We will lose our sense of denial. Being truthful with another person will tear away our denial. We begin to feel clean and honest.

Now that you know what you have to *lose* when you admit your wrongs to another, let me tell you three benefits you will *gain*.

1. We gain healing that the Bible promises. Look at James 5:16 again: "Confess your sins to each other and pray for each other so that you may be healed." The key word here is *healed*. The verse doesn't say, "Confess your sins to one another and you will be forgiven." God *forgave* you when you confessed your sins to *Him*. Now He says you will begin the healing process when you confess your sins to *another*.

2. We gain freedom. Our secrets have kept us in chains—bound, frozen, unable to move forward in any of our relationships with God and others. Admitting our sins *snaps* the chains so God's healing power can start. "They cried to the Lord in their troubles, and he rescued them! He led them from the darkness and the shadow of death and snapped their chains" (Psalm 107:13–14, TLB).

Unconfessed sin, however, will fester. In Psalm 32:3–4 (GNT) David tells us what happened to him when he tried to hide his sins: "When I did not confess my sins, I was worn out from crying all day long.... My strength was completely drained." Remember, "Openness is to wholeness as secrets are to sickness." My grandpa used to say, "If you want to clear the stream, you need to get the hog out of the spring." Admit and turn from your sins. Remember that the only sin God can't forgive is the one that is not confessed.

3. We gain support. When you share your inventory with another person, you get support! The person can keep you focused and provide feedback. When your old friend "denial" surfaces and you hear Satan's list of excuses—"It's really not that bad"; "They deserved it"; "It really wasn't my fault"—your support person can be there to challenge you with the truth. But most of all, you need another person simply to listen to you and hear what you have to say.

How Do I Choose Someone?

Unlike little Jessica, the little girl trapped in the well, whom we talked about in Lesson 12, you can choose the person to come down into your well with you, so choose carefully! You don't want someone to say, "You did what?" or "You shouldn't have done that." You don't need a judge and jury. We already talked about the verdict. Remember Romans 3:23–24 (TLB): "All have sinned; … yet now God declares us 'not guilty' … if we trust in Jesus Christ, who … freely takes away our sins" and 1 John 1:9: "If we confess our sins, he is faithful and just and will forgive us our sins and purify us from all unrighteousness"?

You just need someone to listen. I find that it works best to choose someone who is a growing Christian and is familiar with the eight principles or the 12 Steps.

1. Choose someone of the same sex as you, whom you trust and respect. Enough said!

2. Ask your sponsor or accountability partner. Just be sure they have completed Principle 4 or Steps 4 and 5. The process should go more smoothly if the person is familiar with what you are doing. He or she will also have a sense of empathy, and if the person can share personal experiences, you will have a healthy exchange.

3. Set an appointment with the person, a time without interruptions! Get away from the telephones, kids, all interruptions for at least two hours. I have heard of some inventories that have taken eight hours to share. That's perhaps a little dramatic.

Guidelines for Your Meeting

1. Start with prayer. Ask for courage, humility, and honesty. Here is a sample prayer for you to consider:

   God, I ask that You fill me with Your peace and strength during my sharing of my inventory. I know that You have forgiven me for my past wrongs, my sins. Thank You for sending Your Son to pay the price for me, so my sins can be forgiven. During this meeting help me be humble and completely honest. Thank You for providing me with this program and _____ (the name of the person with whom you are sharing your inventory). Thank You for allowing the chains of my past to be snapped. In my Savior's name I pray, Amen.

2. Read the Principle 4 verses found on page 25 in Participant's Guide 3, *Getting Right with God, Yourself, and Others.*
3. Keep your sharing balanced—weaknesses and strengths!
4. End in prayer. Thank God for the tools He has given to you and for the complete forgiveness found in Christ!

PRINCIPLE 4 TESTIMONY

My name is Marnie, and I am a grateful believer in Jesus Christ who struggles with sexual addiction and food issues.

I wish I could start this story "Once upon a time" or "There once was a little girl." But instead it starts like this: A broken home, tortuous abuse, fits of rage, and being stripped away from those I held dear to my heart. And this was just a fraction of my childhood that began my forbidden lifestyle filled with fantasy, sex, and lust.

My path to recovery started at Saddleback Church in November of 2000. I remember that night well. I crawled in broken and completely unaware of reality. My view on life had become so distorted and my actions had become so out of control, I don't think the Enemy himself could've kept up.

That night I watched as people smiled, hugged, and celebrated, because it happened to be the ninth anniversary of Celebrate Recovery. I arrived an hour early, completely unaware that the worship service didn't start until seven o'clock. So, I sat and listened to the band rehearse.

I remember sitting there, *almost* all alone, with only a handful of people walking around setting things up. As I looked around, tears began to form in my eyes and it was all I could do to blink them back. I didn't know what I was doing there. My thoughts were wandering and had become so disjointed. Everything within me wanted to just get up and walk out. It was evident I was still in denial. I kept hearing the same thoughts repeating themselves in my head: *Whatever is wrong with these people is way worse than anything I could have done!* and *Whatever I've done, I'm sure I can fix it on my own!* But for some reason I just could not bring myself to get up out of that chair and leave.

I was startled as a man came up to me, put his hand on my shoulder, and said, "Excuse me, but this seat is taken." As I looked around the empty room, it took me a while to realize that he was kidding. But you know, just in those few words, I felt a sense of comfort and relief. I felt welcomed and a little less "out of place."

That night I attended Newcomers 101 where, for the first time, I confessed my secrets. I managed to utter the words that had gone unspoken for years — *"I cheated on my husband"* — and moments after that, I began to sob. That was it. That was all I said. The woman, who was leading 101 that night, leaned forward, cupped my hands in hers and told me for the first time "Everything's going to be okay. You've come to the right place." The sincerity in her voice warmed me.

Long before I was born, there was already turmoil brewing in my family. Before my first birthday, my parents had finalized their plan to divorce. My older sister and I were sent to live with my father and grandparents in Hawaii. Once we arrived, my dad conveniently left the scene. My grandparents were unofficially assigned to care for us as if we were their own. My fondest childhood memories are of the years I spent with my grandparents in Hawaii. They taught me about Jesus, and by their example, I learned Christian values. Thankfully, they showed me what it was like to live in a "normal" family. My parents, on the other hand, were diabolical opposites of my grandparents.

My father is a functioning alcoholic, who also has a wandering eye for women. I watched as my dad moved from relationship to relationship and as his addiction to pornography and alcohol grew. His complete disregard for his calling as a father allowed me plenty of time to explore as a young child. I can remember being crouched in a corner with my sister as we attempted to smoke cigarettes and drink some of my dad's beer. As a young girl, curiosity took me by surprise one day when I was snooping around the house and found my dad's *Playboy* collection hidden in his dresser drawers. I felt as though I had just stumbled upon a secret, and I ran out of the room. But at the same time, I was intrigued at the images I saw. Often, my dad would take my sister and me to his girlfriend's house where we were abandoned in the living room and told to watch television while Dad retreated into the bedroom with his girlfriend. Even at such a young age, I was well aware of what they were doing. I viewed this as a totally acceptable lifestyle. My last encounter with my father was when I was in my twenties. That day I wandered onto his patio finding an enraged, drunken man waving a butcher knife in my face.

At the age of five, I moved back to California to live with my mother. She has the personality of a raging alcoholic, minus the alcohol. The movie *Mommy Dearest* comes to mind. She was physically, verbally, and emotionally abusive. One unpleasant incident that sticks with me the most was when I was packing to go on a camping trip with family friends. I walked in on her in one of her fits of rage and she had slapped me in the face so hard that my tooth punctured my lip. Needless to say, I had a huge fat lip and black eye the following day. I told everyone I had been eating and that my fork had slipped. She'd always apologize and say she hated what she had done, but in the next breath, tell me I deserved it. I don't know how many times I ended up in the hospital as a young girl. I remember vividly my mother being sent out of the room and the doctors asking, "Did your mother hit you?" and with a stoic face, my response always being a simple shake of the head "no."

Throughout my childhood, I became my mother's human piñata—often a victim of choking, and dodging mirrors she threw at me. I also was beaten with lamps, hangers, high-heeled shoes, and whatever else was within reach. To cope with my dysfunctional life, I escaped into a fantasy life, filled with lustful thoughts and pornographic images that were embedded in my mind. I would stay in bed for hours fanaticizing about sexual acts, replaying the same dreams over and over again in my head.

My upbringing was so filled with turmoil that I had no choice but to escape the insanity. Just before the start of my senior year of high school, I emancipated myself. At seventeen, legally, I was recognized as an adult. I moved out and was on my own. I was determined to break the cycle of dysfunction I had been living with all of my life. But I had become a product of my environment.

I married my high school sweetheart in June of '98. Marriage started off difficult for us. Although we had dated for eight years prior to getting married, it almost seemed that in an instant we had grown miles apart, as if our years together had somehow been reversed. Our conversations were no longer familiar. Instead, we stuck to superficial topics. Hard times were beginning to materialize. We were struggling financially and we were living with his parents. The enemy sank his fangs into me as I viewed my marriage as a mistake; a "verbal blunder," so to speak; a rural penitentiary. Bitterness, resentment, and hatred started to paint an ugly picture, as my visions of a "normal" lifestyle fell by the wayside. We went through months of arguing and a lot of broken promises. I felt like I was running in place. I felt taken advantage of, disrespected, and unappreciated. I felt like I had no voice and no control. I felt robbed of my dreams. Most of all, I felt emotionally bankrupt. It was then that my behavior exploded into an uncontrollable fury; my solution, adultery. Just ten short months into my marriage, I had cheated on my husband.

As my addictive lifestyle was starting to take shape, I took a new position at work, which would require me to fly to the Bay Area every Monday and fly home every Thursday. All of this free time away from my husband gave me the freedom to make my own choices, which only fueled my unhealthy behaviors. In my denial, life never felt so good. I was getting attention from men I hardly knew and who hardly knew me. Every day, I became more and more independent of my marriage. I felt in control. I was finally doing something I thought I wanted to do instead of having to live by someone else's rules. But in my heart, I knew something was desperately wrong. I struggled with confusion about the Christian values I had been taught as a child versus what the world deems as socially acceptable behavior. I suddenly felt as if I only knew these childhood beliefs intellectually. For the first time in my life, my faith in God had been tried and shaken, because at this point in my life, my relationship with the Lord was nonexistent. I ignored those feelings and instead replaced them with alcohol, anorexia, and adultery. I was now on a suicide mission *devoted to a life of deception."* My life became intertwined with the very women I had been warned against in my childhood Bible teachings: Jezebel, Potiphar's wife, and Delilah. My life had now become a reflection of the woman whose *"greatest accomplishment in life was the destruction of the man who loved her most."* My forbidden lifestyle progressed into a double life. I continued keeping up the variety of appearances that had sustained me throughout the years. At work, I was balanced, poised, and professional. I would walk in with a smile on my face, go to my office, shut the door, and act out with Internet pornography and chat rooms. When I was with my college friends, I was the baby. I played the "innocent" codependent Marnie, the "good girl," the Marnie who never drank, but just took care of the rest of the bunch when they did. At church I was the devout Christian, pseudo listening from the concrete bench outside, but making sure my friends and family all knew I was present and accounted for. But the real Marnie, the uninhibited Marnie, surfaced after work hours where I would spend most of my free time at bars with the "good old boys club." I could tell a good dirty joke or two and just be one of the guys. The more I drank, the more I talked. The more I talked, the more I started blaming my circumstances for my behavior. My drinking buddies got the unvarnished story of how awful life was like for me at home. I became completely cavalier with a total disregard and disrespect for myself and for those around me. My life was a riotous mess.

My insatiable appetite for more manifested itself as I attempted to fill the void within me, only to find out that this beast of ugliness would, in no way, be satisfied. My form of self-punishment and control was to starve my body, both spiritually and physically. Body image became more important to me than anything else in my life, including the people I loved the most. I was now on a quest for the perfect figure, no matter what the cost. Starving myself made me feel like I was making my own decisions. I put myself on a rigid diet which consisted of a handful of grapes each day and excessive amounts of Diet Coke. I decided what I put in my body. I decided what I would look like. I started working out obsessively, running between twelve and fifteen miles a day. This lifestyle, coupled with my sexual addiction, left my body weak and out of fuel. I weighed a mere ninety-two pounds, with a sunken face, and was rapidly self-destructing. My addiction was now in full throttle.

As I saw the scenes of my life unfolding, I became desperate to find freedom from my "web of deception." I picked up the phone and called Saddleback Church and they suggested I try Celebrate Recovery. During that time, I recalled the Christian values taught to me as a child by my grandparents, which I had buried due to my anger and resentment toward God. He had finally gotten my attention. It was then that I realized, *"I don't understand myself at all, for I really want to do what is right, but I can't. I do what I don't want to—what I hate. I know perfectly well that what I am doing is wrong, and my bad conscience proves that I agree with these laws I am breaking. But I can't help myself, because I'm no longer doing it. It is sin inside me that is stronger than I am that makes me do these evil things" (Romans 7:15–20).* At this point, I felt as if I had been hollowed out and the world, as I knew it, was slowly being erased. I didn't know how to reconcile these conflicting pieces of my past. The pain had finally become greater than the fear. I had reached my bottom.

Two months after that first fateful night at Celebrate Recovery, a women's step study group opened. So I picked up a *Celebrate Recovery Bible* and a set of Celebrate Recovery participant's guides and began a pilgrimage through the Christ-centered 12 Steps with women I could relate to and who could also relate to me … and where secrets seemed all but impossible. At first I kept myself at a safe distance. I would guard my secrets so that no one could use what they knew to hurt me. I also felt hideously ugly, and thought the scars that had been left behind were visible to everyone. But, as I began to share, for the first time I saw women who just stayed silent throughout, listening without judgment. I began to grasp that this internal battle I was having was not uncommon. It was then that I started to understand how the pains of my past played a crucial part in my behavior. I started realizing that I was in a cycle of addiction. All my life I viewed men as objects and I was imitating what I had learned in my childhood. I had kept *so* many secrets—childhood secrets, secrets in my adult life, and secrets in my marriage—but by saying them out loud, it brought some truth to my reality. I found comfort in the fact that I could not be perfect—there was no such thing as the perfect marriage or the perfect body. Most importantly, I saw just how far I had fallen away from my relationship with Christ. *"Problems far too big for me to solve are piled higher than my head. Meanwhile my sins, too many to count, have all caught up with me and I am ashamed to look up"* (Psalm 40:12).

Principle 4 says, "Openly examine and confess my faults to myself, to God, and to someone I trust." "Happy are the pure in heart" (Matthew 5:8).

I began exploring this new, unchartered territory at Celebrate Recovery by working this principle, and the true healing began. It was then I heard God's promise of freedom and stopped acting out. *"It was then that I realized that whatever is covered up will be uncovered, and every secret will be made known. So then, whatever you have said in the dark will be heard in broad daylight"* (Luke 12:2–3).

As I laid my sins at the foot of the cross and turned from my addictions, God declared me not guilty. He *"blotted out the charges proved against you, the list of his commandments which you had not obeyed. He took this list of sins and destroyed it by nailing it to Christ's cross"* (Colossians 2:13–15).

I have reconciled my relationship with my husband and today my relationships are built on honesty and trust. My marriage has been restored. The challenges are still there. Marriage takes work. And my view on marriage is that every couple needs to argue every now and then, just to prove that the relationship is strong enough to survive it. We have been blessed with the most precious gifts of all, two beautiful baby girls. My new ministry in life is my family. Where they once played second fiddle to my work and my addictive behavior, they are now my priority. In fact, in this day and age, where people are so accessible with smart phones, iPads, iPods, etc., our family has a rule: "No electronics at the table." Most importantly, I am teaching my children that NOTHING is more important than my time with them. No email, text, tweet, phone call, whatever.

As for my mom and dad, I have found it in my heart to forgive them, although I still do not have a relationship with either of them. Though I have made attempts over the years, I remain steadfast in the fact that neither of them are safe people to have around me, my husband, or my girls. Neither of them has changed their behaviors, and unfortunately, they have been left to live in their own misery. I have learned how to embrace my pain and made the choice to abandon my life of deception and destruction.

As I reflect on my life now, I thank God for His never-failing truth and understanding. I look back at the journey I had to take through Celebrate Recovery to bring balance to the chaos of my life, and now the blessings that come with being able to help people use Celebrate Recovery as a tool to implement peace and joy in their own lives. I have used these same tools to continue my obedience and submission to Christ as a wife, mother, and employee. God has taken my tragedy and used it as a testament of my faith. Most of all, I thank God that, unlike Delilah, mine is not "a life wasted," and that He chose to spare me rather than erase me from history as He did Delilah. I'm no longer defined by my past mistakes and failures. It's only by God's grace that today, when I look at myself in the mirror, I no longer see myself as someone trying to be perfect, or an adulterer, or an alcoholic, or anorexic. I see myself as an incredibly blessed mother, wife, and forgiven child of God.

In corporate America I used to fly every week and find myself in compromising situations because of my husband's absence. Ironically, God is using the very same pattern of flying that was so instrumental in virtually destroying my life to restore me to wholeness. Today I get to serve on the Celebrate Recovery conference team, where it is my privilege to travel every other week to different cities nationally and internationally to help coordinate Celebrate Recovery one-day seminars. My accountability team now spans the nation, as I have filled my life with godly women and men from whom I seek guidance every day. With an accountability partner in almost every state, there's no hiding anymore.

This reminds me of God's promise that says, *"Even though you are at the ends of the earth, the LORD your God will go and find you and bring you back again"* (Deuteronomy 30:4).

You know, *"there was a time when I wouldn't admit what a sinner I was. But my dishonesty made me miserable and filled my days with frustration. All day and all night your hand was heavy on me. My strength evaporated like water on a sunny day until I finally admitted all my sins to you and stopped trying to hide them. I said to myself, 'I will confess them to the LORD.' And you forgave me! All my guilt is gone"* (Psalm 32:3–5).

Thank you for letting me share.

PRINCIPLE 5

Voluntarily submit to every change God wants to make in my life and humbly ask Him to remove my character defects.

"Happy are those whose greatest desire is to do what God requires." (Matthew 5:6)

READY

Principle 5: Voluntarily submit to every change God wants to make in my life and humbly ask Him to remove my character defects.

"Happy are those whose greatest desire is to do what God requires."
(Matthew 5:6)

Step 6: We were entirely ready to have God remove all these defects of character.

"Humble yourselves before the Lord, and he will lift you up."
(James 4:10)

Introduction

Congratulations! If you are ready for Principle 5, you have already taken some major steps on the road to recovery. You admitted you had a problem and were powerless over it; you came to believe that God could and would help you; you sought Him and turned your life and your will over to His care and direction; you wrote a spiritual inventory and shared that with God and another person. You've been busy! That's a lot of work—hard work!

Maybe you're thinking that it's about time to take a breather and relax for a while. Think again!

In some recovery material, Step 6 (Principle 5) has been referred to as the step "that separates the men from the boys"! I would also like to add, "separates the women from the girls"! So tonight we are going to answer the question, "What does it mean to be entirely READY?"

Ready

One of the reasons that Principle 5 "separates the men from the boys"—or the women from the girls—is because it states that we are ready to "voluntarily submit to every change God wants to make in my life."

Most of us, if not all of us, would be very willing to have *certain* character defects go away. The sooner the better! But let's face it, some defects are hard to give up.

I'm an alcoholic, but there came a time in my life, a moment of clarity, when I knew I had hit bottom and was ready to stop drinking. But was I ready to stop lying? Stop being greedy? Ready to let go of resentments? I had been doing these things for a long time. Like weeds in a garden, they had developed roots!

We've formed our defects of character, our hang-ups, our habits over periods of ten, twenty, or thirty years. In this principle you and God—together—are going after these defects. *All* of them!

Tonight's acrostic will show you how to get READY to allow Him to do that.

Release control
Easy does it
Accept the change
Do replace your character defects
Yield to the growth

The first letter tonight stands for RELEASE control. That reminds me of a story I heard.

A man bumped into an old friend in a bar. He said, "I thought you gave up drinking. What's the matter, no self-control?" The friend replied, "Sure I've got plenty of self-control. I'm just too strong-willed to use it!"

God is very courteous and patient. In Principle 3, He didn't impose His will on you. He waited for you to invite Him in!

Now in Principle 5, you need to be "entirely ready," willing to let God into every area of your life. He won't come in and clean up an area unless you are willing to ask Him in.

It has been said that "willingness is the key that goes into the lock and opens the door that allows God to begin to remove your character defects." I love the way the psalmist invites God to work in his life: "Help me to do your will, for you are my God. Lead me in good paths, for your Spirit is good" (Psalm 143:10, TLB).

Simply put, the *R*—release control—is "Let go; let God!"

The *E* in ready stands for EASY does it. These principles and steps are not quick fixes! You need to allow time for God to work in your life.

This principle goes further than just helping you stop doing wrong. Remember, the sin is the *symptom* of the character defect.

Let me explain. The sin is like a weed in a garden: It will keep reappearing unless it is pulled out by the roots. And the roots are the actual defects of character that *cause* the particular sin. In my case, the major sin in my life was abusing alcohol. That was the act, the sin. The defect of character was my lack of any positive self-image. So, when I worked Principle 5, I went after the defect—my lack of a positive self-image—that caused me to sin by abusing alcohol.

That takes time, but God will do it. He promised! "Commit everything you do to the Lord. Trust him to help you do it and he will" (Psalm 37:5, TLB).

The next letter is *A*: ACCEPT the change.

Seeing the need for change and allowing the change to occur are two different things, and the space between recognition and willingness can be filled with fear. Besides that, fear can trigger our old dependency on self-control. But this principle will not work if we are still trapped by our self-will. We need to be ready to accept God's help throughout the transition. The Bible makes this very clear in 1 Peter 1:13–14 (GNT): "So then, have your minds ready for action. Keep alert and set your hope completely on the blessing which will be given you when Jesus Christ is revealed. Be obedient to God, and do not allow your lives to be shaped by those desires you had when you were still ignorant."

As I said, all the steps you have taken on the road to recovery have helped you build the foundation for the "ultimate surrender" that is found in Principle 5.

James 4:10 says, "Humble yourselves before the Lord, and he will lift you up." All we need is the willingness to let God lead on us on our road to recovery.

Let's move on to the *D* in ready, which is extremely important: DO replace your character defects.

You spent a lot of time with your old hang-ups, compulsions, obsessions, and habits. When God removes one, you need to replace it with something positive, such as recovery meetings, church activities, 12th-Step service, and volunteering! If you don't, you open yourself for a negative character defect to return.

Listen to Matthew 12:43–45 (GNT): "When an evil spirit goes out of a person, it travels over dry country looking for a place to rest. If it can't find one, it says to itself, 'I will go back to my house.' So it goes back and finds the house empty, ... Then it goes out and brings along seven other spirits even worse than itself, and they come and live there."

I said that one of my major defects of character was a negative self-image, a nonexistent self-esteem, to be more exact. I wasted a lot of time in bars, attempting to drown it. When I started working the 12 Steps, I found I had lots of time on my hands. I tried to fill it by doing positive things that would build my self-esteem, rather than tear it down.

In addition to working my program and attending meeting after meeting, I fellowshiped and worked with "healthy" people. I volunteered. As the months passed, I got more involved at church too. That's when God called me to start to build Celebrate Recovery. I started going to seminary.

You don't have to start a ministry, but you do have to replace your negative character defect with something positive. There are many, many opportunities to serve and get involved in at church.

The last letter in ready is the *Y*: YIELD to the growth.

At first, your old self-doubts and low self-image may tell you that you are not worthy of the growth and progress you are making in the program. Don't listen! Yield to the growth. It is the Holy Spirit's work within you.

"The person who has been born into God's family does not make a practice of sinning, because now God's life is in him; so he can't keep on sinning, for this new life has been born into him and controls him — he has been *born again*" (1 John 3:9, TLB).

Wrap-Up

The question is, "Are you entirely ready to voluntarily submit to any and all changes God wants to make in your life?"

If you are, then read the Principle 5a verses found in Participant's Guide 3 on page 32, and pray the following prayer:

Dear God, thank You for taking me this far in my recovery journey. Now I pray for Your help in making me be entirely ready to change all my shortcomings. Give me the strength to deal with all of my character defects that I have turned over to You. Allow me to accept all the changes that You want to make in me. Help me be the person that You want me to be. In Your Son's name I pray, Amen.

VICTORY

Principle 5: Voluntarily submit to every change God wants to make in my life and humbly ask Him to remove my character defects.

"Happy are those whose greatest desire is to do what God requires."
(Matthew 5:6)

Step 6: We were entirely ready to have God remove all these defects of character.

"Humble yourselves before the Lord, and he will lift you up."
(James 4:10)

Step 7: We humbly asked Him to remove all our shortcomings.

"If we confess our sins, he is faithful and just and will forgive us our sins and purify us from all unrighteousness." (1 John 1:9)

Introduction

Tonight we are going to look at an overview of Principle 5. We are going to answer the question, How can you have victory over your defects of character?

Victory

We are going to use the acrostic VICTORY.

Voluntarily submit
Identify character defects
Change your mind
Turn over character defects
One day at a time
Recovery is a process
You must choose to change

The *V* is <u>VOLUNTARILY</u> submit to every change God wants me to make in my life and humbly ask Him to remove my shortcomings. The Bible says that we are to make an offering of our very selves to God. "Offer yourselves as a living sacrifice to God, dedicated to his service and pleasing to him. . . . Let God transform you inwardly by a complete change of your mind" (Romans 12:1 – 2, GNT).

When you accepted Principle 3, you made the most important decision of your life by choosing to turn your life over to God's will. That decision got you right with God; you accepted and determined to follow His Son Jesus Christ as your Lord and Savior.

Then you began to work on you. You made a fearless and moral inventory of yourself. The first step in any victory is to recognize the enemy. My inventory showed me that I was my greatest enemy.

You came clean by admitting and confessing to yourself, to God, and to another person your wrongs and your sins. For probably the first time in your life, you were able to take off the muddy glasses of denial and look at reality with a clear and clean focus.

Now you are considering what Step 6 says: that you are "entirely ready to have God remove all these defects of character." You're at the place in your recovery where you say, "I don't want to live this way anymore. I want to get rid of my hurts, hang-ups, and habits. But how do I do it?"

The good news is that *you* don't do it!

Step 6 doesn't read, "You are entirely ready to have you remove all these defects of character," does it? No, it says, "You are entirely ready to have *God* remove all these defects of character."

So how do you begin the process to have God make the positive changes in your life that you and He both desire?

You start by doing the *I* in victory: IDENTIFY which character defects you want to work on first. Go back to the wrongs, shortcomings, and sins you discovered in your inventory. Falling down doesn't make you a failure, staying down does! God doesn't want us just to admit our wrongs, He wants to make us right! He wants to give us a future and a hope! God doesn't just want to forgive us, He wants to change us! Ask God to first remove those character defects that are causing you the most pain. Be specific! "In their hearts humans plan their course, but the LORD establishes their steps" (Proverbs 16:9).

Let's move to the *C*, which stands for CHANGE your mind.

Second Corinthians 5:17 tells us that when you become a Christian, you are a new creation, a brand new person inside. The old nature is gone. The changes that are going to take place are the result of a team effort. Your responsibility is to take the action to follow God's direction for change. You have to let God transform (change) you by renewing your mind.

Let's look at Romans 12:2: "Do not conform to the pattern of this world, but be transformed by the renewing of your mind. Then you will be able to test and approve what God's will is—his good, pleasing and perfect will."

To transform something means to change its condition, its nature, its function, and its identity. God wants to change more than just our behaviors. He wants to change the way we think. Simply changing behaviors is like trimming the weeds in a garden instead of removing them. Weeds always grow back unless they are pulled out by the roots. We need to let God transform our minds!

How? By the *T* in victory: TURNING your character defects over to Jesus Christ. Relying on your own willpower, your own self-will, has blocked your recovery. Your past efforts to change your hurts, hang-ups, and habits by yourself were unsuccessful. But if you "humble yourselves before the Lord, . . . he will lift you up" (James 4:10).

Humility is not a bad word, and being humble doesn't mean you're weak. Humility is like underwear: we should have it, but we shouldn't let it show. Humility is to make the right estimate of one's self or to see ourselves as God sees us.

You can't proceed in your recovery until you turn your defects of character over to Jesus. Let go! Let God!

The next letter is *O*: ONE day at a time.

Your character defects were not developed overnight, so don't expect them to be instantly removed. Recovery happens *one day at a time!* Your lifelong hurts, hang-ups, and habits need to be worked on in twenty-four-hour increments. You've heard the old cliché: "Life by the yard is hard; life by the inch is a cinch." Jesus said the same thing: "So don't be anxious about tomorrow, God will take care of your tomorrow too. Live one day at a time" (Matthew 6:34, TLB).

When I start to regret the past or fear the future, I look to Exodus 3:14 where God tells us that His name is "I AM."

I'm not sure who gets the credit for the following illustration, but it's right on. God tells me that when I live in the past with its mistakes and regrets, life is hard. I can take God back there to heal me, to forgive me, to forgive my sins. But God does not say, "My name is 'I was.'" God says, "My name is 'I AM.'"

When I try to live in the future, with its unknown problems and fears, life is hard. I know God will be with me when that day comes. But God does not say, "My name is 'I will be.'" He says, "My name is I AM."

When I live in today, this moment, one day at a time, life is not hard. God says, "I am here." "Come to me, all you who are weary and burdened, and I will give you rest" (Matthew 11:28).

Let's look at the letter *R*: RECOVERY is a process, "one day at a time" after "one day at a time."

Once you ask God to remove your character defects, you begin a journey that will lead you to new freedom from your past. Don't look for perfection, instead rejoice in steady progress. What you need to seek is "patient improvement." Hear these words of encouragement from God's Word: "And I am sure that God who began a good work within you will keep right on helping you grow in his grace until his task within you is finally finished on that day when Jesus Christ returns" (Philippians 1:6, TLB).

The last letter in victory is *Y*: YOU must choose to change.

As long as you place self-reliance first, a true reliance on Jesus Christ is impossible. You must voluntarily submit to every change God wants you to make in your life and humbly ask Him to remove your shortcomings. God is waiting to turn your weaknesses into strengths. All you need to do is *humbly ask!*

"God gives strength to the humble,... so give yourselves humbly to God. Resist the devil and he will flee from you. And when you draw close to God, God will draw close to you" (James 4:6–8, TLB).

Wrap-Up

To make changes in our lives, all I had to do and all you need to do is to be *entirely* ready to let God be the life-changer. We are not the "how" and "when" committee. We are the preparation committee: all we have to be is *ready*!

Tonight, Jesus is asking you, "Do you want to be healed, do you want to change?" You must choose to change. That's what Principle 5 is all about! Let's close with prayer.

Dear God, show me Your will in working on my shortcomings. Help me not to resist the changes that You have planned for me. I need You to "direct my steps." Help me stay in today, not get dragged back into the past or lost in the future. I ask You to give me the power and the wisdom to make the very best I can out of today. In Christ's name I pray, Amen.

PRINCIPLE 5 TESTIMONY

My name is John, and I am a grateful believer in Jesus Christ who struggles with codependency.

My earliest memories are probably kindergarten and the beginning of grade school. I was a pretty happy and extroverted little fella. I was very active, full of joy and energy, secure and comfortable in my own skin. We were Mom, Dad, my older brother (by three years), and then twin sisters a year younger—all together in Duluth, Minnesota. My parents were saved and belonged to an exciting new independent Pentecostal church. They were young and zealous, and had young and zealous friends, and a young and zealous pastor. My father worked at a men's clothing store and my mom stayed home with us kids. Some of the families from our young and zealous church got together and decided to buy some property just outside the city limits in a lovely, private wooded area. They all wanted to build some homes together, form a Christian neighborhood, with Christian kids riding their Christian bikes on a Christian road, with Christian dogs chasing Christian cats . . .

Our family quickly signed on to that project and soon we were living in a freshly built log home on Morning Star Drive.

I guess I was in the second grade or so when, one by one, each of us four clueless siblings was called upstairs into our parents' bedroom for news of the divorce. This is how Mom wanted to break it to us. This is one of my few branded-in memories. I remember the unfinished texture of the wooden baluster on the balcony, my hand sort of trailing behind me on the railing trying to somehow slow my progress to my father and mother's room. My older brother came out sobbing, and I just kept walking toward their room, straining to look through their cracked door. There was something evil crouched beyond that door: depression, pain . . . unwelcome, unasked-for change.

It was so quiet after the divorce announcement. My parents used to fight a lot before the announcement, but now my dad hadn't the spirit for fighting; he gave up. Again, the realization of past yelling matches came *after* the hush fell on that big log home. My father, one of the heroes, if there are any in this testimony, was so infinitely sad. My mom knew the pain she was causing—I do believe that—but at the same time, I have come to understand that she didn't. She was not making decisions based on the truth. She was lying to herself, and to us, about how much fun her new life would be, *our* new life, would be. It was a fresh start, a new and exciting adventure. Her world was a cleverly constructed fantasy of greener grass.

She packed us up and moved us away from my father, to a farm where a new family was waiting. I remember her turning her head to us in the passenger and back seats while driving and repeating over and over, "Isn't this exciting?"

At the first meeting of the soon-to-be-step-family, I remember lots of dogs and the smell of a dairy farm. I was game; it DID look exciting. My sisters took things in stride as well, but my older brother did not. I *adapted* to this new life. I did whatever I was told; I was compliant; I had fun; I rode motorcycles; I pitched in with the haying; I picked rocks in the fields; I camped out with my stepbrother; I shot a pistol, rode the three-wheeler, grabbed an electric fence on a dare to see who could hold on the longest. I did it. I conformed. My brother did not.

In the midst of my mother's chaotic relationship with this new husband, my brother went a little crazy. Our oldest stepbrother was a bullying beast of a teenager who had his father's temper. He was full of hate, full of rage, and I stayed out of his way, laughed at his dirty jokes, did what I was told. My brother did not laugh, did not do what he was told, did not stay out of anyone's way.

One night, out in the barn, my older brother had enough of our "bully stepbrother" and tried to crush his head with a lead pipe. He whiffed badly. I watched as my brother paid a terrible price for standing up to a bully. It was a terrifying experience, which led to me and my brother both moving back to our dad's. My brother and I carried on a new existence at my father's home in that huge, empty log tomb. Dad was not coping well and we weren't enough to keep him going. He had seen his church collapse a few months earlier in a scandal. His church, his marriage, and his life had been taken from him; the rug had been pulled out; that was his new reality and ours.

Somewhere in the transition from grade school to middle school, depression took me like anesthesia. I remember it coming on, then I remember coming out of it. I ate a lot, I know that. I was like a Hoover vacuum on a very low setting. Whatever food was near me got sucked in, slowly but surely. I stared at whatever TV had to offer for hours after school, when other kids were outside playing. I began to skip school, constantly faking migraines. My mother was divorced again and off the farm. *I didn't care, I was depressed.* She had repented of her foolishness, and my brother and I were going to live with her and my sisters again in a nice little duplex. *I didn't care, I was depressed.* I was back with mom, my sisters, and my brother, and I was put in counseling. Now, I did care about that. I hated that. Maybe my hating counseling shocked me out of my depression. Counseling scared me straight.

When I did awaken from my depressed stupor, I found myself in the body of this scared, fat, introverted older kid. Mom was on welfare trying to get an education so I wore a lot of secondhand clothing. Bullies were a terror to me. I was much larger than most kids my age, but I was afraid of everyone. I was what others said I was. There was no doubt in my mind. I just wanted to disappear. That's how I coped. I began to deal with problems through invisibility. A very big boy willing every part of his being to disappear into thin air best describes me at this time of my life. I was living a life of "quiet desperation." I was tortured and tormented by my classmates, physically and emotionally abused, and I felt like I deserved it.

I was helpless, powerless, and daily frozen with fear, being constantly silenced by crippling insecurity. This overwhelming insecurity at times reclaims its hold on me. A strange residual social fear lingers, but I have learned to trust that it remains for God's purposes. I choose to embrace this weakness and say with Paul: *"His power is perfected in my weakness. When I am weak, I am truly strong."*

One day it all began to change. It started when I stood up to a guy in my class who wanted to take my seat, and what do you know, he backed down. I started lifting weights, then I went by myself and tried out for the football team, and I made it. Then I went to the church youth group, started cracking jokes, starting talking to girls. By my junior year of high school, I was starting for the varsity football team and ENJOYING school for the first time in my life.

My grades stunk, but I was happy and independent. I had been getting more and more involved in the youth group, and I began developing a vibrant relationship with God. I had prayed for salvation at five years of age with my father, but now I was beginning to understand and answer a clear call to His service. At fifteen, I seriously committed myself to Jesus Christ. I made a vow to live for Him for the rest of my life.

I graduated from high school and eventually moved with my mom to the Twin Cities where I was back to being a "nobody." I had been lightly recruited by a couple local colleges for football and had received a small scholarship at a Christian university in Missouri, but that insecurity came back stronger than ever, convincing me all efforts to succeed were hopeless. I began a slow and steady roll back into depression. I was not in church, not in school. I was back to a day-to-day existence without meaning, without purpose, working the graveyard shift at a local gas station. My mom had many relationships over the years following the farm with one deadbeat after the other; but in St. Paul, Minnesota, she picked up their king in a bar one summer evening.

He told her that he was the son of a wealthy CEO, and that he would pay her back if she would spring for a weekend of partying in Duluth. He had no intention of paying for anything; he wasn't the son of a CEO; he was a con man running up her credit cards, depleting her savings, until finally he showed his true colors. One evening he took the rented Cadillac my mother had charged for their lavish weekend fantasy and disappeared. After my mom called the police a few days following his departure, I found him late one night passed out on the seat of the stolen Caddy.

I wanted to save my mom from these guys every time. She was always able to sell me on them, and then when she turned against them, I was right there with her, comforting her, consoling. I was blinded to her responsibility in these situations. I wanted to be somebody's favorite—to save someone—and she was beginning to rely on my shoulder to cry on. No matter what she had done to me, or to the family over the years, I loved her, I still believed in her, she relied on me, and that was what I desperately clung to. So, I called the police on the loser in the Caddy, and I was the hero, until my mom decided to bail the con man out of jail. When she walked through the door with him, I almost fell out of my chair. The king was back. I gave my mom an ultimatum. I was amazed and hysterical with anger when she gave me her answer. No. This man would stay, and I would go. Back to my dad's I went.

Soon after moving back to my father's, I had an opportunity to move north and play football at a community college. It was at this remote, "nowhere" school that I learned about the wonderful numbing effects of alcohol. It was easy to let it all go there in Virginia, Minnesota. I was alone, I was depressed, and I was a waste. My life consisted of football, a meager schedule of classes, alcohol whenever and however I could get it, and a girlfriend hand-picked to put up with my moodiness and drinking. I had plugged into a local church the moment I arrived, but it couldn't hold me; I just was too wrapped up in my pain, in coping. The discovery of alcohol was a revelation. It made me more depressed, but in a bittersweet, self-pitying, brooding sense.

I dropped out of college after my first year, and ended up rooming with my best friend from high school back in Duluth. I began working another graveyard shift cleaning the floors at a grocery store. I was sleeping through the days, stockpiling alcohol on the shelf, working a dead-end job that I could barely hold, picking fights. Now *I* was becoming the bully. I would drink at home, and then go out drinking, drive home drunk, and drink. There was nothing else in my future. This was my life, for the rest of my life.

One night I was alone, and I was sober, or I was drunk, or someplace in between. I do remember the shotgun in my hands. I had my grandfather's double barreled shotgun across my lap. I tried to put it to my head, but fear swept over me. Was I so pathetic that I couldn't even kill myself?

I began playing games with loading it and trying to peek down the barrel to see if I could get up the courage to take this seriously. I wept and screamed on the floor of my room for God to save me, but I was alone. He must have had enough and abandoned me; I couldn't blame Him. I wanted Him to leave me alone; I didn't deserve love. I was going to die, and I was going to be as insignificant in death as I was in life.

I was finally ready. Calm and determined, sniffing away the last of the tears, I said my last half-hearted prayer, "Lord, if You're there, it's time to let me know, or I'm finished." Another ridiculous ultimatum.

But, in that little upstairs apartment, God answered me. The room glossed over, and I was in a cave. Ribs became part of the infrastructure of the room, and I was inside something. It was a vision. The only one I have ever had. And it wasn't angels and harps. It was me clearly in the inner guts of a fish. I grabbed hold of that vision with two desperate hands, finding and opening my old Bible from youth group. I had no idea where the story of Jonah was. It was a book in itself. The story was familiar, but what did that have to do with me? Then I saw it, the prayer in the second chapter. Jonah's prayer is what was in me. My spirit had been speaking this in groans, in the throes of anguish. *"In my distress I called to the LORD, and he answered me. From deep in the realm of the dead I called for help, and you listened to me cry.... I said, 'I have been banished from your sight....'" The engulfing waters threatened me, the deep surrounded me.... To the roots of the mountains I sank down; the earth beneath barred me in forever. But you, LORD my God, brought my life up from the pit. When my life was ebbing away, I remembered you, LORD, and my prayer rose to you.... What I have vowed I will make good. I will say, 'Salvation comes from the LORD'"* (Jonah 2:1–9).

I dedicated myself to the Lord that moment, telling Him that what I had vowed as a committed Christian in my youth, I would make good.

I signed up for the fall to go to the Christian university in Missouri where I had initially, upon graduation, received a seed scholarship for football. I had no idea where the funds would come from, but it was clear that was the place God wanted me. It was where He had wanted me all along. I had been running from a call. Like Jonah.

I was accepted to the school and the money somehow was there for me to attend. Life was so sweet these three years of school. I was away at school, playing football. I had Christ-centered classes, and Christian friends, so why was I still struggling to maintain my sobriety? There were rules against drinking. I had even signed a covenant that I would abstain from alcohol. But that didn't mean opportunities didn't present themselves; it didn't mean opportunities weren't created. My last binge ended late one night after staring into the disappointed eyes of the most beautiful woman God has ever breathed life into. My girlfriend had been able to melt away some of the walls that were again forming around me—we even began talking about marriage, about kids, about everything—but we hadn't talked about this drinking stuff before.

Another stamped-in, burned-in memory is when I stopped by her off-campus apartment after having a few drinks, and then a few more drinks with some friends who lived in the same apartment complex. My girlfriend didn't say so, but it was all over her face when she saw me. She was disappointed. I don't think she ever really thought twice about us—we were in love and flying recklessly and blissfully toward our future—but in that instant, I saw a loss of respect … even some doubt. She loved me for the right reasons—for the Christian man I wanted to be—and this wasn't it. It was in this moment, confronted with this past-and-once-again-present coping strategy, that the double-standard I was keeping between my Christian ascent and my worldly descent came to a head. I was either going to become the man God had created and called *or* go back to despair, loneliness, death, and hell. I chose life, and have never, in over a decade of sobriety, ever regretted my decision.

My girlfriend and I got married, and I received a degree in criminal justice, but ended up enjoying a counseling group I was placed in during my practicum so much that I began to explore counseling and social work as a career. Together we moved to my wife's home state of Delaware where I began working for the state's Division of Family Services as a family crisis therapist.

During my five years in that office, I toiled through a master's program in social work, and began group and individual work at a private counseling agency on the side to earn hours for my clinical licensing. I loved the work, I loved counseling, and I loved group process.

What I didn't realize is that in working two to three jobs ministering to others, I was neglecting my ministry at home to my family. Three jobs at times kept me away constantly, and I was even volunteering any leftover hours at the church. It was exhausting—and a trying time for my marriage.

I tried to convince my wife, unsuccessfully, that this work was my mission field. I was giving my all in answer to "the call." But my absence was wearing on her, on us. We had two girls, and I didn't see much of them. My explanation to them, to myself, and to God was that I was needed out there; people needed me; they needed saving! She had her parents to lean on, my kids had their grandparents. Those I helped didn't have anyone but me. Isn't being a Christian about helping the helpless AT ANY COST?

What I didn't fully realize is that through college, working toward a degree, playing football, and now with my career goals, my master's degree, my striving for success in counseling others, I was succumbing to the pressure of trying to earn back my value. The value I had lost by being a fat, spineless nobody without any answers. My professional life was a tenuous balance of keeping everyone happy with me, spinning anything negative, running from conflict, blaming others, justifying my very existence, running, running to keep that distance . . . keeping the helpless loser I once was far behind me.

One day, God called me to a fast. A one-week fast. I managed to doubt it and fight it for a good month, but I finally relented. When the fast was over, I was incredibly disappointed. No lightning bolts, no giant handwriting on the wall.

What a rip-off! Oh well. It was done and I had been obedient. A few weeks later, my brother-in-law, a youth pastor working in a little church in West Virginia, called and asked if I would travel to West Virginia to talk to his church's men's ministry about outreach.

His pastor had felt God leading the church to do more for those outside their four walls. I said I would be glad to do it, and soon found myself talking to a small group of men in Clarksburg, West Virginia about Celebrate Recovery, and some other outreach programs I was heading up in our church in Delaware.

A week later, I was being asked to consider interviewing in this same church to do outreach ministry full-time. God was orchestrating a miraculous life-change, and soon I was chugging through the mountains in a U-Haul contemplating this new direction in my life and ministry.

Now the recovery program I had started in Delaware was very loosely based on the Celebrate Recovery curriculum, and I had plans in West Virginia to veer even further off the Celebrate Recovery course. I have since discovered why I was reluctant to conform to the program. Running my own program, my way, was all about pride. Tailor-making my own recovery program elevated me to the keeper of all the keys, giving me the illusion of being in complete control and helping me stay aloof in a "therapist" role. It kept people looking to me for the answers. I wanted to be their savior. *"I, even I, am the Lord, and apart from me there is no savior" (Isaiah 43:11).*

After several months of running the "John" recovery program in my new ministerial role in West Virginia, with frustratingly minimal success, my wonderful little church sent me to my first Celebrate Recovery Summit. It was during those three days in August 2006 that I felt challenged to make a commitment to run this ministry by the letter. I had been fighting it, as I was to learn later, mainly because I would rather help "those people," rather than be *one* of "those people."

However, as I listened to the testimonies given at the Summit, as I worshiped with the thousands of lives being transformed by the power of God through the truths of this program, I felt the gentle conviction of the Holy Spirit calling me to submit and SURRENDER. I had been asking everyone to share their lives with me, to open up, be completely transparent so they could find healing and hope for their lives. However, I had never really done that myself. What hypocrisy! During a question-and-answer time at one of the Summit workshops, I made a public confession that I had been using the Celebrate Recovery name, but had not been following the model. It was at that vulnerable place, the giving up of my power, where my own healing began. You could say that my journey of discovery into my own emotional and spiritual DNA finally began when I submitted to the Celebrate Recovery DNA. While I had been trying to construct a new me through meeting the needs of others, God had wanted nothing more than to deconstruct me by exposing my own many hurts, hang-ups, and habits. Through the work of this ministry, especially going through the step study, I finally dared to get honest about my past.

Principle 5 says, "Voluntarily submit to every change God wants to make in my life and humbly ask Him to remove my character defects." "Happy are those whose greatest desire is to do what God requires" (Matthew 5:6).

Finally, I would have to take a real look at myself and either change or continue in my own pride and ego. Then, as I wrote my inventory, I realized something that broke me to a point where I hadn't been broken before. I started to see and feel how much my efforts to replace God with self-sufficiency and self-righteousness had grieved my God and Savior Jesus Christ. After sharing my inventory, with the help of another minister, I made my first heart-wrenching amends. My first amends were offered to God, and through that process I felt His forgiveness, mercy, and love for me like never before.

In that place of grace, He gave me a new awareness of a value I could never earn, and a value I will never lose.

"How deep the Father's love for us, how vast beyond all measure that He would send His only Son, to make a wretch His treasure."

Today I have come to a new realization and reliance on His economy. It is not by my strength, not by man's might, but truly by His Spirit that I (and others) find true recovery. My wife and I celebrated our twelfth anniversary in June. I have four beautiful daughters. (Yes, I am powerless and my life is truly unmanageable.) My family has now become my most important and cherished ministry.

I want to encourage anyone who is feeling the overwhelming weight of insecurity to let go, get vulnerable, and trust in the Lord. In Principle 7 we are taught: *"Reserve a daily time with God for self-examination, Bible reading, and prayer in order to know God and His will for my life and to gain the power to follow His will."* Celebrate Recovery rightly emphasizes this complete dependency on Christ as the only opportunity we have for true peace, security, and salvation.

I thank God for His love, and I thank God for my family; I thank God for this program and for my incredible Celebrate Recovery family; and I thank God for the opportunity to share my testimony with you.

Thank you for letting me share.

PRINCIPLE 6

Evaluate all my relationships. Offer forgiveness to those who have hurt me and make amends for harm I've done to others, except when to do so would harm them or others.

"Happy are the merciful." (Matthew 5:7)
"Happy are the peacemakers." (Matthew 5:9)

—

AMENDS

Principle 6: Evaluate all my relationships. Offer forgiveness to those who have hurt me and make amends for harm I've done to others, except when to do so would harm them or others.

"Happy are the merciful." (Matthew 5:7)
"Happy are the peacemakers." (Matthew 5:9)

Step 8: We made a list of all persons we had harmed and became willing to make amends to them all.

"Do to others as you would have them do to you." (Luke 6:31)

Introduction

This week, we are going to focus on Principle 6. In fact, we are going to spend the next two months on Principle 6. That's how important it is to our recovery. We will use some of the time for teaching and we will celebrate the Lord's Supper next week to help us really understand the true meaning of forgiveness, but I would like to use most of our time for testimonies from you. Please let me know if you would like to share your story of how Principle 6 has positively impacted your recovery and relationships.

Tonight, we are going to give an overview of Principle 6, which is all about making amends. "Forgive me as I learn to forgive" sums it up pretty well.

We started doing repair work on the *personal* side of our lives earlier in our recovery by admitting our powerlessness, turning our lives and wills over to God's care, doing our moral inventory, sharing our sins or wrongs with another, and admitting our shortcomings and asking God to remove them. But now we begin to do some repair work on the *relational* side of our lives. Making your amends is the beginning of the end of your isolation from God and others.

Still, some of us balk at making amends. We think, "If God has forgiven me, isn't that enough? Why should I drag up the past? After all, making amends doesn't sound natural."

The answer to that objection is simple: making amends is not about your *past* so much as it is about your *future.* Before you can have the healthy relationships that you desire, you need to clean out the guilt, shame, and pain that has caused many of your past relationships to fail.

So, in the words of Step 8, it is time to "make a list of persons that we have harmed and become willing to make amends to them all." At this point, you are only looking for the willingness. Step 8 only requires that we identify those to whom we need to make amends or offer forgiveness.

Luke 6:31 reminds us to treat others the way that we want to be treated. For some of you, that may be very difficult. You have been hurt very badly or abused. Many of you had nothing to do with the wrong committed against you.

Often I have counseled people on Principle 6 and on the critical importance of forgiveness, only to have them say, "Never will I forgive! Not after what was done to me!" In these cases, the wrong against the individual was often child molestation, sexual abuse, or adultery. Such sins are deep violations that leave painful wounds, but they also are the root of dysfunction that bring many people into recovery.

Forgiving the perpetrator of such wrongs, even after the one harmed has dealt with the emotional pain, seems impossible. We are going to deal specifically with this issue in the lesson on the three types of forgiveness.

For now, listen to the way Celebrate Recovery rewords this step for those in the sexual/physical abuse groups:

> Make a list of all persons who have harmed us and become willing to seek God's help in forgiving our perpetrators, as well as forgiving ourselves. Realize we've also harmed others and become willing to make amends to them.

Let's look at the second part of Principle 6: "... make amends for harm I've done to others, except when to do so would harm them or others."

Listen as I read Matthew 5:23–24: "Therefore, if you are offering your gift at the altar and there remember that your brother or sister has something against you, leave your gift there in front of the altar. First go and be reconciled to them; then come and offer your gift."

The first part of Principle 6 deals with being willing to consider forgiveness. The second part of Principle 6 calls us to action as we make our amends and offer our forgiveness. Going back to the garden metaphor, we need to pull out the dead weeds in our past broken relationships so that we can clear a place where our new relationships can be successfully planted or restored. That's why Principle 6 is so important.

In Participant's Guide 3, on page 43, you will find the "Amends" list.

Column 1 is where you list the persons to whom you need to be willing to make amends, those whom you have harmed. Column 2 is for the persons that you need to become willing to forgive. List them this week.

During the next two months, add to the lists as God reveals to you other names to include. Remember, all you are doing at this point is writing them down.

Amends

Let's look at tonight's acrostic and answer the question, How do I make AMENDS?

Admit the hurt and the harm
Make a list
Encourage one another
Not for them
Do it at the right time
Start living the promises of recovery

The *A* is ADMIT the hurt and the harm. Principle 4 showed us how important it is to open up to God and to others. Your feelings have been bottled up far, far too long, and that has interfered with all your important relationships. In this step of your recovery you need to once again face the hurts, resentments, and wrongs that others have caused you or that you have caused to others. Holding on to resentments not only blocks your recovery, it blocks God's forgiveness in your life.

Luke 6:37 (GNT) tells us, "Do not judge others, and God will not judge you; do not condemn others, and God will not condemn you; forgive others, and God will forgive you."

The next letter in amends is *M*: MAKE a list.

In addition to the "Amends" worksheet in Participant's Guide 3, you will find the "Celebrate Recovery Inventory" on pages 30 and 31 in Participant's Guide 2. You can also use these sheets to help you make your amends list.

In column 1, on your inventory, you will find the list of people that you need to forgive. These are the people who have hurt you. In column 5, you will find the list of people to whom you owe amends. These are the ones whom you have hurt.

If it has been a while since you did your inventory, God may have revealed others to you that you need to add to your list. That's why it's important to start off with the "Amends" worksheet.

When you are making your list, don't worry about the "how-tos" in making your amends. Don't ask questions like *How could I ever ask my dad for forgiveness? How could I ever forgive my brother for what he did?* Go ahead and put the person on your list anyway. "Treat others as you want them to treat you" (Luke 6:31, TLB).

The *E* in amends stands for ENCOURAGE one another.

It has been said that encouragement is oxygen to the soul. Before you make your amends or offer your forgiveness to others, meet with your accountability partner or sponsor, someone to encourage you and to provide a good "sounding board." That person's objective opinion is valuable to ensure that you make amends and offer forgiveness with the right motives.

Hebrews 10:24 says, "And let us consider how we may spur one another on toward love and good deeds." If you are asked to be an encourager, an accountability partner, or a sponsor, be honored. And remember, you can't hold a torch to light another's path without brightening your own.

The *N* in amends is the reason for making the amends: NOT for them.

You need to approach those to whom you are offering your forgiveness or amends humbly, honestly, sincerely, and willingly. Don't offer excuses or attempt to justify your actions; focus only on your part.

In five words, here's the secret to making successful amends: *Do not expect anything back!* You are making your amends, not for a reward, but for freedom from your hurts, hang-ups, and habits.

Principle 6 says that I am responsible to "make amends for harm I've done to others." Jesus said, "Love your enemies and do good to them; lend and expect nothing back" (Luke 6:35, GNT). God loves us generously and graciously, even when we are at our worst. God is kind; we need to be kind!

Do you know that you can become addicted to your bitterness, hatred, and revenge, just as you can become addicted to alcohol, drugs, and relationships? A life characterized by bitterness, resentment, and anger will kill you emotionally and shrivel your soul. They will produce the "Three Ds":

Depression

Despair

Discouragement

An unforgiving heart will cause you more pain and destruction than it will ever cause the person who hurt you.

Let's move on to the *D* in amends: DO it at the right time.

This principle not only requires courage, good judgment, and willingness, but a careful sense of *timing!*

Ecclesiastes 3:1 (TLB) tells us, "There is a right time for everything." There is a time to *let* things happen and a time to *make* things happen. There is a right time and a wrong time to offer forgiveness or to make amends.

Before making amends, you need to pray, asking Jesus Christ for His guidance, His direction, and His perfect timing.

Principle 6 goes on to say, "... except when to do so would harm them or others."

Listen to Philippians 2:3–4: "In humility value others above yourselves, not looking to your own interests but each of you to the interests of the others."

Don't wait until you *feel* like making your amends or offering your forgiveness; living this principle takes an act of the will! Or perhaps I should say a *crisis* of the will. Making your amends is an act of obedience to Scripture and of personal survival.

The last letter in amends is *S*: START living the promises of recovery.

As we complete this principle, we will discover God's gift of true freedom from our past. We will begin to find the peace and serenity that we have long been seeking. We will become ready to embrace God's purpose for our lives.

God promises, "I will repay you for the years the locusts have eaten" (Joel 2:25).

Wrap-Up

Principle 6 offers you freedom—freedom from the chains of resentment, anger, and hurt; freedom, through your amends for the harm you caused others, to look them in the eye, knowing that you are working with God in cleaning up your side of the street.

In your small groups, I encourage those of you who have completed Principle 6 to share the freedom and the blessings that you have received.

Let's pray.

Dear God, I pray for willingness—willingness to evaluate all my past and current relationships. Please show me the people who I have hurt, and help me become willing to offer my amends to them. Also, God, give me Your strength to become willing to offer forgiveness to those who have hurt me. I pray for Your perfect timing for taking the action that Principle 6 calls for. I ask all these things in Your Son's name, Amen.

FORGIVENESS

⸻

Principle 6: Evaluate all my relationships. Offer forgiveness to those who have hurt me and make amends for harm I've done to others, except when to do so would harm them or others.

"Happy are the merciful." (Matthew 5:6)
"Happy are the peacemakers." (Matthew 5:9)

Step 8: We made a list of all persons we had harmed and became willing to make amends to them all.

"Do to others as you would have them do to you." (Luke 6:31)

Step 9: We made direct amends to such people whenever possible, except when to do so would injure them or others.

"Therefore, if you are offering your gift at the altar and there remember that your brother or sister has something against you, leave your gift there in front of the altar. First go and be reconciled to them; then come and offer your gift." (Matthew 5:23–24)

⸻

Introduction

Tonight we are going to continue to work on evaluating all of our relationships. We will offer forgiveness to those who have hurt us and, when possible, make amends for the harm we've done to others, without expecting anything in return.

We have discussed how to make your amends, but tonight I would like to talk about something that can block, stall, or even destroy your recovery: the inability to accept and offer *forgiveness*.

I think we all agree that forgiveness is a beautiful idea until we have to practice it.

A guy once told me, "John, you won't catch me getting ulcers. I just take things as they come. I don't ever hold a grudge, not even against people who have done things to me that I'll never forgive." Right!

I saw this sign on a company bulletin board: "To err is human; to forgive is not company policy."

There are a lot of jokes about forgiveness, but forgiveness is not something that those of us in recovery can take lightly, because forgiveness is clearly God's prescription for the broken. No matter how great the offense or abuses, along the path to healing lies forgiveness.

We all know that one of the roots of compulsive behavior is pain—buried pain.

In Principle 1 we learned that pretending the hurt isn't there or that it doesn't bother you anymore won't solve your problems. Jeremiah 6:14 (TLB) reminds us that "You can't heal a wound by saying it's not there!"

Facing your past and forgiving yourself and those who have hurt you, and making amends for the pain that you have caused others, is the only lasting solution. Forgiveness breaks the cycle! It doesn't settle all the questions of blame, justice, or fairness, but it does allow relationships to heal and possibly start over.

So tonight let's talk about the three kinds of forgiveness.

Forgiveness

In order to be completely free from your resentments, anger, fears, shame, and guilt, you need to give and accept *forgiveness* in all areas of your life. If you do not, your recovery will be stalled and thus incomplete.

The first and most important forgiveness is extended from God to us. Have you accepted God's forgiveness? Have you accepted Jesus' work on the cross? By His death on the cross, all our sins were canceled, paid in full; a free gift for those who believe in Him as the true and only Higher Power, Savior, and Lord.

Jesus exclaimed from the cross, "It is finished" (John 19:30). No matter how grievously we may have injured others or ourselves, the grace of God is always sufficient! His forgiveness is always complete!

Romans 3:22–25 (GNT) says, "God puts people right through their faith in Jesus Christ. God does this to all who believe in Christ, because there is no difference at all: everyone has sinned and is far away from God's saving presence. But by the free gift of God's grace all are put right with him through Christ Jesus, who sets them free. God offered him so that by his blood he should become the means by which people's sins are forgiven through their faith in him."

Remember, if God wasn't willing to forgive sin, heaven would be empty.

The second kind of forgiveness is extended from us to others. Have you forgiven others who have hurt you? This type of forgiveness is a process. You need to be willing to be willing, but to be truly free, you must let go of the pain of the past harm and abuse caused by others.

Forgiveness is all about letting go. Remember playing tug-of-war as a kid? As long as the people on each end of the rope are tugging, you have a war. You "let go of your end of the rope" when you forgive others. No matter how hard they may tug on their end, if you have released your end, the war is over. It is finished! But until you release it, you are a prisoner of war!

Think about who your anger is hurting most. I'll give you a hint. It's you! Forgiveness enables you to become fully freed from your anger and allows you to move forward positively in those relationships.

The Bible has a lot to say about forgiveness. Romans 12:17–18 says, "Do not repay anyone evil for evil. Be careful to do what is right in the eyes of everyone. If it is possible, as far as it depends on you, live at peace with everyone."

Causing an injury puts you *below* your enemy. Revenging an injury makes you *even* with him. Forgiving him sets you one *above* him. But more importantly, it sets you free!

By the way, on your list of "others to forgive," you might have forgotten about someone you may need to forgive: God. Yes, you heard me right. God.

God cannot and does not sin. His very nature is marked by perfect holiness in every attribute and action. God is perfect in love, mercy, and grace. But remember that He loved us so much that He gave us a free will. He didn't want us to be His puppets. He wanted us to love Him as our choice. You need to understand and believe that the harm others did to you was from their free will. It was their choice, not God's. It was *not* God's will. Once you understand "free will" you will understand that your anger toward God has been misplaced.

His promise is found in 1 Peter 5:10 (PH): "After you have borne these sufferings a very little while, God himself (from who we receive all grace and who has called you to share his eternal splendour through Christ) will make you whole and secure and strong."

If you have been the victim of sexual abuse, physical abuse, or childhood emotional abuse or neglect, I am truly sorry for the pain you have suffered. I hurt with you. But you will not find the peace and freedom from your perpetrators until you are able to forgive them. Remember, forgiving them in no way excuses them for the harm they caused you, but it will release you from the power they have had over you. I have rewritten Steps 8 and 9 of the 12 Steps for you.

> Step 8: Make a list of all persons who have harmed us and become willing to seek God's help in forgiving our perpetrators, as well as forgiving ourselves. Realize we've also harmed others and become willing to make amends to them.

> Step 9: Extend forgiveness to ourselves and to others who have perpetrated against us, realizing this is an attitude of the heart, not always confrontation. Make direct amends, asking forgiveness from those people we have harmed, except when to do so would injure them or others.

To recap, we need to accept God's forgiveness by accepting what Jesus did for us on the cross, and we need to forgive and ask forgiveness of others. The last kind of forgiveness is perhaps the most difficult for us to extend.

We need to forgive ourselves. Have you forgiven yourself? You can forgive others, you can accept God's forgiveness, but you may feel the guilt and shame of your past is just too much to forgive.

This is what God wants to do with the darkness of your past: "Come, let's talk this over! says the Lord; no matter how deep the stain of your sins, I can take it out and make you as clean as freshly fallen snow. Even if you are stained as red as crimson, I can make you white as wool! If you will only let me help you" (Isaiah 1:18–19, TLB).

No matter how unloved or worthless you may feel, God loves you! Your feelings about yourself do not change His love for you one bit.

Let me ask you a question: If God Himself can forgive you, how can you withhold forgiveness from yourself? In fact, I believe that we must forgive ourselves before we can honestly forgive others. The first name on your amends list needs to be God, the second needs to be yours. Why?

The answer is found in Matthew 22:36–40 (TLB), where Jesus was asked,

> "Which is the most important command?" Jesus replied, "'Love the Lord your God with all your heart, soul, and mind.' This is the first and greatest commandment. The second most important is similar: 'Love your neighbor as much as you love yourself.'"

Now how can you love or forgive your neighbor, if you can't love or forgive yourself? If you have not forgiven yourself, your forgiveness to others may be superficial, incomplete, and done for the wrong motives.

Self-forgiveness is not a matter of assigning the blame to someone else and letting yourself off the hook. It's not a license for irresponsibility. It is simply an acknowledgment that you are human like everybody else and that you've reached the stage in your recovery at which you are able to give yourself greater respect.

Wrap-Up

As you take the necessary steps of forgiveness, you will discover that you are letting go of the guilt and shame. You'll be able to say, "I'm not perfect, but God and I are working on me. I still fall down, but with my Savior's help, I can get up, brush myself off, and try again.

We can say, "I forgive myself because God has already forgiven me, and with His help, I can forgive others."

When you forgive yourself, you don't change the past, but you sure do change the future!

GRACE

Principle 6: Evaluate all my relationships. Offer forgiveness to those who have hurt me and make amends for harm I've done to others, except when to do so would harm them or others.

"Happy are the merciful." (Matthew 5:6)
"Happy are the peacemakers." (Matthew 5:9)

Step 9: Made direct amends to such people whenever possible, except when to do so would injure them or others.

"Therefore, if you are offering your gift at the altar and there remember that your brother or sister has something against you, leave your gift there in front of the altar. First go and be reconciled to them; then come and offer your gift." (Matthew 5:23–24)

Introduction

Tonight, we are going to finish discussing Principle 6. We have talked about how to evaluate all our relationships, offer forgiveness to those who have hurt us, and make amends for the harm that we have done to others, when possible, without expecting anything back.

As we grow as Christians and as we grow in our recovery, we want to follow the guidance and directions of Jesus Christ. As we get to know Him better, we want to model His teachings and model His ways. We want to become more like Him. Honestly, if we are going to implement Principle 6 to the best of our ability, we need to learn to model God's grace. But how?

Grace

The key verses of Celebrate Recovery are 2 Corinthians 12:9–10 (NCV): "But he said to me, 'My grace is enough for you. When you are weak, my power is made perfect in you.' So I am very happy to brag about my weaknesses.

Then Christ's power can live in me. For this reason I am happy when I have weaknesses, insults, hard times, sufferings, and all kinds of troubles for Christ. Because when I am weak, then I am truly strong."

Celebrate Recovery is built on and centered in Christ's grace and love for each of us.

Let's look at tonight's acrostic: GRACE.

God's gift
Received by our faith
Accepted by God's love
Christ paid the price
Everlasting gift

The *G* in grace is GOD'S gift.

Grace is a gift. Grace cannot be bought. It is freely given by God to you and me. When we offer (give) our amends and expect nothing back, that's a gift from us to those whom we have hurt.

Romans 3:24 (NCV) tells us, "All need to be made right with God by his grace, which is a free gift. They need to be made free from sin through Jesus Christ."

First Peter 1:13 (NCV) says, "Prepare your minds for service and have self-control. All your hope should be for the gift of grace that will be yours when Jesus Christ is shown to you."

If my relationship with God was dependent on my being perfect, I would have trouble relating to God most of the time. Thank God that my relationship with Him is built on His grace and love for me. He gives the strength to make the amends and offer the forgiveness that Principle 6 requires.

And how do we receive God's gift of grace? That's the *R* in grace: RECEIVED by our faith.

No matter how hard we may work, we cannot earn our way into heaven. Only by professing our faith in Jesus Christ as our Lord and Savior can we experience His grace and have eternal life.

Ephesians 2:8–9 says, "For it is by grace you have been saved, through faith—and this is not from yourselves, it is the gift of God—not by works, so that no one can boast."

Let me share another verse with you. Philippians 3:9 (TLB) states, "No longer counting on being saved by being good enough or by obeying God's laws, but by trusting Christ to save me; for God's way of making us right with himself depends on faith—counting on Christ alone."

You and I tend to be more interested in what we *do*. God is more interested in what we *are*. / who we are

Romans 5:2 says of Jesus, "Through whom we have gained access by faith into this grace in which we now stand. And we boast in the hope of the glory of God."

Just a word of warning: Our walk needs to match our talk. Our beliefs and values are seen by others in our actions. And it is through our faith in Christ that we can find the strength and courage needed for us to take the action Principle 6 requires: making our amends and offering our forgiveness.

The next letter in grace is *A*. We are ACCEPTED by God's love.

God loved you and me while we were still out there sinning. Romans 5:8 says, "God demonstrates his own love for us in this: While we were still sinners, Christ died for us."

We can, in turn, love others because God first loved us. We can also forgive others because God first forgave us. Colossians 3:13 (TLB) says, "Be gentle and ready to forgive; never hold grudges. Remember, the Lord forgave you, so you must forgive others."

Ephesians 2:5 (NCV) reminds us, "Though we were spiritually dead because of the things we did against God, he gave us new life with Christ. You have been saved by God's grace."

I don't know about you, but I know that I do not deserve God's love. But the good news is He accepts me in spite of myself! He sees all my failures and loves me anyway. And the same goes for you.

Hebrews 4:16 (NCV) tells us, "Let us, then, feel very sure that we can come before God's throne where there is grace. There we can receive mercy and grace to help us when we need it."

Let's move on to the *C* in grace: CHRIST paid the price.

Jesus died on the cross so that all our sins, all our wrongs, are forgiven. He paid the price, sacrificed Himself for you and me so that we may be with Him forever.

When we accept Christ's work on the cross, we are made a new creation. We can then rely on God's strength and power to enable us to forgive those who have hurt us. We can set aside our selfishness and speak the truth in love. We focus only on our part in making amends or offering our forgiveness.

Ephesians 1:7 (NCV) says, "In Christ we are set free by the blood of his death, and so we have forgiveness of sins. How rich is God's grace."

The last letter in grace is *E*: God's grace is an EVERLASTING gift.

Once you have accepted Jesus Christ as your Savior and Lord, God's gift of grace is forever.

Let me read a quote from the Big Book of AA, pages 83–84: "Once you have completed Step Nine, you will know a new freedom and a new happiness.... You will comprehend the word serenity and know peace.... You will suddenly realize that God is doing for you what you could not do for yourself."

And here's a quote from the *real* Big Book—the Bible: "And I am sure that God who began the good work within you will keep right on helping you grow in his grace until his task within you is finally finished on that day when Jesus Christ returns" (Philippians 1:6, TLB).

Also, 2 Thessalonians 2:16 (NCV) states, "May our Lord Jesus Christ himself and God our Father encourage you and strengthen you in every good thing you do and say. God loved us, and through his grace he gave us a good hope and encouragement that continues forever."

My life verse is 1 Peter 2:9–10 (TLB), where God says, "For you have been chosen by God himself—you are priests of the King, you are holy and pure, you are God's very own—all this so that you may show to others how God called you out of the darkness into his wonderful light. Once you were less than nothing; now you [John Baker] are God's own. Once you knew very little of God's kindness; now your very lives have been changed by it."

I stand before you as a product of God's grace. Everyone here this evening who has let Christ into his or her life is also a product of God's grace. As we model this grace, we will be able to do the work that Principle 6 requires.

Let's close tonight with Colossians 1:6: "The gospel is bearing fruit and growing throughout the whole world—just as it has been doing among you since the day you heard it and truly understood God's grace."

PRINCIPLE 6 TESTIMONY

My name is Linda, and I am a grateful believer in Jesus Christ who struggles with sexual, physical, and emotional abuse and codependency.

I was born in Iowa and raised in a Christian home. My family moved to California when I was four years old, and so I have spent most of my life in Southern California. My dad read the Bible and we prayed together every night after dinner. I attended Sunday school, sang in the church choirs, attended catechism, and went to a Christian school until my junior year of high school.

I was one of six children, born in the middle of the pack. Our parents took us to church twice every Sunday. I learned from a very early age that God was my friend. I memorized a lot of Bible verses and always talked directly to Him.

During my high school years, my dad and mom worked hard and left us girls in charge of taking care of the house and getting dinner ready every night. Since I was the oldest of the girls at home, I felt responsible for organizing the workload so everyone would get along. I thought it was my job to make everything perfect and make everyone happy. I used my organizational skills to my advantage to control my siblings. I also learned to be a people-pleaser. I did what I thought would make people happy, like me, and accept me. I didn't know that codependency would become a crippling issue in my life. My family may have looked good when we went to church, but everybody ignored the real "elephant" that was in the middle of the room.

My dad had serious anger issues that made us young girls run to our room in fear at times. My mom was the perfect codependent who taught us to wear our masks wherever we went and that we should not talk about things that happened in our house.

I met my first boyfriend when I was a freshman in high school. He came from a very dysfunctional family, where his dad was both verbally and physically abusive. His mother was another model of codependency. What a perfect candidate for me to "fix"!

For the next four years, I tried to rescue my boyfriend as he struggled with his dad and his family issues. I thought I could fix him into what I wanted—"the perfect boyfriend"—and I even thought I could make him stop smoking pot. While he was away serving in the Army, he proposed to me, and we were married in 1974. After the wedding, we immediately moved to Colorado Springs, Colorado, where he was stationed.

Our first few months seemed to be going along okay until I found out that my new husband was still smoking pot with his Army buddies. I felt betrayed, lied to, disappointed, and I was ready to "pack up" and move back to California. As I was making final plans to leave, I found out I was pregnant with my first daughter. I thought, *Now I am really stuck!* I called out to God to help me through this. My husband begged me to stay, so I set up what I thought would be some realistic boundaries: We would go to church; he could *not* use family funds to continue in his drug addiction; and he could *not* stash his drugs around the house or bring them around me or the baby.

Although now I realize I was continuing to enable his addiction to illegal drugs, at the time I thought that I was in complete control of the situation. Wow, what a codependent I had become, just like my mom. I thought this was going to be the best situation, and at that point, I was able to "let go and let God."

Deuteronomy 31:6 says, "Be strong and courageous. Do not be afraid or terrified because of them, for the LORD your God goes with you; he will never leave you nor forsake you."

Over the next eighteen years we relocated back to Southern California where we had three more children. I became a stay-at-home mom with my kids. I had two girls and two boys, three years apart in age, just like I had planned—again the insanity of my control issues. These years were spent "covering up" and "enabling" my husband's drug addiction. I was constantly making excuses for his missing work, not attending family functions, and not going to church.

His drug addiction became completely out of control, but whenever I brought it up, it triggered anger in him and fear in me. Essentially, denial took over our lives. I was "settling" for his excuses, because I didn't want my four kids to have divorced parents. I wanted the perfect family and finally realized that I was living a double life.

There was our life at church where everyone thought our family was perfect. This was the picture that I wanted them to see. Then there was the life at home where nothing was perfect. My denial had completely consumed me and my life! I felt powerless, that there was no hope for me beyond the life I was living. The daily verbal and emotional abuse was overwhelming. This was the same pattern that I had seen many years before.

Then one day, while in a drug-induced rage, my husband attacked and raped me. I told him the kids were in the room, to which he replied, "Good, they can stand and watch." I felt ashamed, powerless, completely embarrassed and humiliated.

A loving friend said to me, "Look what you are doing to your kids. What you are exposing them to will cause them to end up hating and blaming you one day." Which it did.

But as I've heard at Celebrate Recovery, "It takes three things to cause change: Fear, Pain, and Catastrophe."

My life had become one in which I *feared* my husband; I was in *pain* due to the abuses.

And the rape—that was the *catastrophe*! Now I had the perfect storm, but still it was hard for me to make the final decision to end the marriage.

I suggested we go for counseling. We always went together for one or two sessions, but then he stopped and said I was the one with the problem. We went through four different counselors and heard the same answer from them all: "Until he is ready to change, nothing will be different." I finally understood that this was the end of our marriage. It was time for *me* to change, but how?

I did follow through on the divorce, but life was not easy for years afterward. I became independent and worked both a full-time job and any extra house-cleaning jobs I could find to provide for me and the kids. I was filling my life with resentments over all of my issues and all of the denial that I had lived with for so long. Guilt was taking over.

Well, my life started to change for the better. I changed churches and got involved again doing things that I knew would connect me back to a better life and provide structure for the kids, such as singing in the choir and joining a Bible study.

In May 1996, I met a man while working for a company in Orange County. We seemed to get along and had a great relationship over the phone. In my lack of self-esteem, I started to think something was wrong with me because he didn't ask me out until five months later.

We dated for four years and during that time we shared some of our own challenges, including interference from our respective ex-spouses and the influences they had on our children. We even got to the point of breaking up a couple of times during our dating.

We attended a remarriage workshop and found that our compatibility was strong. We learned how blended families work and how we needed to support each other in our roles. We also each had a strong personal relationship with God, and I was encouraged that our relationship was what God had planned.

During this time, he explained a lot of his past and was very open about his family dysfunction as well as his former alcohol and drug abuse. I wondered why I was attracted to another alcoholic and drug addict. But I decided that I was back in my comfort zone of being in control again!

I believe that I was actually becoming an encouragement in his walk. After all, he must be okay because he had gone over ten years without using drugs or alcohol.

We married on September 16, 2000. Now life was perfect! NOT!

My husband was working and traveling out of town a lot. Our "honeymoon" came to a screeching halt one evening in April 2001, just seven months after our wedding, when we got custody of my four grandkids. This caused, over time, a lot of stress in our marriage.

In January 2002, just thirty days after moving into our new home in Chino, California, my husband had his first heart attack. This could not be happening. I thought that this move would be perfect for the grandkids and wanted to have this guy around for a while! Now I was facing major health issues with him. Again, I thought that I could fix this. He recovered and we were doing well.

And then just six weeks after my husband was released to go back to work, he had his second heart attack. I stood and watched as the ER team shocked him three times to bring him back! I was overwhelmed with emotion; my whole life was turning upside down!

I didn't know where to turn for help as we had just moved into this new home and didn't know anyone. And then it got worse—he lost his job. Why was this happening to me?

All of this turmoil and then a few months later, in 2003, my husband dropped the "bomb." He told me that he didn't want to be married anymore. I was hurt and overwhelmed with questions. What did I do wrong? What could I do differently? How was I going to make it through this one? I certainly didn't know how to fix it! All of the "old" feelings of self-esteem, doubt, fear, and guilt were back.

We tried counseling, and during a session one evening he actually told me that he didn't love me anymore. He was disconnected from everything: the grandkids, church, recovery, me, everything that I thought mattered to both of us. I was devastated and I needed help to get through this time. I had to turn back to trusting God.

Romans 15:13 says, "May the God of hope fill you with all joy and peace as you trust in him, so that you may overflow with hope by the power of the Holy Spirit."

I spoke with my pastor, who helped set up a meeting for my husband with someone from Celebrate Recovery. After meeting with his sponsor and continued Christian counseling, my husband's attitude began to change. And, praise God, over a period of time, the man I married was back! This whole experience helped me to understand more about Celebrate Recovery, but I still didn't know how important it would become in our lives together. I realized that this was not just my husband's problem; I had a role in it too! We both needed the connection with community that we had stopped when we moved out of the area.

Coming to Celebrate Recovery and going through the step study groups has shown me that it is okay not to be perfect. God loves me just the way He created me. He helped me to heal from the fear and pain of my past and also to show me how to forgive those who have hurt me.

Ephesians 4:31–32 says, "Get rid of all bitterness, rage and anger, brawling and slander, along with every form of malice. Be kind and compassionate to one another, forgiving each other, just as in Christ God forgave you."

God continues to show me how to trust Him with everything in my life. When things get tough, I'm relearning how to let go and let God. I have also learned that being submissive in my marriage means to duck so that God can hit my husband over the head, that God will get his attention and do the fixing and I don't have to.

Each week I get the opportunity to watch miracles happen: relationships restored, marriages rebuilt, and lives changed. God is the Great Miracle Worker and Great Healer. I look forward to every Wednesday when I go to Celebrate Recovery. I know that it is a safe place for me. I know that even though there is this tough thing called life that continues to "show up," I have a place where I can share my experience, strength, and hope with others.

Romans 15:4 says, "For everything that was written in the past was written to teach us, so that through the endurance taught in the Scriptures and the encouragement they provide we might have hope."

God has given me the opportunity to serve as the Encourager on the Celebrate Recovery TEAM, as a leader for step study groups and Wednesday Celebrate Recovery open share groups.

Thirteen years ago when I became involved with Celebrate Recovery, I had no idea that the tools that I would be learning would help me deal with the issues that would continue to come up in life and issues that I had not yet dealt with.

I wish that I could tell you that my story ends here, but I am still in recovery for a purpose. Remember that I introduced myself as struggling with sexual, physical, and emotional abuse. In July 2011, I was going to be faced again with, yes, the "elephant" that was still in the middle of the room. It never went away; it just got bigger.

This time I dropped the "bomb" on my husband. One afternoon, after a weekend away with my sisters, I asked him to talk with me. I had something I wanted to share: I had buried the issue that I was molested by a family member when I was a young girl.

I didn't know what to expect from my husband, but I was afraid it was going to mess up our relationship and get ugly. Instead, I was met with love, support, and an attitude of understanding. He stated that he would do whatever it took to get through this newest challenge in our marriage.

I had assumed a level of guilt as a result of the molestation, because I thought that if I had only said something earlier in life, the molestation of others may not have continued. (This same perpetrator continued the sexual abuse with several other female family members and was also hurting other relationships.) I did try to explain these issues a few years ago to my mom, but received no support from her.

Principle 6 states, "Evaluate all my relationships. Offer forgiveness to those who have hurt me and make amends for harm I've done to others except when to do so would harm them or others." "Happy are the merciful" (Matthew 5:7). "Happy are the peacemakers" (Matthew 5:9).

I have since confronted my perpetrator and have expressed forgiveness toward him, something I never would have been able to do without the tools that I have learned in Celebrate Recovery. I have also learned that I "get to" release the shame and guilt that came with being molested and I no longer let that rule me or my decisions.

Colossians 3:13 says, "Bear with each other and forgive one another if any of you has a grievance against someone. Forgive as the Lord forgave you."

I still have a long way to go — more healing is necessary — but I know there is a safe place where I can go to share my issues with others who have similar hurts in their pasts. I desire to be an example of hope for others who struggle with abuses like these.

Another key area where Celebrate Recovery has played a huge role is when I lost my sister Bonnie, who went to heaven to be with Jesus in 2011. The outpouring of love and support from Celebrate Recovery has allowed me to grieve appropriately. I am always being made aware that my Forever Family continues to grow beyond what I ever thought it could be.

Today, I "get to" serve side by side with my husband, as we share the passion for recovery and try to be the best examples of God's mercy, grace, and love toward others. It is my desire to be the best wife, mother, nana, and leader that I can be.

I walk with the joy that is in me and with the hope that others will step out of denial and into God's grace.

In closing, God never wastes a hurt and He wants us to share our victories and to be an example of His unending mercy and grace to others.

Thank you for letting me share.

Principle 7

Reserve a daily time with God for self-examination, Bible reading, and prayer in order to know God and His will for my life and to gain the power to follow His will.

CROSSROADS

Principle 7: Reserve a daily time with God for self-examination, Bible reading, and prayer in order to know God and His will for my life and to gain the power to follow His will.

Step 10: We continued to take personal inventory and when we were wrong, promptly admitted it.

"So, if you think you are standing firm, be careful that you don't fall!"
(1 Corinthians 10:12)

Introduction

You have arrived at a very important junction. You have traveled a long road, which required facing your denial; surrendering your life to Jesus Christ; taking an honest look at your life; listing, confessing, and sharing all your wrongdoing; being humble enough to allow God to make major changes in you; becoming willing to forgive or make amends; offering your forgiveness to those that have hurt you; making amends for all the harm that you have caused to others...

WOW! That's quite a journey! Not too long ago, most of us would have said that it was an impossible journey, that we could never have changed or grown so much, that we could never have done the work that the first six principles ask of us.

And we would be right. We could never have made it through by ourselves on our own power. In fact, the only reason we have made it this far is because we made a decision way back in Principle 3 to turn our lives and wills over to the care of God.

Jesus explains it this way in John 8:32: "You will know the truth, and the truth will set you free." Then in John 14:6 He defines Truth by saying, "I am the way and the truth and the life. No one comes to the Father except through me." We have been set free from our addictions and our obsessive/

compulsive behaviors because of the "Truth" we have asked into our hearts, Jesus Christ.

Because of this life-changing decision you made, Jesus has come in—at your invitation—and rebuilt the foundation of your life! You will undoubtedly see major changes, if you haven't already!

Principle 7 and Step 10 are a crossroads of your recovery. It is not a place to stop and rest on past accomplishments. We need to thank God for getting us this far on our road to recovery, praise Him for the many victories over our hurts, hang-ups, and habits we have seen in working the first nine steps, but we also need to continue working the last three steps with the same devotion and enthusiasm that got us to this point in our recoveries.

First Corinthians 10:12 puts it this way: "So, if you think you are standing firm, be careful that you don't fall!"

Most recovery material refers to Steps 10 through 12 (Principles 7 and 8) as the "maintenance steps." I disagree with the use of the word *maintenance*.

I believe that it is in these steps and principles that your recovery, your new way of living, really takes off, really bears the fruit of all the changes that God and you have been working on together.

It is in Principles 7 and 8 where you and I will live out our recoveries for the remainder of our time here on this earth—one day at a time! That's much, much more than "maintenance," folks!

Step 10

As we begin to work Step 10[7], we will see that it is made up of three key parts.

1. The *what*: "We continued to take personal inventory . . ."
2. The *why*: ". . . and when we were wrong . . ."
3. The *then what*: ". . . promptly admitted it."

Tonight we are going to spend a little time looking at each of these parts of Step 10. Of course, we need an acrostic. Tonight the word is TEN.

Take time to do a daily inventory
Evaluate the good and the bad
Need to admit our wrongs promptly

The *T* answers the "what" question: TAKE time to do a daily inventory. To inventory something is simply to count it. Businesses take inventory all

---

7. Please note that though Step 10 and Principle 7 differ somewhat in their focus, both point toward the same result: the character and image of Christ in our daily life. This lesson will emphasize the step more than the principle, but in no way do we intend to discount the many benefits of daily living Principle 7.

the time. Principle 7 reminds us to "reserve a daily time with God for self-examination, Bible reading, and prayer." This gives us quiet time to count the good and bad things we did during a particular period of time. Lamentations 3:40 exhorts us to "examine our ways and test them, and ... return to the LORD."

We need to ask ourselves these questions:

- What good did I do today?
- In what areas did I blow it today?
- Did I do or say anything that hurt anyone today?
- Do I owe anyone amends?
- What did I learn from my actions today?

I do this on a daily basis. I reflect on my day to see if I harmed someone, acted or reacted out of fear or selfishness, or went out of my way to show kindness.

As we stressed in Principle 4, our daily inventories need to be balanced. We need to look at the things we did right as well as the areas in which we missed the mark and blew it! Believe it or not, by the time we get to Principle 7, we actually start doing a lot of things right. But if we are not careful, we can slowly slip back into our old habits, hang-ups, and dysfunctions, so we need to take regular, ongoing inventories.

The *E* in our acrostic answers the "why" question: EVALUATE the good and the bad.

The step doesn't say, "... *if* we're wrong." That's what I *wish* it said. *If* I'm ever wrong ... *if* perhaps I blew it ... No. The step says *when* I'm wrong.

Sometimes, I really do not want to work this step. It forces me to admit that, on a daily basis, I'm going to be wrong and I'm going to make mistakes. I struggled with this for years in my early recovery, until one day I saw a sign that was hanging in a meeting room in downtown Los Angeles. The sign read: "Would you rather be right ... or well?"

Would *you* rather be right or well?

First John 1:8–10 (TLB) says: "If we say we have no sin, we are only fooling ourselves, and refusing to accept the truth. But if we confess our sins to him, he can be depended on to forgive us and to cleanse us from every wrong. (And it is perfectly proper for God to do this for us because Christ died to wash away our sins.) If we claim we have not sinned, we are lying and calling God a liar, *for he says we have sinned.*"

In John 3:21 Jesus tells us, "Whoever lives by the truth comes into the light." Step 10 brings us, on a daily basis, into the light.

Once we see the light, we have a choice. We can ignore it or we can act on it. If we act, we are living the last part of Step 10 and answer the "then what" question. We NEED to admit our wrongs promptly.

For years I couldn't admit it when I was wrong. My wife can vouch for that! I couldn't admit my mistakes. My refusal to offer amends blocked all my relationships, especially with my family. As I grew and matured in the Word and recovery, I discovered that I had to *own* my mistakes and take responsibility for my actions. I couldn't do that if I didn't take time daily to allow God to show me where I missed the mark.

There's another word that I wish had been left out of Step 10, the word *promptly.* It's easier for me to admit the mistakes I made ten years ago than the mistakes I just made today. But Step 10 says promptly! As soon as I realize that I blew it I need to promptly admit it!

In Matthew 5:23 – 24 (MSG), Jesus tells us, "This is how I want you to conduct yourself in these matters. If you enter your place of worship and, about to make an offering, you suddenly remember a grudge a friend has against you, abandon your offering, leave immediately, go to this friend and make things right. Then and only then, come back and work things out with God."

In other words, admit your wrongs … promptly!

Wrap-Up

One way to easily keep track of your good and bad behavior is to keep a journal. Participant's Guide 4 has space on pages 19 – 25 for you to practice using a journal for one week. Now, your journal is not for you to record the calories that you had for lunch today or your carpool schedule for school. Your journal is a tool for you to review and write down the good and the bad things you did today.

Look for negative patterns, issues that you are continually writing down and having to promptly make amends for — again and again. Share them with your sponsor or accountability partner, and set up an action plan for you, with God's help, to overcome them.

Try to keep your journal for seven days. Start out by writing down one thing that you are thankful for from your experiences from the day. That will get you writing.

If you haven't used a journal so far in your recovery, I believe you will find this recovery tool a great help! I encourage you to make journaling a daily part of your program.

Next week we will talk about the how-tos of Step 10 and ways of avoiding constantly needing to offer your amends.

Daily Inventory

Principle 7: Reserve a daily time with God for self-examination, Bible reading, and prayer in order to know God and His will for my life and to gain the power to follow His will.

Step 10: We continued to take personal inventory and when we were wrong, promptly admitted it.

"So, if you think you are standing firm, be careful that you don't fall!"
(1 Corinthians 10:12)

Introduction

Tonight we want to focus on the how-tos of Step 10. But first, I would like to see how you did with your seven days of Step 10 journaling. I know for many of you it was the first experience in writing down your thoughts on a daily basis. I thought it would be interesting to randomly call on some of you to come up here and read them for the whole group. Just kidding!

But, it is important to recap our day in written form — the good and the bad, the successes and the times when we blew it. Here's why:

1. When you write down areas in which you owe amends, it will help you to see if patterns are developing, so that you can identify them and work on them with the help of Jesus Christ and your sponsor.

2. You can keep the amends you owe to a very "short list." As soon as you write down an issue you can make a plan to PROMPTLY offer your amends. After you make the amends you can cross it off in your journal.

Inventory

Some of you may have had trouble getting started writing in your journal. Let me give you three hints that will help you get started putting the ink on the paper.

1. Start off by writing down just one thing that happened that particular day for which you are thankful. Just one thing can get you started, and it will also help you sleep better that night.

2. Ask your accountability partner/sponsor to hold you accountable for writing in your journal each night.

3. This is the one that really works for me! Memorize Galatians 5:22–23, the "fruit of the Spirit": "The fruit of the Spirit is love, joy, peace, forbearance, kindness, goodness, faithfulness, gentleness and self-control."

Daily ask yourself any of these questions to prompt your writing, starting each question with the word "today":

- How did I show *love* to others? Did I act in an unloving way toward anyone?

- Did others see in me the *joy* of having a personal relationship with the Lord? If not, why not?

- How was my serenity, my *peace*? Did anything happen that caused me to lose it? What was my part in it?

- Was I *patient* (forbearing)? What caused me to lose my patience? Do I owe anyone amends?

- Would anyone say that I was *kind/good*? In what ways did I act unkind?

- How was my *faithfulness*? Did I keep my word with everyone?

- How was my *gentleness* and *self-control*? Did I lose my temper, speak a harsh or unkind word to someone?

As we work Step 10 and Principle 7, we begin the journey of applying what we have discovered in the first nine steps. We humbly live daily—in reality, not denial. We have done our best to amend our past. Through God's guidance, we can make choices about the emotions that affect our thinking and actions. We start to take action—positive action—instead of constant *reaction*.

In Principle 7 we desire to grow daily in our new relationship with Jesus Christ and others. Instead of attempting to be in control of every situation and every person we come in contact with, or spinning out of control ourselves, we are starting to exhibit self-control, the way God wants us to be. Remember "self under control" is what we are seeking. Self under *God's* control is what we are striving for.

God has provided us with a daily checklist for our new lifestyle. It's called the "Great Commandment," and it is found in Matthew 22:37–40 where Jesus said, " 'Love the Lord your God with all your heart ... soul and ... mind.' This is the first and greatest commandment. And the second is like it: 'Love your neighbor as yourself.' All the Law and the Prophets hang on these two commandments."

When you do your daily personal inventory, ask yourself, "Today, did my actions show what the second greatest commandment tells me to do? Did I love my neighbor (others) as myself?"

As we live the two commandments by putting the principles and steps into action in our lives, we will become more like Christ. We will become doers of God's Word, not hearers only. James 1:22 says, "Do not merely listen to the word, and so deceive yourselves. Do what it says." Our actions need to be consistent with our talk. You may be the only Bible someone ever reads. That's being a real "Living Bible." That's how the apostle Paul lived. He says in 1 Thessalonians 1:5 (TLB), "Our very lives were further proof to you of the truth of our message." Others should see God's truth shown in our lives.

Step 10 does not say how often to take an inventory, but I would like to offer three suggestions that can help us keep on the right road, God's road to recovery.

Do an Ongoing Inventory

We can keep an ongoing inventory throughout the day. The best time to admit we are wrong is the exact time that we are made aware of it. Why wait? Let me give you an example.

Yesterday afternoon, I snapped at my son. I was immediately faced with a choice. I could admit that I was wrong ("I shouldn't have snapped at Johnny; all he wanted to do was play catch") and make amends with him ("Johnny, I'm sorry for speaking so sharply; I was wrong"), or I could wait until later and risk rationalizing it away ("He saw I was busy; he had no right to ask me to play at that time").

You don't have to wait until you go home, cook dinner, watch TV, and then start your journal. If you do an ongoing inventory during the day, you can keep your amends list very short!

Do a Daily Inventory

At the end of each day, we look over our daily activities, the good and the bad. We need to search where we might have harmed someone or where we acted out of anger or fear. But once again, remember to keep your daily inventory balanced. Be sure to include the things that you did right throughout the day. The best way to do this is to journal.

I spend about fifteen minutes just before I go to sleep, journaling my day's events, asking God to show me the wrongs that I have committed. Then, as promptly as I can the next morning, I admit them and make my amends.

Do a Periodic Inventory

I take a periodic inventory about every three months. I get away on a "mini retreat"! I would encourage you to try it. Bring your daily journal with you, and pray as you read through the last ninety days of your journal entries. Ask God to show you areas in your life that you can improve on in the next ninety days and *celebrate the victories* that you have made.

By taking an ongoing, a daily, and a periodic inventory we can work Step 10 to the best of our abilities. With God's help we can keep our side of the street clean.

Here are a few key verses to learn and follow for Step 10.

*"Intelligent people think before they speak; what they say
is then more persuasive" (Proverbs 16:23, GNT).*

*"Let no foul or polluting language, nor evil word nor unwholesome or
worthless talk [ever] come out of your mouth, but only such [speech] as is
good and beneficial to the spiritual progress of others"
(Ephesians 4:29, AB).*

*"A wise, mature person is known for his understanding.
The more pleasant his words, the more persuasive he is"
(Proverbs 16:21, GNT).*

"A word of encouragement does wonders!" (Proverbs 12:25, TLB)

*"If I had the gift of being able to speak in other languages
without learning them, and could speak in every language there is
in all of heaven and earth, but didn't love others, I would only
be making noise" (1 Corinthians 13:1, TLB).*

Step 10 Daily Action Plan

1. Continue to take a daily inventory, and when you are wrong, promptly make your amends.
2. Summarize the events of your day in your journal.
3. Read and memorize one of the Principle 7a verses on page 33 of Participant's Guide 4.
4. Work all steps and principles to the best of your ability.

The key verse for this lesson is Mark 14:38: "Watch and pray so that you will not fall into temptation. The spirit is willing, but the flesh is weak." Let's close in prayer.

Dear God, thank You for today. Thank You for giving me the tools to work my program and live my life differently, centered in Your will. Lord, help me to make my amends promptly and ask for forgiveness. In all my relationships today help me to do my part in making them healthy and growing. In Jesus' name I pray, Amen.

RELAPSE

Principle 7: Reserve a daily time with God for self-examination, Bible reading, and prayer in order to know God and His will for my life and to gain the power to follow His will.

Step 11: Sought through prayer and meditation to improve our conscious contact with God, praying only for knowledge of His will for us and power to carry that out.

"Let the message of Christ dwell among you richly." (Colossians 3:16)

Introduction

(Note: At Saddleback Church, we start with Lesson 1 in January. Therefore, we are teaching Principle 7 in November. That's why this lesson begins with a reference to Christmas.)

Tonight, we are going to start working on Principle 7. We are going to look specifically at how to maintain the momentum of your recovery during the approaching holidays!

Holidays can be tough, especially if you are alone, or if you are still hoping your family will live up to your expectations. This is a key time of the year to guard against slipping back to your old hurts, hang-ups, or habits. A key time to guard against relapse!

Therefore, tonight we are going to talk about how you can prevent RELAPSE. You don't have to start your Christmas shopping yet, but it's not too early to start working on a relapse-prevention program.

Preventing Relapse

Tonight's acrostic is RELAPSE:

Reserve a daily quiet time
Evaluate
Listen to Jesus
Alone and quiet time
Plug in to God's power
Slow down
Enjoy your growth

The first letter in relapse stands for Principle 7 itself: RESERVE a daily quiet time with God for self-examination, Bible reading, and prayer in order to know God and His will for my life and gain the power to follow His will.

As I said, during the holidays, it's easy to slip back into our old hurts, hang-ups, and habits. The alcoholic goes back to drinking, the overeater gains back the weight, the gambler goes back to "lost wages" (Las Vegas), the workaholic fills up his schedule, the codependent goes back to an unhealthy relationship. The list goes on and on.

The first step in preventing a relapse is to admit that you will be tempted, that you are not above temptation. Jesus wasn't, why should you be?

We find the account of Jesus' temptation in Matthew 4:1–11 (TLB):

Jesus was led out into the wilderness to be tempted there by Satan.... For forty days and forty nights he ate nothing and became very hungry. Then Satan tempted him to get food by changing stones into loaves of bread.

"It will prove you are the Son of God," he said.

But Jesus told him, "No! For the Scriptures tell us that bread won't feed men's souls: obedience to every word of God is what we need."

Then Satan took him to Jerusalem to the roof of the Temple. "Jump off," he said, "and prove you are the Son of God."

Jesus retorted, "It also says not to put the Lord your God to a foolish test."

Next, Satan took him to the peak of a very high mountain and showed him the nations of the world and all their glory. "I'll give it all to you," he said, "if you will only kneel and worship me."

"Get out of here, Satan.... The Scriptures say, 'Worship only the Lord God. Obey only him.'"

Then Satan went away, and angels came and cared for Jesus.

The test was over; the devil left. Jesus was tempted. He never sinned, but He was tempted.

Mark 14:38 tells us: "Watch and pray so that you will not fall into temptation. The spirit is willing, but the flesh is weak."

Remember, being tempted isn't a sin. It's falling into the action of the temptation that gets us into trouble. You know it's odd, temptations are different from opportunities. Temptations will always give you a second chance!

Temptation is not a sin; it is a call to battle. When we are tempted to fall back into our old hurts, hang-ups, and habits we need to say to Satan as Jesus did in Matthew 4:10 (TLB): "Get out of here ... The Scriptures say, 'Worship only the Lord God. Obey only him.'"

The next word in our acrostic reminds us of Step 10: EVALUATE.

Let me just recap what we have talked about in the last two lessons. Your evaluation needs to include your physical, emotional, relational, and spiritual health.

As Pastor Rick (Warren) says, don't forget the value of doing a "H-E-A-R-T" check. Ask yourself daily if you are

Hurting
Exhausted
Angry
Resentful
Tense

If you answer yes to any of the above, just use the tools you have learned in recovery to help get you back on track. We find specific instructions for this step in Romans 12:3–17 (NLT): "Be honest in your estimate of yourselves.... Hate what is wrong. Stand on the side of the good. Love each other.... Be patient in trouble.... Do things in such a way that everyone can see you are honorable."

Daily practice of Step 10 maintains your honesty and humility.

The *L* is LISTEN to your Higher Power, Jesus Christ.

We need to take a time-out from the world's "rat race" long enough to listen to our bodies, our minds, and our souls. We need to slow down enough to hear the Lord's directions. "Test everything that is said to be sure it is true, and if it is, then accept it" (1 Thessalonians 5:21, TLB). I like that verse in *The Message*: "Don't be gullible. Check out everything, and keep only what's good. Throw out anything tainted with evil."

Let's look at the letter *A*, which stands for ALONE and quiet time.

The first part of Step 11 says: "We sought through prayer and meditation to improve our conscious contact with God."

In Principle 3, we made a decision to turn our lives and our wills over to God's care; in Principle 4, we confessed our sins to Him; and in Principle 5, we humbly asked Him to remove our shortcomings.

Now, in Principle 7 in order to keep your recovery growing, you need to have a daily quiet time with Jesus. Even He spent time alone with His Father; you need to do the same. Set a daily appointment time to be alone with God, so that you can learn to listen carefully, learn how to hear God!

In Psalm 46:10 God tells us to "be still, and know that I am God."

Step 11 uses the word *meditation*. Meditation may be new to you, and you may feel uncomfortable. The definition of *meditation* is simply "slowing down long enough to hear God." With practice, you will begin to realize the value of spending time alone with God.

The Enemy will use whatever he can to disrupt your quiet time with God. He will allow you to fill your schedule with so many good things that you burn out or do not have the time to keep your appointment with God. The Enemy loves it when he keeps us from growing and from working on the most important relationship in our lives—our relationship with Jesus.

Psalm 1:1–3 (GNT) tells us: "Happy are those who … find joy in obeying the Law of the Lord, … they study it day and night. They are like trees that grow beside a stream, that bear fruit at the right time."

The next letter is *P*: PLUG in to God's power through prayer.

I can't tell you the number of people who, in counseling, have asked me, "Why did God allow that to happen to me?"

I reply, "Did you pray and seek His will and guidance before you made the decision to get married, before you made the decision to change jobs?" or whatever their issue might be.

You see, if we don't daily seek His will for our lives, how can we blame Him when things go wrong?

Some people think their job is to give God instructions. They have it backward. Our job is to daily seek His will for our lives. You see, God's guidance and direction can only start when our demands stop.

Don't misunderstand me here. I'm only suggesting that we must stop *demanding* things of God, not stop *asking* things of Him. Specific prayer requests are another way to be plugged in to God's power.

In Philippians 4:6 (TLB), Paul tells us to pray about everything asking for God's perfect will in all our decisions: "Don't worry about anything; instead, pray about everything; tell God your needs and don't forget to thank him for his answers."

The verse says *His* answers, *His* perfect will—not mine or yours. Ours are imperfect and most often self-centered. We often use prayer as a labor-saving device, but I need to remind myself daily that God will not do for me what I can do for myself. Neither will God do for you what you can do for yourself.

Let's look at the *S* in our acrostic: SLOW down long enough to hear God's answer.

After you spend time praying to God, you need to slow down long enough to hear His answers and direction. We can become impatient. We want God's answer now! But, we need to remember our timing can be flawed and God's timing is always perfect! After we pray and ask, we need to listen. God said to Job, "Listen to me. Keep silence and I will teach you wisdom!" (33:33, TLB).

Philippians 4:7 (TLB) tells us: "If you do this [present your requests to God] you will experience God's peace, which is far more wonderful than the human mind can understand. His peace will keep your thoughts and your hearts quiet and at rest as you trust in Christ Jesus."

Finally, the last letter in relapse is *E*: ENJOY your growth.

You need to enjoy your victories. Rejoice in and celebrate the small successes along your road to recovery! First Thessalonians 5:16–18 (GNT) tells us to "be joyful always, pray at all times, be thankful in all circumstances. This is what God wants from you in your life in union with Christ Jesus." And don't forget to share your victories, no matter how small, with others in your group. Your growth will give others hope!

With daily practice of these principles and with Christ's loving presence in your life, you will be able to maintain and continue to grow in recovery!

Wrap-Up

Honestly, sometimes I wish I could take a vacation from my recovery, especially during the holidays. I'm sure you all have felt that way at one time or another. But let me assure you that relapse is real. It does happen! And it can be very costly. I urge you to take the actions that we talked about tonight to prevent relapse.

Let's get practical. Here are some things to do to prevent relapse during the holidays:

1. Pray and read your Bible daily. Establish a specific time of day to have your "quiet time."
2. Make attending your recovery meeting a priority. Stay close to your support team. If you find yourself saying, "I'm too busy to go to Celebrate Recovery tonight," make time. Flee from whatever you are doing and come share your recovery.
3. Spend time with your family if they are safe. If they are not, spend time with your church family. We are going to have Celebrate Recovery every Friday night throughout the holidays. You do not have to be alone this holiday season.

4. Get involved in service. Volunteer! You don't have to wait until you get to Principle 8 to start serving.

These are just a few ideas and suggestions. Share tonight in your small groups on ways that you, with God's help, can prevent relapse in your recovery.

GRATITUDE

Principle 7: Reserve a daily time with God for self-examination, Bible reading, and prayer in order to know God and His will for my life and to gain the power to follow His will.

Step 11: We sought through prayer and meditation to improve our conscious contact with God, praying only for knowledge of His will for us and power to carry that out.

"Let the message of Christ dwell among you richly." (Colossians 3:16)

Introduction

Tonight we are going to focus our attention outward rather than inward. We have taken many steps on our road to recovery. Our first step was to admit that we were (and are) powerless. Our second step led us to choose, once and for all, a power by which to live. We took our third and most important step when we chose to turn our lives and wills over to the only true Higher Power, Jesus Christ.

As we continue our journey, we grow in our conscious contact with God and He begins to unfold in our lives. And, as we begin to grow in our understanding of Him, we begin to live out the decision we made in Principle 3. We keep walking now, in peace, as we maintain inventories on a regular basis and as we continue to deepen our relationship with Christ. The way we do this according to Principle 7, is to "reserve a daily time with God." During this time we focus on Him by praying and meditating.

Prayer is talking to God. Meditation is listening to God on a daily basis. When I meditate I don't get into some yoga-type position or murmur, "om, om, om." I simply focus on and think about God or a certain Scripture verse or maybe even just one or two words. This morning I spent ten or fifteen minutes just trying to focus on one word: *gratitude.*

I need to meditate every morning, but I don't. Some mornings my mind wanders and I find it very difficult to concentrate. Those old familiar friends will come back. You know, that old familiar committee of past dysfunction. The committee will try to do everything it can to interrupt my quiet time with God. Through daily working the principles to the best of my ability, however, I've learned to shut them up most of the time.

I've learned to listen to God, who tells me that I have great worth. And He will say the same to you — if you will listen.

When I start my day with Principle 7 and end it by doing my daily inventory, I have a pretty good day — a reasonably happy day. This is one way I choose to live "one day at a time" and one way I can prevent relapse.

Another way to prevent relapse, especially during the holidays, is by maintaining an attitude of gratitude.

Gratitude

This week, the week before we celebrate Thanksgiving, I suggest that your prayers be focused on your gratitude in four areas of your life: toward God, others, your recovery, and your church. I'm going to ask you to write them down on your "gratitude list." This is an interactive lesson.

> **Teacher's note:** Make copies and hand out the "Gratitude List" found in Appendix 10. After you present each of the four areas on the list, pause and give the participants a couple of minutes to complete each of the sections.

We are going to take some time now for you to build your gratitude list for this Thanksgiving.

First, for what are you thankful to *God*? Offer prayers of gratitude to your Creator.

In Philippians 4:6, we're told, "Do not be anxious about anything, but in every situation, by prayer and petition, with thanksgiving, present your requests to God."

Psalm 107:15 encourages us to "give thanks to the LORD for his unfailing love and wonderful deeds for mankind." What wonderful deeds they are! What are at least two areas of your life in which you can see God's work and that you are thankful for this holiday season?

You can reflect on the last eleven months or on what God has done for you this week or even today. Then take a moment to list just a few of the special things for which you are thankful to your Higher Power.

The next area is to list the individuals whom God has placed in your life to walk alongside you on your road of recovery. We need to be thankful for *others*.

"Let the peace of Christ keep you in tune with each other, in step with each other. None of this going off and doing your own thing. And cultivate thankfulness. Let the Word of Christ—the Message—have the run of the house" (Colossians 3:15–16, MSG).

Who are you thankful for? Why? Take a moment to list them.

The third area we can be thankful for is our *recovery*.

"As for us, we have this large crowd of witnesses around us. So then, let us rid ourselves of everything that gets in the way, and of the sin which holds on to us so tightly, and let us run with determination the race that lies before us" (Hebrews 12:1, GNT).

What are two recent growth areas of your recovery for which you are thankful? Again, list them now.

The fourth and final area to be thankful for is your *church*.

"Enter the Temple gates with thanksgiving" (Psalm 100:4, GNT).

What are two things for which you are thankful to your church?

Wrap-Up

Take your "gratitude list" home with you tonight and put it in a place where you will see it often. It will remind you that you have made progress in your recovery and that you are not alone, that Jesus Christ is always with you.

Using your gratitude list, going to your recovery meetings and making them a priority, and getting involved in service in your church are the best ways I know to prevent relapse during the holidays.

Let's close in prayer.

Dear God, help me set aside all the hassles and noise of the world to focus and listen just to You for the next few minutes. Help me get to know You better. Help me to better understand Your plan, Your purpose for my life. Father, help me live within today, seeking Your will and living this day as You would have me.

It is my prayer to have others see me as Yours; not just in my words but more importantly, in my actions. Thank You for Your love, Your grace, Your perfect forgiveness. Thank You for all those You have placed in my life, for my program, my recovery, and my church family. Your will be done, not mine. In Your Son's name I pray, Amen.

PRINCIPLE 7 TESTIMONY

My name is Monty, I am a grateful believer in Jesus Christ who struggles with gambling.

I was born in a little town called Okemah, Oklahoma. My dad met my mom after he returned from World War II; he was in the Army, where he drove tanks. My mom, on the other hand, was one of seven siblings raised on a farm not far from Okemah. I came into this world at about one o'clock in the morning January 2, 1951, and just nine months later we were living in Richmond, California, across the bay from San Francisco.

I entered into the first grade in Richmond, but my dad had so many different jobs, we moved so many times, and I attended so many schools that I didn't stay long enough to pass the first grade. That's right, I flunked the first grade. I remember feeling very stupid and not like other kids who had no problem passing the easiest grade in school. This affected my educational outlook for most of my first twelve school years. My grades were barely passing all the way until I graduated from high school. But I got my diploma!

At my graduation, when they were calling out each of the names of my classmates to receive their rolled-up reward for twelve long years of both good teachers and bad, it was my turn to be handed my diploma. Over the loud speaker came someone else's name, not mine.

I know my face must have shown an expression of failure because at that moment I went back in time to being a five-year old again. I was being told by a loudspeaker—to all my friends, family, and everyone in the bleachers—"YOU FLUNKED."

I was dumbfounded and embarrassed, but the wise teacher who was giving out the diplomas held my right hand in a very tight adult handshake, looked at me and my horrified expression, and then whispered in a calm voice, "Just wait!"

The next name, read loud and clear, was mine. Wow, close call! But I made it, and now it was time for the next step in my education: "finally" off to college in the fall.

In college, I had professors and instructors teaching everything from math, science, and logic to history, English, and world religions including Christianity, Hinduism, Islam, Buddhism, and Atheism. I met students who claimed to be witches and followers of Scientology, Mormonism, Jehovah's Witness, and other cults. Of course, I had my own brand of homemade religion that I believed which I called Monty-theism.

This religion was made up in my own mind, not from any Bible or any formal religion, just my own way of believing. But it was this very belief system that formed my understanding about God and just who He was. *Proverbs 14:12 says, "There is a way that appears to be right."*

It was while I was attending Cerritos College in 1976, studying to become an accountant, that Jesus changed my life and this wrong way of thinking. I was going to school during the day and working part-time in a small machine shop in Paramount, California. I was going to parties and lots of dance clubs all over Southern California almost every night, drinking cheap wine and smoking marijuana. My friends and I were completely caught up in the culture of the '70s. One of the standard sayings of that day was, "Keep on truckin'." That is exactly what we were doing: living and loving this carefree lifestyle.

The Vietnam War was the only threat to my college commitment. I was ready any day to be drafted and sent off to fight for our country. I was living at home with my parents rent-free. My parents paid my auto insurance, most of my school expenses, food, and even the gas for my car, a 1962 Ford van that they had also purchased. I had it all.

I never gave much thought to things like religion, church, growing up, and being an adult. Pretty much all I cared about was myself and a few close friends.

My first girlfriend in school was my first love and brought me to my life's big crossroad—I emphasize the "CROSS" in the road. She and I were together through most of junior high and some of senior high school, but broke up just before my junior year. My friends used to tease me because I talked about her all the time.

Do you remember your first love? They say "Your first car is like your first love, you will never forget them!" We experimented with pot together while we were going steady. Except for a couple of tries of a very strong drug called angel dust, which I was told afterward is some kind of animal tranquilizer that stays in your brain for years, I never went on to use any other drugs. However, my girlfriend did go on to stronger and more dangerous drugs.

One morning in January, I got up to go to work and my mother told me that my former girlfriend was very sick and in the hospital. I decided to go after work and pay her a visit, not aware of how sick she really was. When I got there she was tied to the bed, tubes in every part of her body, hooked up to all kinds of machines with lights, bells, and beeping sounds. She was in the final stages of Hepatitis C. Her eyes and skin were yellow and she could barely speak. I could not believe what I was seeing. My very first love was dying right in front of me. There was nothing I could do; I was totally help-less to help her.

I did not know how to pray, and I didn't know God in any way, shape, or form. She was barely able to communicate, but through her slurred words she asked me to read to her. I was fresh out of reading material, so I grabbed the book that is in most hospital rooms: a Gideon Bible. So with all the expertise of a "not-so-great first-year Bible student," I opened to a book called John. I can't remember much of what I read, but it seemed to give her some comfort.

After I left the room, I completely came apart. Totally uncontrolled tears ran down my face and a feeling of being more lost than I have ever felt in my life overcame me.

The next day when I went to see her, I stopped first at a flower shop across the street from the hospital. I was weeping so much that the lady couldn't understand what I was asking for. She guessed my emotion and cried herself at my grief. I come by these tears naturally and I am in good company as Jeremiah was known as the "Weeping Prophet," and John tells of Jesus weep-ing for Lazarus at his death.

As I walked into the room with flowers in hand, I was surprised to see that my ex-girlfriend was sitting up in a chair, not as yellow or as sick. She seemed to be getting better. Our communication was clearer, and we visited a couple of hours. She wanted me to read to her again. Again, I got the Bible and read some more, not understanding it one bit better. Two unbelievers reaching out to God for help, and we wouldn't have known what to do with that divine help if we got it. God would save both of us, although not in a way either of us could or would understand for some time. Jesus, in His infinite wisdom, knew perfectly what each of us needed.

Her salvation came the next day, by way of her death, mine after her funeral. A young man shared the gospel with me after her funeral. He said he had remembered seeing my girlfriend at several services before she got sick. He thought she had told him that she had asked Jesus into her life and that may be why she wanted me to read from the Bible. Only God knows. This young man took the time to explain to me that God sent His son into the world in human form to save mankind—and me. He patiently answered my questions about the Bible, God, death, and most importantly, my grief.

That night when I was alone with all the thoughts of that dark and terrible day, I prayed, "Jesus, I don't know if I can live this new life with You, but if You will forgive me, I promise to trust You with all my heart." At that very moment on my bed in the middle of the night, I felt the weight of that dread-ful day and my whole life lift up from my soul. It felt like I rose up from my bed and floated when Jesus came into my life. I've never been the same and never wanted to return to the past life. I started reading the Bible the next day in the weirdest place for a new Christian to start reading.

God's plan was for me to read a very special verse, *Revelation 2:4: "Nevertheless I have this against you, that you have left your first love."* God came into my life because I thought I had lost my very first love. God in His Bible was telling me two things: my first love is really Jesus Christ and He loves me much more than I could ever love anyone else in my life.

The next step in my life was entering into the family of God by way of the church. About six months later, I was asked by my brother to go on a blind date. My date's family went to a church in Bell Gardens.

The next day was Sunday, and I asked her if I could meet her at her church, and she said yes; so I went to my first Sunday school class and a worship service. This became my home church and is to this day.

We dated for two years and during that dating time, we got engaged. I would come to find that my new wife was the perfect example of a Proverbs 31 woman. We got married September 16, 1978, in our home church and have been married for over thirty-four years! I can't believe that she has been able to put up with me for all these years. God did not bless us with children of our own, but He provided many opportunities for us to work with the youth groups from the church and community.

In fact, I became a junior high Sunday school teacher and then started working as a youth pastor with the junior high kids. I eventually became the senior high youth pastor and an associate pastor.

Wow, what a great story of salvation—so far.

But like the famous Paul Harvey would say: And now, the rest of the story . . .

My addiction to gambling started very slowly. One night after our Wednesday youth meeting, I asked my new assistant youth leader to go to dinner with me at a restaurant in Downey, California. While we were seated at a table waiting for our waitress to take our order, I noticed a numbered game panel on one of the TV screens near our table. As we watched the graphics, little white balls would float across the multicolored game board and light on one number at a time, a lot like BINGO. I asked my friend what it was and he said it was called Keno, a legal gambling game new to California. I had been to Las Vegas a few times in my life, and even played Keno there along with many other games of chance. I always lost my money pretty easily, but had a lot of fun.

I never realized how much my need to gamble was addicting, because it was always so far to go to Vegas to play. I was never comfortable in the local poker casinos, so I didn't consider them to be a temptation for me. But these local restaurants and 7-Elevens were right up my alley, so to speak. They were simple and easy gambling establishments, fun places to get involved in a very wrong way of spending my hard-earned money. Slowly but surely, I spent more and more money for my addiction. Some of that money was supposed to be for bills and everyday expenses. I started getting money out of our checking and saving accounts. I actually depleted our savings account two times. I was caught by my wife many times and, of course, I promised I would stop. My "stopping" was really my sick way of thinking "getting money without being caught" by my wife.

I was a textbook example of a full-blown addict; I needed my "gambling fix" just like a person hooked on any other kind of habit. And I exhibited all the behaviors that go along with addictions: stealing, lying, denial, and just plain being too proud to admit I had an out-of-control habit.

My life was in a downward spiral. While at work, church, or home, I made out that I was living up to the principles taught from the Bible. But in my alone times, with no accountability, I was in the uncontrolled addiction of my struggle. I was spending money and using funds that were meant to buy food, gas, and pay bills. I was in love with trying to be the next winner, no matter how much it cost.

In 2008, my wife called me at work and asked the deadly question, "Have you been gambling again? There is a lot of money missing from our accounts." I admitted how out-of-control I was, and how sorry I was, and that it would never happen again. Translated: "I'll try to control my gambling and hide it better to not get caught." In *1 John 1:8–10* the Bible reminds me, *"If we say we have no sin, we are only fooling ourselves, and refusing to accept the truth. But if we confess our sins to him, he can be depended on to forgive us and cleanse us from every wrong. If we claim we have not sinned, we are lying and calling God a liar, for he says we all have sinned."* Although I admitted to my wife that I had messed up, I was not willing to admit it to God or to confess my sins to Him.

As you can imagine, my wife saw right through this lame excuse because she had a very close friend who was in Anonymous meetings and could tell when an addict was lying. My wife informed me she had found a Gamblers Anonymous meeting on Saturday nights in Downey, and I needed to attend or else. I went and was involved with that organization for about a year. My accountability to the meeting was enough to make me stop for over a year, but it was just another "white-knuckle experience." I truly spoke every Saturday night about my struggle by saying "Hi, my name is Monty and I haven't placed a bet in over a year." Accountability really works, but after a year, I felt like I was cured. So, I stopped going to the meetings and within a few weeks, I would spend two or three dollars on scratchers or a couple of games of Keno. In just a short time, I was back in as deep as before. Still being a practicing Christian and a practicing gambler every chance I got.

On April 9, 2010, I got that bitter call from my wife. Again! I knew this time it was the "or else." But after many strong warnings and a time of clarity, we decided it was time to look for a Christian recovery program.

This time, she located a Christ-centered recovery program called Celebrate Recovery. I was informed that my choice was: to go on Friday, or I could go on Friday. She left it up to me.

I went to Celebrate Recovery that Friday. I started going to the groups, and the change came almost from the first night when I told my wife this is truly a Christ-involved program. I was welcomed, loved on, and felt the presence of the Holy Spirit when I entered those rooms the first time!

Since coming to Celebrate Recovery, my life has been changed in more ways than I could have ever dreamed of or hoped for. The program was filled with many helpful tools to guide me into a wonderful transition from guilt, lying, and bad behaviors to forgiveness, honesty, good habits, new friendships, and a brand-new relationship with our God, His church, and the Bible.

After attending a few meetings, my new friends told me about another great tool in Celebrate Recovery called a step study group and how it had changed their lives both physically and more importantly, spiritually. I decided to take the leap of faith and began attending a step study group at Emmanuel Church. The real teacher is God's Holy Spirit. Through the Word of God and the step study participant's guides, which are based upon the eight principles, I've learned more about God's great love and care for my hurts, hang-ups, and habits.

Principle 7 says, "Reserve a daily time with God for self-examination, Bible reading, and prayer in order to know God and His will for my life and gain the power to follow His will."

I've learned to trust the wisdom of my heavenly Father to make me into a new creature filled with truth, love, and grace, and to walk in the newness of life promised by our wonderful Redeemer.

Second Corinthians 5:17 states, "Therefore, if anyone is in Christ, the new creation has come: The old has gone, the new is here!"

As the weeks and months passed, the step study became more and more a part of my everyday life. My friends, family, and coworkers have noticed the changes in me, and I didn't have to tell them. By the grace of God and applying the eight principles based on the Beatitudes in the Bible, I have not gambled since April 9, 2010. This is a miracle and now I know what people mean when they say, "Don't leave before the miracle happens." God has replaced my need to gamble with a need to know Him and His Word. The Holy Spirit is leading me "one day at a time," and I am definitely "enjoying every moment at a time."

I would like to share a Scripture that has helped me on this road to recovery: *"For as many as are led by the Spirit of God, these are sons of God. For you did not receive the spirit of bondage again to fear, but you received the Spirit of adoption by whom we cry out, 'Abba, Father.' The Spirit himself bears witness with our spirit that we are children of God, and if children, then heirs — heirs of God and joint heirs with Christ, if indeed we suffer with him, that we may also be glorified together"* (Romans 8:14 – 17).

I know that God is on this road to recovery with me, and He is helping me every day to stay out of my mess. My work in the church is one area that has benefitted because of my attendance at Celebrate Recovery. I'm much more effective as an assistant pastor, teacher, and shepherd. Even in my home I am becoming the kind of man my wife deserves by being the husband God wanted me to be all along.

God bless you and God bless Celebrate Recovery!

Thank you for letting me share.

PRINCIPLE 8

Yield myself to God to be used to bring this Good News to others, both by my example and by my words.

"Happy are those who are persecuted because they do what God requires." (Matthew 5:10)

GIVE

Principle 8: Yield myself to God to be used to bring this Good News to others, both by my example and by my words.

"Happy are those who are persecuted because they do what God requires." (Matthew 5:10)

Step 12: Having had a spiritual experience as the result of these steps, we try to carry this message to others and to practice these principles in all our affairs.

"Brothers and sisters, if someone is caught in a sin, you who live by the Spirit should restore that person gently. But watch yourselves, or you also may be tempted."
(Galatians 6:1)

Introduction

I think that if God had to choose his favorite principle, He would choose Principle 8: "Yield myself to God to be used to bring this Good News to others, both by my example and by my words."

Why do I think Principle 8 is God's favorite? Because it is putting our faith into action. God's Word tells us in James 2:17, "Faith by itself, if it is not accompanied by action, is dead." Active faith is important to God!

Don't get me wrong, works are not going to save you. Only faith in Jesus Christ as your Lord and Savior can do that. It is through our actions, however, that we demonstrate to God and others the commitment we have to our faith in Jesus Christ.

So tonight, we are going to begin to work on Principle 8. The corresponding step is Step 12, the "carrying the message" step, the "giving back" step.

What is "giving back" all about? What does it truly mean to give?

To answer that question, I did a word study on the meaning of *give* or *giving*. In the New Testament, the word *give* has seventeen different Greek words with seventeen different meanings. So tonight, I thought you would find it interesting for me to do a thirty-minute lecture on each of the uses of the word *give*. Just kidding!

Perhaps we'll take a more practical look at the meaning of the word *give* as it relates to Principle 8, since that's what this principle is really all about.

Principle 8 does not tell us to give in unhealthy ways, ways that would hurt us or cause us to relapse into our codependent behaviors. No, Principle 8 is talking about healthy, non-codependent giving of oneself without the slightest trace of expecting to receive back. Remember, no person has ever been honored for what they have received. Honor has always been a reward for what someone gave.

Matthew 10:8 sums up Principle 8: "Freely you have received; freely give."

In Principle 8, we *yield* ourselves to be used by God to bring this good news to others, both by our example and our words.

Give

It is in Principle 8 we learn what it means to truly GIVE.

God first
I becomes we
Victories shared
Example of your actions

The *G* stands for GOD first.

When you place God first in your life, you realize that everything you have is a gift from Him. You realize that your recovery is not dependent or based on material things, it is built upon your faith and your desire to follow Jesus Christ's direction.

Romans 8:32 (GNT) says that God "did not even keep back his own Son, but offered him for us all! He gave us his Son—will he not also freely give us all things?"

We are never more like God than when we give—not just money or things but our very selves. That's what Jesus did for us. He gave us the greatest gift of all—Himself.

The second letter in give is *I*. When we give, the I becomes we.

None of the steps or principles begin with the word *I*. The very first word in Step 1 is *we*. In fact, the word *we* appears in the 12 Steps fourteen times. The word *I* never appears even once in any of the 12 Steps. The road to recovery is not meant to be traveled alone. This is not a program to be worked in isolation.

Jesus said, " 'Love the Lord your God with all your heart and with all your soul and with all your mind.' This is the first and greatest commandment. And the second is like it: 'Love your neighbor as yourself' " (Matthew 22:37–39).

When you have reached this step in your recovery and someone asks you to be a sponsor or to be an accountability partner, do it! The rewards are great, and being a sponsor or an accountability partner is one way to carry the message!

Ecclesiastes 4:9–12 (GNT) makes this concept of giving very clear: "Two are better off than one, because together they can work more effectively. If one of them falls down, the other can help him up. But if someone is alone … there is no one to help him. … Two people can resist an attack that would defeat one person alone."

The third letter stands for VICTORIES shared.

God never, never, never, ever wastes a hurt! He can take our hurts and use them to help others. Principle 8 gives us the opportunity to share our experiences, victories, and hopes with one another.

Deuteronomy 11:2 tells us to remember what we've learned about the Lord through our experiences with Him. We start off by saying, "This is how it was for me; this is the *experience* of what happened to me. This is how I gained the *strength* to begin my recovery, and there's *hope* for you."

Second Corinthians 1:3–4 (GNT) encourages us to "give thanks to the God and Father of our Lord Jesus Christ, the merciful Father, the God from whom all help comes! He helps us in all our troubles, so that we are able to help others who have all kinds of troubles, using the same help that we ourselves have received from God."

All the pain, all the hurt that my twenty years of abusing alcohol caused, all the destruction that I caused to myself and those I loved, finally made sense when I got to Principle 8. I finally understood Romans 8:28 (TLB): "We know that all that happens to us is working for our good if we love God and are fitting into his plans."

He called me according to His plans, and because I answered God's call, I can stand here as an example that God works all things for good according to His purpose.

To God be the glory!

I want to spend the rest of my life doing recovery work. You know, though, it's not really work. It's service, a service of joy.

This thought leads us to the last letter in give: EXAMPLE of your actions.

You all know that your actions speak louder than your words. Good intentions die unless they are executed.

In James 1:22 we are exhorted to be "doers of the word." But, in order to be of help to another, we are to "bring the Good News to others."

That's what Step 12 says. It doesn't say to bring a little good news or to bring good news only to others who are in recovery.

You have all heard the term "Sunday Christians." Let us not become just "Friday night recovery buffs."

Works—actions, not words—are proof of your love for God and another person. Faith without works is like a car without gasoline. First John 3:18 (NEB) says, "My children, love must not be a matter of words or talk; it must be genuine, and show itself in action."

Giving and serving is a thermometer of your love. You can give without loving. That's what we sometimes do in a codependent relationship. Or we give because we feel we have to. You can give without loving, but you can't love without giving.

Wrap-Up

The Lord spreads His message through the eight principles and the 12 Steps. We are the instruments for delivering the Good News. The way we live will show others our commitment to our program, to our Lord, and to them!

I would like to leave you with Luke 8:16 from *The Message*: "No one lights a lamp and then covers it with a washtub or shoves it under the bed. No, you set it up on a lamp stand so those who enter the room can see their way."

We're not hiding things; we're bringing everything out into the open. So be careful that you don't become misers ... generosity begets generosity. Bring the Good News with joy!

YES

———————⌒———————

Principle 8: Yield myself to God to be used to bring this Good News to others, both by my example and by my words.

"Happy are those who are persecuted because they do
what God requires." (Matthew 5:10)

Step 12: Having had a spiritual experience as the result of these steps, we try to carry this message to others and to practice these principles in all our affairs.

"Brothers and sisters, if someone is caught in a sin, you who live
by the Spirit should restore that person gently. But watch yourselves,
or you also may be tempted."
(Galatians 6:1)

———————⌒———————

Introduction

Modern technology is something else! Take an old, beat-up Diet Coke can—dirty, dented, holes in it. A few years ago, it would have been thrown in the garbage and deemed useless, of no value. Today it can be recycled, melted down, purified, and made into a new can—shiny and clean—that can be used again.

We're going to talk about recycling tonight—recycling your pain by allowing God's fire and light to shine on it, to melt down your old hurts, habits, and hang-ups so they can be used again in a positive way. They can be recycled to show others how you worked the principles and steps with Jesus' healing into the solution and how you have come through the darkness of your pain into Christ's glorious freedom and light.

Society tells us that pain is useless. In fact, people are coming to believe that *people* in pain are useless! At Celebrate Recovery, we know that pain has value, as do the people who experience it. So while the world says no, tonight we say yes!

Yes

Tonight's acrostic couldn't be any more positive! It is the word YES.

Yield myself to God
Example is what is important
Serve others as Jesus Christ did

The *Y* is Principle 8 itself: YIELD myself to God to be used to bring this Good News to others, both by my example and by my words.

To truly practice this principle, we must give God the latitude He needs to use us as He sees fit. We do that by presenting everything we have — our time, talents, and treasures — to Him. We hold loosely all that we call our own, recognizing that all of it comes from His hand. When we have yielded to Him, God can use us as His instruments to carry the message to others in word and action.

Galatians 6:1 – 2 (TLB) tells us: "If a Christian is overcome by some sin, . . . humbly help him back onto the right path, remembering that the next time it might be one of you who is in the wrong. Share each other's troubles and problems, and so obey our Lord's command."

People take your example far more seriously than they take your advice.

That leads us to the *E* in yes: EXAMPLE is what is important!

Your walk needs to match your talk. We all know that talk is cheap, because the supply always exceeds the demand.

If you want someone to see what Christ will do for them, let them see what Christ has done for you.

Here is a question to ask yourself when you get to this principle: Does my lifestyle reflect what I believe? In other words, does it show others the patterns of the world — selfishness, pride, and lust — or does it reflect the love, humility, and service of Jesus Christ?

"Arouse the love that comes from a pure heart, a clear conscience, and a genuine faith" (1 Timothy 1:5, GNT).

This year, we have all been blessed by some outstanding and courageous testimonies at Celebrate Recovery. I would like all those who gave their testimonies this year to stand. These people believe in Principle 8! They believe in it enough to share not only in the safety of their small groups but also with the whole recovery family. They believe in Jesus Christ enough to share their lives with others. They stood up here and shared their weaknesses and strengths with others who are suffering from similar pain, hurts, hang-ups, and habits. They gave others a piece of their heart — not a piece of their mind.

Our goal again for next year is to have two testimonies each month as we work on each step. So, if you have been in recovery for a while and haven't shared your story as yet, get busy, write it out, and get it to me. We need to hear and you need to share your miracle in the coming year.

The last letter in yes is *S*: SERVE others as Jesus Christ did.

When you have reached Principle 8, you are ready to pick up the "Lord's towel," the one with which He washed the disciples' feet in the upper room the night before He was crucified.

Jesus said, "And since I, the Lord and Teacher, have washed your feet, you ought to wash each other's feet. I have given you an example to follow: do as I have done to you" (John 13:14–15, TLB).

You don't all have to give your testimonies to three hundred people to do service. All service ranks the same with God. You can say "y-e-s" to Principle 8 in many ways!

1. *Be an accountability partner.* Find someone in your small group who agrees to encourage and support you as you work through the principles. You agree to do the same for that person. You hold one another accountable for working an honest program.

2. *Be a sponsor.* Sponsors are people who have worked the steps. Their job is to guide newcomers on their journey through the steps, to give a gentle nudge when they are procrastinating or to slow them down when they are rushing through a step. Sponsors do so by sharing their personal journey on their road to recovery.

3. *Become a greeter.* Greeters get to Celebrate Recovery at 6:45 p.m. They welcome and provide directions for newcomers. They provide the newcomer with the important first impression of Celebrate Recovery!

4. *Help with the Solid Rock Cafe.* You need to arrive by 6:00 p.m. to help set up. If you can't get here early, stay a few minutes after to help clean up. You can bake a cake.

5. *Help with the Bar-B-Que.* We'll be starting in the spring. We need help with set-up, clean-up, and everything in between.

6. *Invite someone to church.* Ask someone from your secular groups or a neighbor, a friend, or a coworker!

The world is full of two kinds of people—givers and takers. The takers eat well and the givers sleep well. Be a giver. There are many, many more areas to serve! Make suggestions! Get involved!

Principle 8 comes down to this: Do what you can, with what you have, where you are.

Make your life a mission, not an intermission!

Wrap-Up

The road to recovery leads to service. When you reach Principle 8, the road splits. Some of you will choose to serve at Celebrate Recovery. Others will choose to serve in other areas of the church. The fact is, we need both.

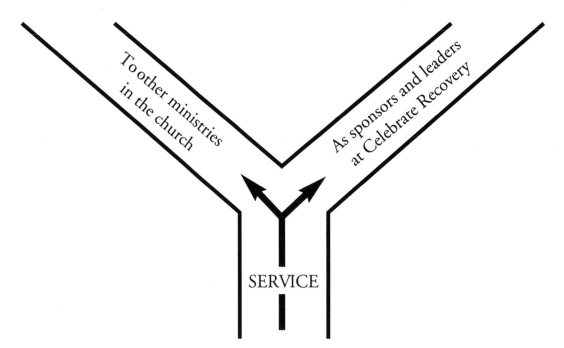

We need you to share your experiences, strengths, and hopes with newcomers here on Friday nights. You do that as leaders, sponsors, and accountability partners. But the church also needs your service. As you serve outside of Celebrate Recovery, you can share with others and get them into recovery when they are ready to work on their hurts, hang-ups, and habits.

Every morning, before I get out of bed I pray this Principle 8 prayer:

Dear Jesus, as it would please You, bring me someone today whom I can serve. Amen.

Will you pray it this week?

PRINCIPLE 8 TESTIMONY

My name is Mac, and I am a grateful believer in Jesus Christ who struggles with drug and alcohol addiction. I have lived to see a milestone in my recovery. After twenty-four years in recovery, I've finally been sober longer than I was using.

My childhood was pretty uneventful in terms of abuse. My parents loved me and set good standards to live by. So I can't look back to blame others for my actions, actions that brought great shame. Today because of Jesus Christ, I don't have to live in the past anymore. I am free!

Ironically though, I spent a lifetime searching for freedom in all the wrong things. My dad was in the military, so by the time I was fifteen, I had moved eight times. I learned to blend in and make friends quickly.

My dad preached wherever he was stationed. So I knew about God, heaven, and hell. I was taught that unless you were a Christian you would go to hell. I remember fear being the motivating factor for being baptized when I was twelve. I appeared to enter a relationship with God, but for all the wrong reasons. Two weeks later at summer camp, I was introduced to marijuana by one of the counselors. I found a group of people who looked like they were having a lot of fun, so I decided, "Who needs to live in fear? These people aren't worrying about anything!" I became fearless and believed I was invincible, not realizing I had set the pace for eventual destruction.

My dad retired from the military and went to seminary to become a full-time pastor, so we moved to Louisiana when I was fifteen. I hated the fact that we were moving and I wondered how I would ever find friends who liked doing what I liked to do now. Amazingly within the first week, I found the same people there. I never ran out of drugs, and acceptance was immediate.

Once we arrived, my parents sent me to church summer camp to straighten me out and that's where I met Mary.

Mary: My name is Mary. I am a grateful believer in Jesus Christ who struggles with codependency.

I grew up an elder's kid. My parents lived out the Deuteronomy verse: "to tie God's word as symbols around your hands and teach them to your children as you walk by them day after day." There were always guests at the dinner table in our home. Missionaries from foreign countries stayed with us for recharging, while others flocked to our home seeking wise counsel, Bible study, and to repair wrecked marriages.

During my childhood, my mother would write Bible verses on three-by-five cards and tape them up all over our bathroom walls. As I would get dressed in the morning, there staring me in the face would be several verses I would read over and over. It just became a habit without me even realizing it. My sister and I would throw our heads under the covers at night and giggle, thinking how silly it was having our mama reciting those verses to us, never realizing the impact they would have on me in years to come.

I confessed Jesus as Lord of my life when I was twelve years old and was baptized, telling myself I would *never* sin again! I wanted to please God with all my heart.

Mac: A new school year began; Mary was a senior and I was a junior. Life was great! After a few months of dating, I talked her into having sex, the first time for both of us, by using the manipulative "if you love me" line. Two weeks later, she didn't start her period, but we thought, *No way; surely one time can't get you pregnant.*

Mary: Four months later I finally consulted a doctor and, yes, I was pregnant. No one had been pregnant outside of marriage in our church, so we had a secret. I felt alone and was convinced Mac couldn't support us. He was only sixteen at the time.

By the time I was five months pregnant, I decided it was confession time to my dad. During my childhood, my mother had a mental illness. Doctors put her through experimental procedures such as electric shock treatments. She suffered in mental hospitals and was a test subject for drugs that often kept her debilitated. So needless to say, my sweet mother who loved me the best she knew how didn't notice I had a growing belly.

I had always been able to talk to my dad, and I knew I couldn't keep it from him any longer. I walked into the den where my dad was taking a nap. I had snuggled up next to him many times throughout the years on that big old flowered sofa, while he read Bible stories to me and we talked about God's love. I knelt down next to him, eye to eye, and said softly, "We need to talk, Daddy."

I was prepared for him to point his finger and say all kinds of harsh words.

But tears began streaming down his cheeks as he said he would support and love me always. I told him my plans for moving out of town and giving my baby up for adoption.

I left home for my secret summer trip. Three months later it was August 17, 1975. That date is significant later in our story. The doctor left me in a tiny room all alone. Labor lasted for twelve hours with no anesthesia and no family. As they rushed me into the delivery room, a nurse shoved a gas mask over my face. I thought they were suffocating me to punish me for what I had done.

I awoke later in bed sheets soaking wet from perspiration and tears. I experienced emotions that were alien to me. A time that was supposed to be the happiest time of my life was my saddest. I moved to a Christian college out of state. My dad was hoping to get me away from Mac.

Mac: But I followed her there. My parents thought by sending me to a Christian college, they would fix me. Guess what? I found the people who loved to party my first day on campus. In fact, I found the guy who first introduced me to pot six years earlier at church camp. Halfway through the semester, I was kicked out of college after sneaking out of the dorm past curfew to smoke a joint with a friend. Mary and I both went home and married three weeks later.

Married life was great. We partied all the time. Later we would come to understand it helped us to mask the guilt of giving up our baby. When we had been married three years, we started trying to have another baby. Mary told me she was quitting the partying. I said, "Go ahead, but I'm not." Even in the midst of my addiction, I set a boundary and decided to quit everything except smoking pot. I convinced myself that marijuana wasn't so bad.

As I continued down the road of drug addiction, the conflict began between us. Our two daughters were born during this time. However, we lived separate lives under the same roof while growing further apart. I stayed away from the house as much as possible, working overtime to pay for my drug habit. By this time, meth had become my drug of choice.

Mary: In time, I came to the realization that our marriage was totally unmanageable, and I couldn't survive without turning my life and hurts over to God. I had to quit trying to be Mac's Holy Spirit and fix him and instead work on my own shortcomings. I started seeking the pathway to peace while Mac continued to run down the path to destruction. This pattern continued for seven years.

I held on to the verses I remembered reading as a child on my bathroom wall. *In Isaiah 55:11, it says when God's word is spoken, it does not come back empty but will accomplish what He desires and achieve the purpose for which He sent it.*

I would also repeat *Isaiah 41:10* to myself the way I remembered my mother quoted it slowly and distinctly. I felt God was speaking to me.

"Do not fear for I am with you. Do not be afraid for I am your God. I will strengthen you and help you. I will uphold you with my righteous right hand."

All those Scriptures I heard as a child were coming back to me, comforting me during the dark and lonely nights. Now I had two secrets I carried. We had a son we would never know and I had an insane husband! I say insane because I didn't know all the drugs he was doing and their effects.

So I walked on eggshells to keep peace. I wore my mask to church every Sunday. I just wanted my insides to feel like everyone else looked on the outside, perfect, I thought.

Mac: Amazingly enough, even as a drug addict, there was a line I said I would never cross. The last two years of my addiction I was shooting up ten to twelve times a day. I wore long-sleeve shirts all the time so no one would notice the marks on my arms. I slept only about sixteen hours a week. One Sunday morning, God gave me a great gift at the time and I didn't even realize it. It was a moment of clarity.

I was crashed out in the bed, and our four-year-old daughter stood beside the bed and said to her mother, "Why doesn't Daddy go to church with us anymore?" Mary said, "He's been working hard. He needs sleep." Our daughter replied, "If he doesn't go to church, then I'm not either!" I pretended to be asleep and not hear what she said.

They left for church and then all of a sudden I felt like I ran into a brick wall. God used a little girl to break my heart. I realized I was killing everybody I claimed to love. It was as if my eyes were opened for the first time seeing the insanity of it all. So I collected all my drugs and paraphernalia and burned them.

Mary: I was crushed realizing our children were being affected. That Sunday the sermon was on confession and how good it is for the soul. I remember the song "It Is Well with My Soul." The words hung in my throat. I couldn't breathe. I wanted to just run out of the building. Arriving home, I found Mac sitting in his recliner with tears in his eyes.

Mac: I was raised to believe that men shouldn't cry or show any weakness. But what I found in those tears that morning was relief like I'd never known. I told Mary all that I had done and that I wanted to start a new life. For the first time, Mary stepped out of her codependency and said,

Mary: "Who are you going to call? I'm tired of keeping secrets."

Mac: "I told you I'm through with that life. What more do you want?"

Mary: "We need someone to help us. Would you talk to our pastor?"

Mac: Our pastor had been coming to my cabinet shop for years, getting me to build things for him, only to find out later they were things he really didn't need. He saw something in me that nobody else did. So he came over to pray with us. He said I didn't have to confess before the church, but I might help someone else if I did. I knew I needed to be held accountable.

Mary and I responded to an altar call that Sunday night, expecting to be shunned by people. The whole church came down afterward and cried with us. They didn't know what to do with me—I was their first drug addict—but they loved me and said to keep coming back.

There was one lady who said I needed to go to AA. I thought she was talking about some kind of car club. She said, "Not triple A, but double A—Alcoholics Anonymous."

Mary wanted me to talk to someone at a rehab center the next day. I told her I wasn't crazy and didn't need that. I finally agreed to talk but nothing more. After much discussion with the head guy, he asked if I would stay. I said, "Okay, I guess I'll stay. But I've got to go home and get my stuff."

Mary: "That's okay; your stuff is in the trunk!"

Mac: Our life became a whirlwind with rehab, ninety meetings in ninety days, Bible studies, and making new friends. A whole new life had begun for us. We started Overcomers two years later, which we led for fourteen years. We had approximately twenty to thirty people who came on a regular basis.

Mary: The only other people who knew about our son were my dad, my brother, and his wife. Fast-forward to spring 1988, one month after Mac yielded to God, when God gave us a surprise gift. Our church youth group was going to a rally five hours away and my sister-in-law was one of the chaperones.

They were assigning groups to stay in homes and by the time they got to my sister-in-law's group, they had run out of homes. So they were asked if they would mind staying in a town close by. As the suitcases were being loaded into the car of a friendly couple, my sister-in-law asked if they had any children. When the woman said they had a son named Heath, a funny feeling came over my sister-in-law. So she asked his age. Heath's mother said he was twelve. So my sister-in-law went one step further and asked, "When is his birthday?" Heath's mother said August 17—the date our firstborn, Heath, arrived on August 17, 1975!

At 2:00 a.m. our phone rang. My sister-in-law whispered, "You'll never imagine where I am." I said sleepily, "Where?" She replied, "Heath's bed!" A family at our church has the last name, Heath, so I questioned her, "What are you doing in Mr. Heath's bed?" She exclaimed, "No, no—Heath, *your son!*" Mac and I feel God gave us that gift at that time in our lives to reassure us our son was loved and cared for in a Christian home.

After waiting seven more years, in August 1994 we got the call we always hoped we would get. When Heath was about to turn nineteen, his parents contacted us that he would like to meet us on his birthday. My dad was in charge of videoing the momentous occasion, but as we sat down later to view it, the whole first part of the reunion video was showing the ground. My dad was so excited he forgot he was holding the camera!

It's been seventeen years now since we first met Heath. We didn't get to see Heath's natural birth, but we were blessed with witnessing his spiritual birth as Mac baptized him! In 2005, Heath's parents moved to our city and Heath's mother and my mom became best friends as she took care of my mom after my dad died. We also attend the same church and celebrate holidays together. Our family continues to grow as God has blessed us now with eight grandchildren!

Mac: After leading Overcomers for thirteen years, Mary's brother "happened" to be at Saddleback Church and told me about a ministry called Celebrate Recovery and said I ought to check it out. So in 2004, we attended the Summit. During the second day I told Mary, "We're stopping what we're doing and starting this! Look how many more people we can help—more than just drug addicts and alcoholics, anyone with a hurt, hang-up, or habit!" After 120 days of prayer and preparation, we started Celebrate Recovery at our church on New Year's Eve 2004! During this preparation time, I learned about Principle 8 and realized that this is exactly what God had in mind for us.

Principle 8 states: "Yield myself to God to be used to bring this Good News to others, both by my example and by my words." "Happy are those who are persecuted because they do what God requires" (Matthew 5:10).

This is why we went through all of these trials and then we found out there was more!

I love watching God's plan for our life unfold. A few years ago, a pastor of forty years tried to commit suicide. The "Pharisees" in the church finally got to him. And the only way he could get through his week was by doing something he said he would never do—take a drink. That one drink turned into every Monday. He had been drinking the last ten years and nobody knew except his wife. Finally he couldn't take the hypocrisy of his own life anymore and that's when he attempted suicide. Along with the bottle, he took a handful of pills. He was moved from pastor to one of "those" people. So I got the call to go visit him.

I visited him in ICU and even though he was unconscious, I prayed over him and said, "Don't give up. God still has a plan for you." Over the next few weeks, I was able to share with him about the hope that God still had for him. He later became a part of our Celebrate Recovery ministry. While at one of our small groups, he shared with me that he had just met our son's parents at church on Sunday. I said, "Everybody has; they go to church here now!" And he said, "No, no, you don't understand. Forty years ago when I first became a pastor I performed their marriage ceremony!" Before our son was conceived, God had a plan to use this man to marry the couple that would adopt our son! And then later, allow me to be instrumental in giving him the hope that his relationship could not only be restored, but also that God would continue to use him! God always sees the big picture, and He is always right on time!

Mary: We went from the twenty to thirty people attending our Overcomers' group, a ministry that was already working, to an average attendance of over 250 every Friday night at Celebrate Recovery. Our children are a part of

Celebrate Recovery. They serve in roles of state rep, ministry leader, training coach, open share group leaders, nursery worker, videographer, and youth minister.

Twenty-four years ago, I prayed God would just keep Mac awake in church. God has truly taken the ashes of our lives and turned them into something beautiful. I believe when God said in *Joel 2:25, "I will repay you for the years the locusts have eaten."*

We can't keep quiet about what the Lord has done in our lives and in the lives of our Celebrate Recovery Forever Family! If there is restoration for us, there is hope for you too! Don't give up; put your faith in action by making life's healing choices.

Mac: Being on the front line of what I believe is THE outreach ministry of the church, we are able to bind up the brokenhearted, to proclaim freedom for the captives of sin in Jesus' name, and release from darkness the prisoners of hurts, hang-ups, and habits.

Celebrate Recovery has helped us reach more hurting people to find healing than we could've ever imagined. How can we repay the Lord for His goodness! We share the hope we've found in Jesus! Today we are making life's healing choices and that's Celebrate Recovery!

Thank you for letting us share.

THE SEVEN REASONS WE GET STUCK

Introduction

Tonight, I want to call a time-out. Let's take a week to have you discuss and evaluate where you are on your individual roads to recovery. I believe it is valuable for us all to take a breath, pause, and review our program. We need to stop for a moment and thank God as we look back on our progress and our growth. We need to make sure we are still moving forward through the principles, that we are not hung up on a particular one.

Some of you may have just begun the journey through the principles. Others are somewhere in the middle. It really doesn't matter which one you're on. Anyone can get off track and stuck.

Seven Reasons

Tonight we are going to talk about the seven reasons we get "stuck" in our recoveries!

1. You Have Not Completely Worked the Previous Principle

Perhaps you are trying to move through the principles too quickly. Slow down! Give God time to work! Just moving forward isn't always progress. Did your brakes ever go out when you were driving down a hill? You may be going fast, but it's not progress. It's panic! Remember, this program is a process. It's not a race to see who finishes first.

Galatians 5:25 says, "Since we live by the Spirit, let us keep in step with the Spirit."

Take your time with each principle. Work it to the best of your ability. Remember, many people get lost while trying to find an easier route for the straight and narrow.

2. You Have Not Completely Surrendered Your Will and Your Life to the Lord

Remember, there are two parts to Principle 3. The first is to ask Jesus Christ into your heart as your Higher Power, your Lord and Savior. The second is to seek to follow His will for your life in all your decisions. Perhaps you are trusting Jesus with the "big" things, but you still think you can handle the "small" things.

Proverbs 3:5–6 (TLB) tells us, "For good judgment and common sense, . . . trust in the Lord completely; don't ever trust in yourself. In everything you do, put God first, and he will direct you and crown your efforts with success."

What part of your life are you still holding on to? What areas of your life are you withholding from God? What don't you trust Him with?

3. You Have Not Accepted Jesus' Work on the Cross for Your Forgiveness

You may have forgiven others, but you think your sin is too big to be forgiven.

First John 1:9 (TLB) tells us, "If we confess our sins to him, he can be depended on to forgive us and cleanse us from every wrong." Every wrong! Not just some of our wrongs, but all of them! Believe me, your sin isn't that special, isn't that different.

"So overflowing is his kindness towards us that he took away all our sins through the blood of his Son, by whom we are saved" (Ephesians 1:7, TLB). The verse says "all our sins." Not some of these and some of those, but all of our sins. Period.

I think the real question here is "Have you forgiven yourself?" That's where I see most people getting stuck in their recoveries.

This is what God wants you to do with the darkness of your past: " 'Come now, let us settle the matter,' says the LORD. 'Though your sins are like scarlet, they shall be as white as snow; though they are red as crimson, they shall be like wool' " (Isaiah 1:18).

Remember, "Therefore, there is now no condemnation for those who are in Christ Jesus" (Romans 8:1).

4. You Have Not Forgiven Others Who Have Harmed You

You must let go of the pain of past harm and abuse. Until you are able to release it and forgive it, it will continue to hold you as its prisoner.

It has been said that forgiveness is the key that unlocks the door of resentments and removes the handcuffs of hate. It is the power that breaks the chains of bitterness and the shackles of selfishness.

God's Word promises in 1 Peter 5:10 – 11 (TLB): "After you have suffered a little while, our God, who is full of kindness through Christ, will give you his eternal glory. He personally will pick you up, and set you firmly in place, and make you stronger than ever."

Do you know that you may need to ask forgiveness for blaming God? Let Him off the hook for what others chose to do to you.

There is God's will, the Devil's will, and your free will all at work on the earth. Remember, the harm others did to you was from their free will, not God's will.

5. You Are Afraid of the Risk in Making the Necessary Change

It may be fair to say that some people here tonight put off change and procrastinate as long as they can. There can be several reasons for delaying positive change.

You may be paralyzed by the fear of failure.

Remember, falling down doesn't make you a failure. It's staying down that makes you one. This is where your faith and trust in Jesus Christ comes into play.

You may fear intimacy because of the fear of rejection or being hurt again.

This is why it is so important to move slowly in a new relationship, taking time to seek God's will, develop realistic expectations, and establish proper boundaries.

You may resist change (growth) because of the fear of the unknown.

My life is a mess, my relationships are a mess, but at least I know what to expect. All together now — "a mess!" If you really try working the steps and principles on that hurt, hang-up, or habit, your life will change.

Some people change jobs, mates, and friends, but never think of changing themselves. What does God's Word tell us?

"Fear not, for I am with you. Do not be dismayed.... I will strengthen you; I will help you; I will uphold you with my victorious right hand" (Isaiah 41:10, TLB).

"We can say without any doubt or fear, 'The Lord is my Helper and I am not afraid of anything that mere man can do to me'" (Hebrews 13:6, TLB).

6. You Are Not Willing to "Own" Your Responsibility

None of us is responsible for all the things that have happened to us. But we are responsible for the way we react to them. Let me give you some examples.

In the case of abuse, in no way is the victim at fault or responsible for the abuse.

Step 8 in our sexual/physical abuse 12 Steps reads as follows:

Made a list of all persons who have harmed us and became willing to seek God's help in forgiving our perpetrators as well as forgiving ourselves. Realize that we have also harmed others and become willing to make amends to them.

My kids are not responsible for being children of an alcoholic, but they are responsible for their own actions and recovery. You need to take the responsibility for your part in a broken relationship, a damaged friendship, or with a distant child or parent.

"Examine me, O God, and know my mind; test me, and discover ... if there is any evil in me and guide me in the everlasting way" (Psalm 139:23–24, GNT).

We increase our ability, stability, and responsibility when we increase our accountability to God.

7. You Have Not Developed an Effective Support Team

Do you have a sponsor or an accountability partner? Do you have the phone numbers of others in your small group? Have you volunteered for a 12-Step commitment to your support group?

There are a lot of opportunities to get involved at Celebrate Recovery:

Bar-B-Que team
Solid Rock Cafe team
Bulletin stuffers
Greeters
Sponsors
Accountability partners
Much more...

All you have to do is ask!

"Be with wise men and become wise. Be with evil men and become evil" (Proverbs 13:20, TLB).

"Dear brothers, you have been given freedom: not freedom to do wrong, but freedom to love and serve each other" (Galatians 5:13, TLB).

"Share each other's troubles and problems, and so obey our Lord's command" (Galatians 6:2, TLB).

Remember, the roots of happiness grow deepest in the soil of service.

Wrap-Up

Now you know the seven areas in which we can get bogged down, stuck in our recoveries. How do I know? Because somewhere along my own personal road to recovery, I visited them all.

Take time this week and reflect on your progress, your growth. If you are stuck, talk to your accountability partner, your sponsor, or your small group leader. Find out which of the seven reasons you are hung up on, and together, implement a plan of action and move ahead on your journey.

Keep Celebrate Recovery's Daily Action Plan for Serenity (printed here as well as on page 63 in Participant's Guide 4) where you can see it and review it daily.

Celebrate Recovery's Daily Action Plan for Serenity

1. Daily, continue to take an inventory. When you are wrong, promptly admit it.
2. Daily, study God's Word and pray asking God to guide you and help you apply His teaching and will in your life.
3. Daily, work and live the eight principles to the best of your ability, always looking for new opportunities to help and serve others—not just at your recovery meetings but in all areas of your life.

CLOSING THOUGHTS

Oh, how kind our Lord was, for he showed me how to trust him and become full of the love of Christ Jesus. How true it is, and how I long that everyone should know it, that Christ Jesus came into the world to save sinners—and I was the greatest of them all. But God had mercy on me so that Christ Jesus could use me as an example to show everyone how patient he is with even the worst sinners, so that others will realize that they, too, can have everlasting life. Glory and honor to God forever and ever. He is the King of the ages, the unseen one who never dies; he alone is God, and full of wisdom. Amen. (1 Timothy 1:14–17, TLB)

We have come to the end of this leader's guide, and you are now ready to begin the most exciting part—the actual stepping out and starting one of the most important and significant ministries in your church.

Romans 12:10–13 (NCV) is my prayer for you and your new recovery program.

Love each other like brothers and sisters. Give each other more honor than you want for yourselves. Do not be lazy but work hard, serving the Lord with all your heart. Be joyful because you have hope. Be patient when trouble comes, and pray at all times. Share with God's people who need help. Bring strangers in need into your homes.

Please visit our website, *www.celebraterecovery.com*, for ongoing and updated information.

I am looking forward to learning about all the lives that will be changed and families reunited because of your decision to start Celebrate Recovery.

In His steps,
John Baker

APPENDICES

Celebrate Recovery®
Leadership Covenant

- I have read and agree to follow the *Celebrate Recovery Leader's Guide*.
- I will attend monthly Celebrate Recovery leaders' meetings.
- I will uphold Celebrate Recovery's five small group guidelines in my small group meetings.
- I will pray for each person in my group.
- I will pray for the unity, health, and growth of the church.
- I will squelch gossip and resolve conflict with the truth by applying Matthew 18:15–17.
- I will continue working on my personal recovery and support team.
- I will develop another person to be my coleader.

Signed

_____ Leader _____ Ministry Leader

Date_____

—

Sample Celebrate Recovery®
Leader Information Sheet

Name: _____ Date: _____

Address: _____

City: _____ Zip: _____

Phone: _____ Email: _____

I have completed:

*101 ____ 201 ____ 301 ____ 401 ____ 501 ____ Shape Interview ____

(*Indicates you are a member of Saddleback Church)

I agree to develop my testimony: Yes ____ No ____ If yes, when _____

Open share group I attend: _____

I have been in recovery since: _____

Attended CR since: _____ My sobriety date is: _____

Date completed CR step study: _____

I have had a Celebrate Recovery leader's interview: Yes or No (circle)

I have completed CR information meeting/orientation: Yes or No (circle)

I have completed open share group training: Yes or No (circle)

I have completed step study training: Yes or No (circle)

I have completed sponsor training: Yes or No (circle)

I have completed testimony writing workshop: Yes or No (circle)

I have served in the following areas of ministry or CR service:

_____

_____

_____

The following area of ministry brings me the most joy in my life:

_____

_____

_____

I am interested in getting involved in service at CR because:

_____

_____

_____

_____

I would like to help out at the following campus and areas:
- ❏ Lake Forest Campus
- ❏ San Clemente Campus
- ❏ Irvine Campus
- ❏ San Juan (The Ranch) Campus

Areas of interest:
- ❏ Pizza or Bar-B-Que dinner team
- ❏ Prayer team
- ❏ Prisons or missions
- ❏ CR praise team
- ❏ Solid Rock Cafe
- ❏ Greeter
- ❏ Offering
- ❏ Information table (general meeting night)
- ❏ Open share group leader/step study group leader
- ❏ Kid's Rock

Names of my step study leaders   Recovery references (please list at least two)

_____   _____

_____   _____

For office use only:

CR Interview	101	201	301	Shape	401
Orientation	Open Share	Step Study	4th Step	Sponsor	Testimony

Sample Celebrate Recovery© Leader's Interview Questions

- How are you continuing to grow in your own recovery?
- In what areas do you need further training and growth?
- Who will you ask for accountability or mentoring?
- Do you struggle with being vulnerable? Why or why not?
- What impact has vulnerability made on your group?
- How do you think God sees you?
- Do you ever feel unworthy OR prideful? Why?
- How do you feel about accepting responsibility?
- How will your relationship with God help you carry out these responsibilities?
- What areas are easy for you to serve in and which ones are difficult?
- What would "stepping out of your comfort zone" be for you?
- Do you feel confident in your abilities to uphold the small group guidelines in your group? Why or why not?
- What has been your experience with loving confrontation?
- What will you do to get to know the needs of your group?
- What can you do to encourage your group?

Sexual, Physical, and Emotional Abuse
Women's Group

12 STEPS FOR SEXUAL, PHYSICAL, AND EMOTIONAL ABUSE

STEP ONE—We admit we are powerless over the past and as a result our lives have become unmanageable.

STEP TWO—Believe God can restore us to wholeness, and realize this power can always be trusted to bring healing and wholeness in our lives.

STEP THREE—Make a decision to turn our will and our lives to the care of God, realizing we have not always understood His unconditional love. Choose to believe He does love us, is worthy of trust, and will help us to understand Him as we seek His truth.

STEP FOUR—Make a searching and fearless moral inventory of ourselves, realizing all wrongs can be forgiven. Renounce the lie that the abuse was our fault.

STEP FIVE—Admit to God, to ourselves, and to another human being the exact nature of the wrongs in our lives. This will include those acts perpetrated against us as well as those wrongs we perpetrated against others.

STEP SIX—By accepting God's cleansing, we can renounce our shame. Now we are ready to have God remove all these character distortions and defects.

STEP SEVEN—Humbly ask Him to remove our shortcomings, including our guilt. We release our fear and submit to Him.

STEP EIGHT—Make a list of all persons who have harmed us and become willing to seek God's help in forgiving our perpetrators, as well as forgiving ourselves. Realize we've also harmed others and become willing to make amends to them.

STEP NINE—Extend forgiveness to ourselves and to others who have perpetrated against us, realizing this is an attitude of the heart, not always confrontation. Make direct amends, asking forgiveness from those people we have harmed, except when to do so would injure them or others.

STEP TEN—Continue to take personal inventory as new memories and issues surface. We continue to renounce our shame and guilt, but when we are wrong promptly admit it.

STEP ELEVEN—Continue to seek God through prayer and meditation to improve our understanding of His character. Praying for knowledge of His truth in our lives, His will for us, and for the power to carry that out.

STEP TWELVE—Having a spiritual awakening as we accept God's love and healing through these steps, we try to carry His message of hope to others. Practice these principles as new memories and issues surface claiming God's promise of restoration and wholeness.

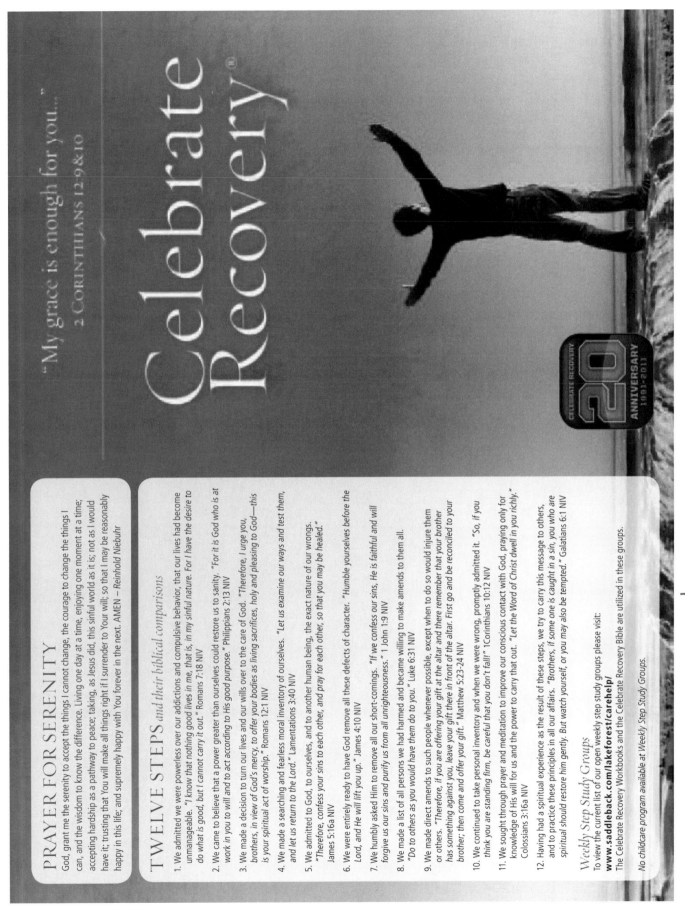

"My grace is enough for you..."
2 CORINTHIANS 12:9&10

Celebrate Recovery®

CELEBRATE RECOVERY 20 ANNIVERSARY 1991-2011

PRAYER FOR SERENITY

God, grant me the serenity to accept the things I cannot change, the courage to change the things I can, and the wisdom to know the difference. Living one day at a time, enjoying one moment at a time; accepting hardship as a pathway to peace; taking, as Jesus did, this sinful world as it is; not as I would have it; trusting that You will make all things right if I surrender to Your will; so that I may be reasonably happy in this life; and supremely happy with You forever in the next. AMEN – *Reinhold Niebuhr*

TWELVE STEPS *and their biblical comparisons*

1. We admitted we were powerless over our addictions and compulsive behavior, that our lives had become unmanageable. *"I know that nothing good lives in me, that is, in my sinful nature. For I have the desire to do what is good, but I cannot carry it out." Romans 7:18 NIV*

2. We came to believe that a power greater than ourselves could restore us to sanity. *"For it is God who is at work in you to will and to act according to His good purpose." Philippians 2:13 NIV*

3. We made a decision to turn our lives and our wills over to the care of God. *"Therefore, I urge you, brothers, in view of God's mercy, to offer your bodies as living sacrifices, holy and pleasing to God—this is your spiritual act of worship." Romans 12:1 NIV*

4. We made a searching and fearless moral inventory of ourselves. *"Let us examine our ways and test them, and let us return to the Lord." Lamentations 3:40 NIV*

5. We admitted to God, to ourselves, and to another human being, the exact nature of our wrongs. *"Therefore, confess your sins to each other, and pray for each other, so that you may be healed." James 5:16a NIV*

6. We were entirely ready to have God remove all these defects of character. *"Humble yourselves before the Lord, and He will lift you up." James 4:10 NIV*

7. We humbly asked Him to remove all our short-comings. *"If we confess our sins, He is faithful and will forgive us our sins and purify us from all unrighteousness." 1 John 1:9 NIV*

8. We made a list of all persons we had harmed and became willing to make amends to them all. *"Do to others as you would have them do to you." Luke 6:31 NIV*

9. We made direct amends to such people whenever possible, except when to do so would injure them or others. *"Therefore, if you are offering your gift at the altar and there remember that your brother has something against you, leave your gift there in front of the altar. First go and be reconciled to your brother; then come and offer your gift." Matthew 5:23-24 NIV*

10. We continued to take personal inventory and when we were wrong, promptly admitted it. *"So, if you think you are standing firm, be careful that you don't fall!" 1Corinthians 10:12 NIV*

11. We sought through prayer and meditation to improve our conscious contact with God, praying only for knowledge of His will for us and the power to carry that out. *"Let the Word of Christ dwell in you richly." Colossians 3:16a NIV*

12. Having had a spiritual experience as the result of these steps, we try to carry this message to others, and to practice these principles in all our affairs. *"Brothers, if some one is caught in a sin, you who are spiritual should restore him gently. But watch yourself, or you may also be tempted." Galatians 6:1 NIV*

Weekly Step Study Groups

To view the current list of our open weekly step study groups please visit:
www.saddleback.com/lakeforest/carehelp/
The Celebrate Recovery Workbooks and the Celebrate Recovery Bible are utilized in these groups.

No childcare program available at Weekly Step Study Groups.

THE ROAD TO RECOVERY

8 Recovery Principles, based on the Beatitudes, by Pastor Rick Warren

1. Realize I'm not God; I admit that I am powerless to control my tendency to do the wrong thing and my life is unmanageable.

   "Happy are those who know they are spiritually poor." Matthew 5:3

2. Earnestly believe that God exists, that I matter to Him, and that He has the power to help me recover.

   "Happy are those who mourn, for they shall be comforted." Matthew 5:4

3. Consciously choose to commit all my life and will to Christ's care and control.

   "Happy are the meek." Matthew 5:5

4. Openly examine and confess my faults to myself, to God, and to someone I trust.

   "Happy are the pure in heart." Matthew 5:8

5. Voluntarily submit to every change God wants to make in my life and humbly ask Him to remove my character defects.

   "Happy are those whose greatest desire is to do what God requires." Matthew 5:6

6. Evaluate all my relationships. Offer forgiveness to those who have hurt me and make amends for harm I've done to others except when to do so would harm them or others.

   "Happy are the merciful." Matthew 5:7 "Happy are the peacemakers." Matthew 5:9

7. Reserve a daily time with God for self-examination, Bible reading, and prayer in order to know God and His will for my life and gain the power to follow His will.

8. Yield myself to God to be used to bring this Good News to others, both by my example and by my words.

   "Happy are those who are persecuted because they do what God requires." Matthew 5:10

Small Group Guidelines

1. Keep your sharing focused on your *own* thoughts and feelings. Please limit your sharing to 3-5 minutes.

2. There will be no cross talk, please. Cross talk is when 2 individuals engage in a dialogue, excluding all others. Each person is free to express their feelings without interruption.

3. We are here to support one another. We will not attempt to "fix" another.

4. Anonymity and confidentiality are basic requirements. What is shared in the group stays in the group! The only exception is when someone threatens to injure themselves or others.

5. Offensive language has no place in a Christ-centered recovery group. Including no graphic descriptions.

CELEBRATE RECOVERY PURPOSE

The purpose of Saddleback Valley Community Church's "Celebrate Recovery" is to fellowship and celebrate God's healing power in our lives through the 12 Steps and 8 Recovery Principles. This experience allows us to "be changed." We open the door by sharing our experiences, strengths and hopes with one another. In addition, we become willing to accept God's grace in solving our lives' problems. By working and applying these Biblical principles, we begin to grow spiritually. We become free from our addictive, compulsive, and dysfunctional behaviors. This freedom creates peace, serenity, joy, and most importantly, a stronger personal relationship with God and others. As we progress through the program we discover our personal, loving and forgiving Higher Power – Jesus Christ.

Welcome to an Amazing Spiritual Adventure!

Pastor John Baker

FRIDAY NIGHT LINE-UP

6–7 p.m. CR BBQ
- Enjoy a BBQ Dinner & Periodic Entree Specials

7–8 p.m. Large Group Session
- Lesson, Personal Testimony or Special Guest Speaker

8–9 p.m. Open Share Small Groups
- **NEWCOMERS "101"** If you are new to Celebrate Recovery, have questions or just need to get connected, this is the group for you!

- **Adult Children of Family Dysfunction (ACA)** Men's & Women's Groups

- **Anger** Men's & Women's Groups

- **Chemically Dependent** Men's & Women's Groups

- **Codependent** Men's & Women's Groups

- **Codependent Women In A Relationship With A Sexually Addicted Man**

- **Financial Issues** Men's Groups

- **Food Addiction** Men's & Women's Group

- **Grupo de Hombres y Mujeres** En Español

- **Hurts, Hang-ups, & Habits** Women's Group

- **Love And Relationship Addiction** Women's Group

- **Sexual Addiction** Men's & Women's Group

- **Women in Recovery from Sexual/Physical/Emotional Abuse**

9–10 p.m. Solid Rock Cafe
- Great Fellowship, Great Coffee, Great Desserts

Children & Youth programs available. Please turn off cell phones during large and small group sessions.

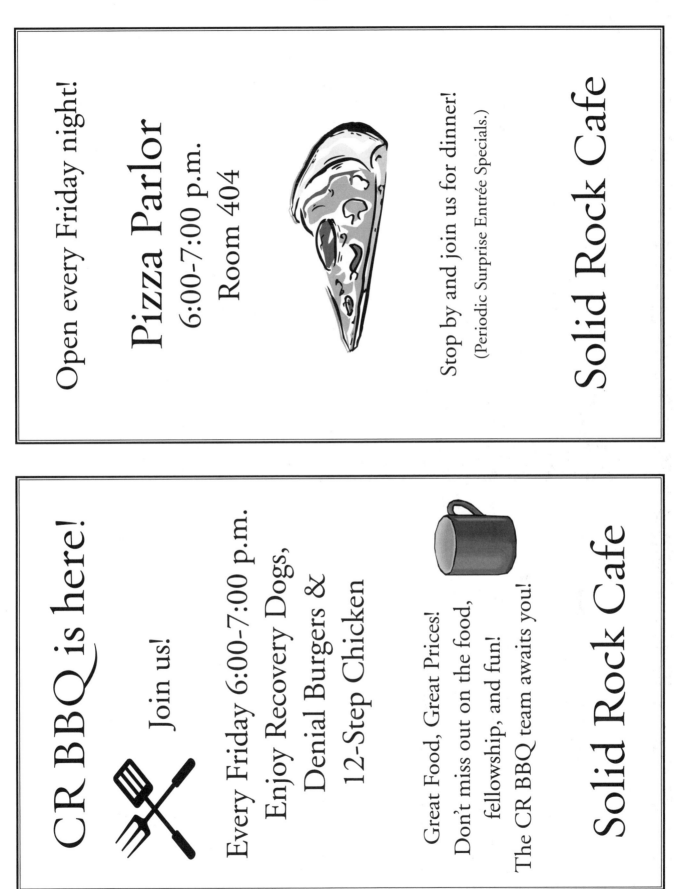

Open every Friday night!

Pizza Parlor

6:00–7:00 p.m.

Room 404

Stop by and join us for dinner!

(Periodic Surprise Entrée Specials.)

Solid Rock Cafe

CR BBQ is here!

Join us!

Every Friday 6:00–7:00 p.m.

Enjoy Recovery Dogs,
Denial Burgers &
12-Step Chicken

Great Food, Great Prices!
Don't miss out on the food,
fellowship, and fun!

The CR BBQ team awaits you!

Solid Rock Cafe

Celebrate Recovery®
Special Dinner

French
"Dip into Your Denial"
Sandwiches

- Hot roast beef, sliced thin and piled high
- Bakery fresh roll
- Served with au jus
- Salad and soda

Dinner starts at 6:00 p.m. in Room 404!
Bring a friend or bring the family!

Celebrate Recovery®

ROOM ASSIGNMENTS

SMALL GROUPS FROM 8-9PM

NEWCOMERS 101 ....PLAZA BLDG, 202

ADULT CHILDREN OF CHEMICALLY ADDICTED - MEN 308

ANGER - MEN'S GROUP 405-407
ANGER - WOMEN'S GROUP 305

CHEMICALLY ADDICTED - MEN'S GROUP ....Tent 3
CHEMICALLY ADDICTED - WOMEN'S GROUP 411

CODEPENDENT - MEN'S GROUP ....Tent 1
CODEPENDENT - WOMEN in relationship with Chem. Addicted 302
CODEPENDENT - WOMEN'S GROUP 304

CODEPENDENT WOMEN 306
in a relationship with a Sexually Addicted man

EXITING A LIFESTYLE OF RISK - MEN'S GROUP 204

EATING DISORDERS - WOMEN'S GROUP 208

GRUPO DE HOMBRES EN ESPANOL - ....Plaza 102
Cualquier area de recuperacion

FINANCIAL RECOVERY - WOMEN'S GROUP 409
FINANCIAL RECOVERY - MEN'S GROUP 301-303

FOOD ADDICTION - WOMEN'S GROUP 307
FOOD ADDICTION - MEN'S GROUP 312

LOVE & RELATIONSHIP ADDICTION - WOMEN'S GROUP............403

SEXUAL ADDICTION - MEN'S GROUP.........................Tent 2
SEXUAL ADDICTION - WOMEN'S GROUP 310

SEXUAL/PHYSICAL/EMOTIONAL ABUSE - WOMEN'S GROUP 401

SOLID ROCK CAFE..... 9:00–10:30 pm............401

Celebrate Recovery®
PRAYER & PRAISE

Welcome!

Whether tonight is your first night or you have been here for years, we have a great group of men and women that love to pray here at Celebrate Recovery and they would like to pray for YOU. You may ask for prayer or share praises on anything: your recovery, your family, your friends.

All your requests will be kept absolutely confidential. Just fill out the back of this card and drop it into the prayer box located at the back resource table. We also have a prayer voicemail where you can leave your prayer requests: (949) 609-8008

If you enjoy praying for others and would like to serve in this ministry, please make a note on this card. We would love to have you be a part!

We're glad you are here! "Give all your worries to him because he cares about you." 1 Peter 5:7

Side 2

Prayer / Praise

Date: _____

Writing a Celebrate Recovery® Testimony

Our greatest resources in Celebrate Recovery are our one true Higher Power Jesus Christ, the indwelling Holy Spirit, and the Scriptures. All Celebrate Recovery curriculum and meetings depend upon these vital resources. Beyond these, the next most powerful resource available to us is a personal testimony of recovery. The importance of the testimony is seen in the prominent role it plays in the annual schedule of large group meetings. Twenty-two of the fifty-two meetings feature a recovery testimony.[1] Because testimonies are so important, there are guidelines for preparing and presenting a recovery testimony. Many will enter your large group meetings with life-and-death issues. Often they are looking for an excuse to leave and not return. This is not the time to have someone "shoot from the hip." You need to be sure that those who attend hear a Christ-centered recovery testimony that is based on real experiences and filled with hope.

One recommendation of Celebrate Recovery training is that recovery testimonies be written and reviewed before being read in the large group time or in other venues.[2] Long testimonies (12–20 minutes) to be shared in the large group meetings should be submitted to the ministry leader for review at least two weeks before presentation. Some of the most frequently asked questions at Celebrate Recovery events or by those visiting our local ministry include:

- **Why is it necessary to have testimonies written and reviewed?**
- **What are the reasons for reading a testimony from a script?**
- **Isn't it boring to hear testimonies read?**

The last question is the easiest to answer and includes both a principle and experience. **The principle is: The excitement and appeal of a Celebrate Recovery testimony comes from clearly conveying how God has powerfully rescued and transformed one of His children. God's power is to be showcased, not the presentation skills of the individual.** When you attend the Summit at Saddleback or a one-day seminar, you will notice that John and Cheryl Baker read their testimonies. It is safe to say that no two people have shared their recovery testimonies more than John and Cheryl. They do so because there are some distinct advantages to reading a carefully written testimony. Thousands of testimonies have been read at the annual Summit, at our one-day

---

1. See pages 48–50 in this leader's guide.
2. This would include church worship services, networking events with other Celebrate Recovery ministries, your local training events, etc. The Trademark Statement of Celebrate Recovery points out the advantages in using the Celebrate Recovery name and establishes minimal requirements for the use of this name under the heading, "The DNA of Celebrate Recovery." There are additional advantages in going beyond the minimal requirements toward the model provided through Celebrate Recovery's official training events and materials. This is the model developed through more than fifteen years of experience at Saddleback's Celebrate Recovery ministry and confirmed in the experience of hundreds of other churches for many years. Experience indicates that the most effective means of ensuring quality testimonies in your meetings is to have them written, reviewed by leadership, and read in the meeting.

conferences, and at local Celebrate Recovery programs. People have been inspired, deeply moved, convicted, and encouraged—but never bored!

Why Is It Necessary to Have Testimonies Written and Reviewed?

1. It helps the presenter prepare with confidence.

You will find that many of your Celebrate Recovery attendees doubt both the value of their story to others and their ability to communicate their story. Many may need help with grammar, wording, and overall composition. Having them write their testimony provides an opportunity for ministry leaders to mentor, guide, and encourage those who are reluctant to share. As you work with individuals through the review process, you have the opportunity to build their confidence.

2. It avoids triggers.

One of the most important promises you make to those who attend your Celebrate Recovery program is that it is a "safe place." Part of keeping Celebrate Recovery a safe place is ensuring that what is shared in a testimony does not trigger unhealthy responses. Writing out a testimony that is reviewed ensures there will be no graphic descriptions and/or inappropriate language in what is shared. What can be appropriately shared in an open share group that is gender- and issue-specific might not be appropriate to voice in the large group meeting.

3. It prevents unnecessary offense.

Many who enter your program have had a negative experience with church earlier in life. Resentment voiced toward particular denominations or groups could deeply offend other participants if these are mentioned by name. By reviewing a testimony, you can help people share their experience without attaching negative labels to secular recovery groups, specific churches, or denominations.

4. It eliminates "churchy" language.

The audience in your large group meeting will include individuals who have little or no experience with the church. They may not know what "redemption" means, but they can understand that Jesus has the power to set them free from their addictions, their harmful habits, and their shame and guilt.

5. It ensures that the testimony focuses on recovery principles and experiences.

It is not enough to describe how one was saved from hell to gain heaven. Recovery testimonies need to zero in on hope that God can deliver us from specific hurts, hang-ups, and habits during our lives on the earth. Testimonies need to *offer evidence* that the principles and steps taught in Celebrate Recovery really work.

6. It helps in adapting each testimony to focus upon a particular recovery principle or step.

As your ministry matures and your participants mature in their recovery, they will be able to see more clearly how each step or principle worked in their own experience. Working from their original written testimony with a reviewer makes it easy to zero in on particular recovery principles or steps. This will move your testimonies toward the ideal of presenting a testimony reinforcing the previous week's lesson.

In Board meetings — in The Echo's — wherever I
tell stories of redemption — wherever   *11*

7.   **It provides a working text for preparing short testimonies for other venues.**

One of the most powerful tools you can employ in expanding the impact of Celebrate Recovery within your own church membership is to have Celebrate Recovery testimonies read on Sunday mornings or in other weekend services. Usually these need to be 5–6 minutes in length. Working from a script of the long testimony makes this much easier. Preparing to share in a worship service where children and youth are present also means adapting the testimony to be appropriate for such an audience.

What Are the Reasons for Reading a Testimony from a Script?

1.   It places the focus on what God has done.

Some people may be tempted to try to be clever or entertaining. The objective of the testimony is to clearly communicate how God sets us free from our hurts, hang-ups, and habits. Simply reading the testimony ensures the good communication of the story. "Playing to the audience" could divert presenters, to the point that they fail to finish their account of recovery.

2.   It ensures that what has been approved is what is shared.

All the advantages of leadership reviews of testimonies will be lost if the presenter is not directed to read what has been approved.

3.   It expands the number who can share testimonies.

Many individuals with powerful testimonies may not share if they believe they have to have a talent for public speaking. Some of the most powerful testimonies come from the most fearful individuals. Without a script to read from they would never be able to share these vital stories of God's transforming power.

4.   It frees the emotions of the presenter.

Time and again, individuals are understandably overcome by emotion in telling their stories. With a script they can let the tears flow for a few moments and then get back on track.

5.   It controls the length of the presentation.

Even the most skilled and experienced communicator can lose track of time. Many who share a testimony may be far from experienced or skilled. Reading from a script helps them finish within the allotted time.

Many who hear the recommendation that testimonies be written, reviewed, and read may feel that this quenches the Spirit during the presentation. If that is a deep, personal theological conviction held in concert with your congregation, tradition, or denomination, then you must work within the framework of authority in your local church. However, we believe that the guidance of the Holy Spirit can be just as powerful during the process of preparation as He can during the presentation itself.

Because the leaders of our own Celebrate Recovery ministry have consistently enforced these guidelines, we have never been caught by surprise or embarrassed by a testimony shared in our large group meeting or during a church worship service. Take advantage of what the Celebrate Recovery leaders at Saddleback have learned "the hard way" by experience. Test it in your own church and we are confident you will blessed as one wonderful story of recovery after another is shared to the glory of God.

Celebrate Recovery®
Welcome Newcomers!

The purpose of Celebrate Recovery is to fellowship and celebrate God's healing power in our lives through the eight recovery principles found in the Beatitudes and Christ-centered 12 Steps. This experience allows us to be changed. We open the door by sharing our experiences, victories, and hopes with one another. In addition, we become willing to accept God's grace in solving our life problems.

By working the Christ-centered steps and applying their biblical principles found in the Beatitudes, we begin to grow spiritually. We become free from our addictive, compulsive, and dysfunctional behaviors. This freedom creates peace, serenity, joy, and, most importantly, a stronger personal relationship with God and others.

As we progress through the principles and the steps we discover our personal, loving, and forgiving Higher Power—Jesus Christ.

Welcome to an Amazing Spiritual Adventure!

Celebrate Recovery Small Groups WILL:

- Provide you a safe place to share your experiences, victories, and hopes with others who are going through a Christ-centered recovery.
- Provide you with a leader who has gone through a similar hurt, hang-up, or habit, who will facilitate the group as it focuses on a particular principle each week. The leader will also keep Celebrate Recovery's "Five Small Group Guidelines."
- Provide you with the opportunity to find an accountability partner or a sponsor.
- Encourage you to attend other recovery meetings held throughout the week.

Celebrate Recovery Small Groups Will NOT:

- Attempt to offer any professional clinical advice. Our leaders are not counselors.
- Allow its members to attempt to fix one another.

—

Celebrate Recovery®

Things We Are, Things We Are Not

Things We ARE:

A safe place to share
A refuge
A place of belonging
A place to care for others and be cared for
Where respect is given to each member
Where confidentiality is highly regarded
A place to learn
A place to grow and become strong again
Where you can take off your mask
A place for healthy challenges and healthy risks
A possible turning point in your life

Things We Are NOT:

A place for selfish control
Therapy
A place for secrets
A place to look for dating relationships
A place to rescue or be rescued by others
A place for perfection
A long-term commitment
A place to judge others
A quick fix

Celebrate Recovery®
Codependency Description

- My good feelings about who I am stem from being loved by you.
- My good feelings about who I am stem from receiving approval from you.
- Your struggle affects my serenity. My mental attention focuses on solving your problems or relieving your pain.
- My mental attention is focused on pleasing you.
- My mental attention is focused on protecting you.
- My self-esteem is bolstered by solving your problems.
- My self-esteem is bolstered by relieving your pain.
- My own hobbies and interests are put aside. My time is spent sharing your interests and hobbies.
- Your clothing and personal appearance are dictated by my desires, as I feel you are a reflection of me.
- Your behavior is dictated by my desires, as I feel you are a reflection of me.
- I am not aware of how I feel. I am aware of how you feel.
- I am not aware of what I want—I ask what you want. I am not aware—I assume.
- The dreams I have for my future are linked to you.
- My fear of rejection determines what I say or do.
- My fear of your anger determines what I say or do.
- I use giving as a way of feeling safe in our relationship.
- My social circle diminishes as I involve myself with you.
- I put my values aside in order to connect with you.
- I value your opinion and way of doing things more than my own.
- The quality of my life is in direct relation to the quality of yours.

Celebrate Recovery®
Chemical Addiction Description

If, when you honestly want to, you find you cannot quit drinking or using entirely, or if you have little control over the amount you consume, you are probably an alcoholic and/or an addict. If that is the case, you may be suffering from a problem which only a spiritual solution will conquer.

If you are as seriously alcoholic or addicted as we were, we believe there is no middle-of-the-road solution. We were in a position where life was becoming impossible, and we had passed into the region from which there is no return through human resources. We had but two alternatives: One was to go on to the bitter end, blotting out the consciousness of our intolerable situation as best as we could; and the other was to accept Jesus Christ as our Higher Power.

Romans 7:15–25

"I do not understand what I do. For what I want to do I do not do, but what I hate I do. And if I do what I do not want to do, I agree that the law is good. As it is, it is no longer I myself who do it, but it is sin living in me. For I know that good itself does not dwell in me, that is, in my sinful nature. For I have the desire to do what is good, but I cannot carry it out. For I do not do the good I want to do, but the evil I do not want to do—this I keep on doing. Now if I do what I do not want to do, it is no longer I who do it, but it is sin living in me that does it. So I find this law at work: Although I want to do good, evil is right there with me. For in my inner being I delight in God's law; but I see another law at work in me, waging war against the law of my mind and making me a prisoner of the law of sin at work within me. What a wretched man I am! Who will rescue me from this body that is subject to death? Thanks be to God, who delivers me through Jesus Christ our Lord! So then, I myself in my mind am a slave to God's law, but in my sinful nature a slave to the law of sin."

There Is a Solution

By working through the eight recovery principles found in the Beatitudes with Jesus Christ as your Higher Power, you can and will change! You will begin to experience the true peace and serenity you have been seeking, and you will no longer have to rely on your dysfunctional, compulsive, and addictive behaviors as a temporary "fix" for your pain.

By applying the biblical principles of conviction, conversion, surrender, confession, restitution, prayer, quiet time, witnessing, and helping one another, which are found within the eight principles and the Christ-centered 12 Steps, you will restore and develop stronger relationships with others and with God.

Celebrate Recovery®

Gratitude List
Principle 7-Step 11

I'm thankful to God:

_____
_____
_____

I'm thankful to God for placing others in my life:

_____
_____
_____

I'm thankful for my recovery program:

_____
_____
_____

I'm thankful for my church:

_____
_____
_____

Remember, maintaining an "attitude of gratitude" is the best prevention against relapse.

"Do not worry about anything, but pray and ask God for everything you need, always giving thanks. And God's peace, which is so great we cannot understand it, will keep your hearts and minds in Christ Jesus" (Philippians 4:6–7, NCV).

Celebrate Recovery Revised Edition Participant's Guides

John Baker

Recovery is not an overnight phenomenon, but more like a journey. The purpose of Celebrate Recovery is to allow us to become free from life's hurts, hang-ups, and habits. By working through the eight principles of recovery based on the Beatitudes, we will begin to see the true peace and serenity that we have been seeking.

The four participant's guides in the Celebrate Recovery program are:

- Guide 1: Stepping Out of Denial into God's Grace
- Guide 2: Taking an Honest and Spiritual Inventory
- Guide 3: Getting Right with God, Yourself, and Others
- Guide4: Growing in Christ While Helping Others

The participant guides are essential to the person in recovery to take part in because it makes everything personal.

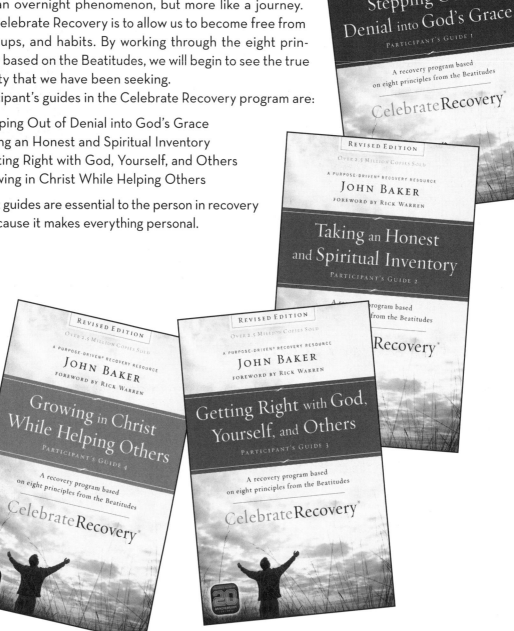

Available in stores and online!

Celebrate Recovery Bible

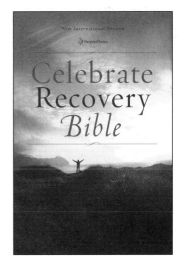

The *Celebrate Recovery Bible* offers everyone hope, encouragement, and the empowerment to rise above their hurts, hang-ups, and habits. This life-changing Bible is based on the proven and successful Celebrate Recovery program developed by John Baker and Rick Warren.

With features based on eight principles Jesus voiced in his Sermon on the Mount, this insightful Bible is for anyone struggling with the circumstances of their lives and the habits they are trying to control.

- Articles explain eight recovery principles and the accompanying Christ–centered twelve steps
- 112 lessons unpack eight recovery principles in practical terms
- Recovery stories offer encouragement and hope
- Over 50 full-page biblical character studies illustrate recovery principles
- 30 days of devotional readings
- Side-column reference system keyed to the eight recovery principles and topical index
- Complete text of the New International Version

Celebrate Recovery Journal

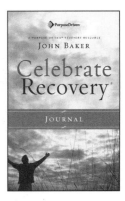

This journal is specially designed to complement the Celebrate Recovery program. The content guides you through the recovery process in a step-by-step fashion. Includes tips on how to benefit from journaling, specific Scriptures pulled from the Celebrate Recovery program, a section to help facilitate a 90-day review of your journaling progress, and a prayer request area to document God's answer to prayer.

*Available in stores
and online!*

Share Your Thoughts

With the Author: Your comments will be forwarded to the author when you send them to *zauthor@zondervan.com*.

With Zondervan: Submit your review of this book by writing to *zreview@zondervan.com*.

Free Online Resources at

www.zondervan.com

Zondervan AuthorTracker: Be notified whenever your favorite authors publish new books, go on tour, or post an update about what's happening in their lives at www.zondervan.com/authortracker.

Daily Bible Verses and Devotions: Enrich your life with daily Bible verses or devotions that help you start every morning focused on God. Visit www.zondervan.com/newsletters.

Free Email Publications: Sign up for newsletters on Christian living, academic resources, church ministry, fiction, children's resources, and more. Visit www.zondervan.com/newsletters.

Zondervan Bible Search: Find and compare Bible passages in a variety of translations at www.zondervanbiblesearch.com.

Other Benefits: Register yourself to receive online benefits like coupons and special offers, or to participate in research.

ZONDERVAN®

ZONDERVAN.com/
AUTHORTRACKER
follow your favorite authors